Through No Fault Of Their Own

Systems for handling redundancy in Britain, France and Germany

Dedicated, in gratitude
to my parents
Suruchibala and
Promode Lal Mukherjee

Santosh Mukherjee

Through No Fault Of Their Own

Systems for handling redundancy in Britain, France and Germany

A PEP REPORT

MACDONALD · LONDON

Copyright © PEP 1973

First published in Great Britain in 1973 by
Macdonald and Company (Publishers) Ltd.,
St. Giles House, 49 Poland Street,
London W.1.

Made and printed in Great Britain by
Redwood Press Limited, Trowbridge, Wiltshire

Paper: ISBN 0 356 04497 1
Cased: ISBN 0 356 04496 3

Contents

Programmes and outcome
A concept of redeployment

List of Tables

Appendix

List of Figures

Acknowledgements

A programme of research on manpower policies in Britain and other industrial countries is being carried out at PEP with financial support from the Ford Foundation and the Leverhulme Trust. This book is part of the series of publications arising from that work.

Officials of the Department of Employment have responded patiently and with generosity to requests for information; the researchers making the study, and PEP are grateful for that help.

Professor M. Rustant (University of Lyons) has provided information for Chapter 12, and Chapter 13 draws on material prepared by Dr. U. Engelen-Kefer (Wirtschaftswissenschaftliches Institut der Gewerkschaften Gmbh).

Miss Carla Standing has assisted with assembly and analysis of material at all stages of the project; the Tables and Figures in particular are largely her work. Mrs Ann Eccles has had charge of the preparation of the manuscript and of all the typing that had to be done before that stage was reached.

PEP is grateful to Oxford University Department for External Studies for enabling Santosh Mukherjee to undertake research for this book.

Foreword

Readers may wish to pick out quickly parts of this book which are relevant to their specific interests. This note, therefore, outlines the scope and layout of the work.

Chapter 1 contains proposals for changes in British policy and practice for handling redundancies. These suggestions come out of an examination of policy in Britain as well as in France and Germany.

British experience before the enactment of redundancy legislation in 1965 is discussed in Chapters 2–5; Chapters 5–11 go on to review the working of the Redundancy Payments Act. The money flows resulting from that legislation are the subject of Chapter 6, and the other main issues are then considered, including the incidence of redundancy in different age groups (Chapters 7 and 8) and the effects of the Act on industrial relations in Britain (Chapter 9). Chapters 10 and 11 draw out the policy implications of the weaknesses arising from the concepts on which the 1965 Act was founded. These chapters also discuss the case for improved data collection, and ways in which better information could enable more serious forecasting and analytical techniques to be worked out.

The last two chapters compare the findings for Britain with systems for dealing with redundancy evolved in France and Germany. One way of approaching this book is to read Chapter 1, then move on to Chapters 12 and 13 to get a picture of French and German experience, and then return to Chapters 2–11 for the details of the current British system.

1 Policy matters

Redundancy is a man-made phenomenon. It is not some spon-
taneous act of nature with a trail of disaster marking its passage. Yet
in Britain at least that is how redundancies seem to appear to those
who are affected as much as to the spectator. In a mature industrial
economy with the reputation of being a welfare state, the extinction
of jobs, still more the effect of that on people, cannot be treated as
hazards simply to be borne with fortitude. Redundancies must have
a clear purpose. The gain from them must be seen to be greater than
the loss so that the disruption of the lives of the people whose
employment is terminated is justified. If redundancies are the
consequence of a rational process, then it should be possible to
develop reasoned concepts and criteria for tackling them. Such
criteria would have to take account of economic and social goals and
the inter-relationship between them.

A reasoned framework of ideas about redundancies and what
should be done about them is half the job. Institutions and
machinery are needed to bring these ideas to fruition. Clearly the
institutions and administrative machinery will be shaped by
reference to the ideas which they are to put into practical effect.
These things need to be done because work is central to the pattern
of life in all Western industrial communities. Redundancy strikes at
this core of a person's relationship with his community.

Purpose of this study

This study is about systems for dealing with redundancy in Britain
since the late 1950s. In analysing the approach during the earlier
period and throughout the more detailed look at the system since

1965, the study focuses on policy matters. Though the detail of the analysis concerns how well or badly a particular institution is working, or the achievements or shortcomings of an administrative set-up, the purpose throughout is to look closely at the policy objects sought through practical means. Criteria for assessment are derived partly from systems in operation in France and Germany, while another part of the evaluative framework of what should be done about redundancies comes from public and Parliamentary discussion in Britain.

In this chapter an attempt is made to bring together points which have policy significance in the detailed discussion in the chapters that follow.

Property rights

At the root of Britain's statutory redundancy policy is the belief that a worker has property rights in his job. From this it follows that on grounds of equity, compensation should be made to someone who loses his job. Hence the British system of statutory severance compensation. It is a scheme without parallel in Western industrial communities. Its uniqueness lies in the right given the worker to the receipt of a cash lump-sum payment solely on grounds that his job has come to an end. Nothing can infringe this entitlement. Even if the man (or woman) goes straight into another job, the cash compensation is paid on the nail.

Not only does the British scheme establish this unconstrained individual right to compensation for loss of employment, the scheme does this across the board for all people in full-time, or near full-time, employment. So far the policy has great clarity. No other country does this kind of thing quite so comprehensively, nor with such generosity. As will be seen in Chapters 12 and 13, neither French nor German systems for handling redundancy provide a comprehensive cash-compensation scheme. That remains true even though in particular industry agreements workpeople in Germany get higher levels of cash compensation than their counterparts in Britain, where the sole exception to the scheme is the worker with less than the two-year minimum length of service. Exclusions in the German schemes spring not only from the piecemeal arrangements that exist there, but also because entitlement to cash compensation does not normally come until after ten years of continuous service with an employer.

So far the reasoning underlying British policy is straightforward. Where the waters begin to muddy is in the United Kingdom scheme's special provision for higher rates of compensation for older workers. The implications of this are considered more fully later. At this point the important issue is the difference in policy between Britain and other Western industrial countries this demonstrates. And here the important question concerns the cause of this difference, and the consequences for other aspects of policy for dealing with the whole issue of redundancy in Britain. In laying the main emphasis on cash compensation (and deploying large resources to that end) the British policy leaves big gaps in the system for diffusing the adverse effects of redundancies. In France and Germany, on the other hand, the framework is much more complex. Where in Britain the thrust of policy is towards cash compensation for the worker and then to leave him to his own devices, other countries in Europe have tried to build systems in which the maximum effort is put into getting him another job. Hence the contrast between Britain's expenditure of £381 million, spread over six years, on individual cash compensation as opposed to about £100 million on adult retraining and public employment services for the dynamic process of redeployment. By contrast, cash compensation to the redundant worker in France and Germany has been substantially less, while provision of employment services and training facilities has attracted the lion's share of funds.

With only a little over-simplification, it is possible to describe the French and German approaches as aiming to secure continuity of employment for the individual in the face of redundancy. In Britain, on the other hand, the largest part of the effort has gone into paying the individual cash for the lost job. Guesswork is involved in attempts to explain how these differences arose, and the factors influencing the formulation of policy in each country. One major influence on British policy-making is the structure of trade unions. Through their institutional behaviour, as much as the intangible feel which they created in industry, British trade unions have contributed to a rigid approach about jobs. Within a firm's internal labour market, individual unions have employed protective practices to preserve jobs for their members at the expense, if necessary, of the jobs of members of other unions. On the occupational labour market too Britain's union attitudes have been closely geared to safeguarding the interests of those already in, against those outside who wanted to get in.

Security of employment to organized workpeople in Britain was a matter of holding on to jobs: security was synonymous with rigidity. All the talk, the accusations and counter-accusations throughout the 1950s about demarcation and restrictive practices, had their origin in this. Observers who have claimed that the technique of productivity bargaining was nothing more or less than buying out restrictive practices in a firm's internal labour market have been wrong in being too categorical. A big part of the productivity bargaining process was indeed about that, just as a substantial element in the reasoning for the British statutory severance-compensation scheme was about buying out the rigidity in workpeople's attitudes towards jobs. But the analogy is far from complete. Flexibility in the internal labour market within a firm was bought in productivity agreements only partly through cash. An equal – some would claim bigger – part in the transformation was played by the new set of negotiating relationships established between employer and workpeople and by the thorough and expensive retraining which was an integral element of the more soundly based productivity agreements. On the national plane, the United Kingdom severance-compensation scheme set out to buy out rigidity, but equal efforts to redeploy the increased supply of manpower were not made. That, taken together with rising unemployment associated with low rates of economic growth, amply justified trade-union pessimism about the foolhardiness of giving up the security of rigidity.

Should employer be sole judge?

While giving the employee an unconstrained right to compensation for loss of employment through redundancy, the statutory scheme in Britain left the employer as the sole judge of the need for redundancies. Here too Britain's policy differs from that of France, Germany and other European countries. Again the chain of causation stretches back to the traditional pattern which prevailed before the 1965 legislation. In the 1950s some employers in Britain were already voluntarily paying cash compensation to workpeople whose jobs they brought to an end. These were unilateral, *ex gratia* cash payments. The employer alone decided who was to be given the sack, and took the decision about the sum of money he would hand out to the workers dismissed. Workpeople's representatives had no say about the need for redundancy, or the amount of the cash payments.

Neither at that stage nor, much more remarkably, since the introduction of the comprehensive statutory scheme, have Britain's public authorities had any direct part in the employer's decision about the necessity for redundancies. Moreover the introduction of the comprehensive compensation scheme was not made the occasion for involving either the public authorities or workpeople's represent-atives in considering the need for a collective dismissal. At another level too the scheme did not provide for joint consideration about how to implement the employer's decision to go ahead with a redundancy. Neither workpeople, nor the public authorities in Britain, have an established right to participate in arrangements for handling the redundancy, once the employer has reached his unilateral decision about its necessity.

Concepts and criteria

These then are the principal characteristics of the British approach to redundancy. Two principles appear to underlie policy in Britain which are not present in French and German policies and pro-grammes. The more explicit of these principles is that redundancies are entirely a matter for the individual employer. And the second, less explicit, but flowing from the basic principle, is that all redundancies are useful from the wider community viewpoint. Both these conceptual items in Britain's system for dealing with redun-dancies are open to question and criticism, in the light of experience of the working of the statutory scheme, and by reference to what is done elsewhere.

Can it be right that all employers should have complete freedom to decide that they will extinguish the livelihoods of part or whole of the labour force they employ? An affirmative answer requires adherence to the view that all redundancies decided on by employers contribute to the greater economic and social good of the community as a whole. It is of course the simplest, and in practice the easiest, posture to adopt. Public authorities do not become embroiled in private decision taking. Employers are not faced by the difficulty of having to persuade either their workforce or the community of the rightness of their action. Yet the consequences of their decisions affect the whole community. While in Brtain, by implication at least, it appears to be the authorities' view that the economic advance of the country is best served by letting employers make their own independent decisions about the size of their labour force, in Germany, that epitome of free enterprise, firms are compelled by law to consult their employees as well as the public authorities.

But to say that public authorities in Britain always take the view that the employer can do no wrong when it comes to redundancies is not entirely true. There is good evidence to show the existence of something of a dual standard for public- and private-sector employers in the United Kingdom. In coalmining, on the railways and, more recently, in British Steel, redundancy procedures have been humane and generous. More effort has gone into finding the least troublesome methods of slimming down these industries' payrolls than is common among private-sector organizations. Apart from paying quite large sums of money to employees dismissed on grounds of redundancy, public-sector enterprises have bent over backwards to moderate the social and psychological disagreeableness of collective dismissals. Where the public sector has scored time and again is in terms of deliberation and long-term preparation. From this have sprung elements of positive redeployment which are strikingly unusual in arrangements made by private firms in Britain.

There are many reasons why redundancy is handled differently by nationalized industries and the private sector. Open though this is to debate, one basic reason probably lies in the nationalized sector's obligation to be publicly accountable for all its actions. Privately owned firms do not of course have this kind of accountability and indeed are exonerated from blame on grounds of their alleged responsibility to owners of capital, for whom profit maximization is of paramount importance. But that is by no means the end of the story.

In particular private-sector industries public authorities have taken a hand in arranging the cutback of manpower made inevitable by technological change or shrinking markets. Employers did not work to their own cost calculations alone. Total (community) economic and social costs entered the calculations at the same time as the public authorities joined in the process of handling the redundancies.

Yet, over the flow of redundancies in the economy as a whole, British public authorities have enjoined a self-denying role to themselves. That this is not a sustainable position was demonstrated by the concern of the public authorities about the age structure of people being made redundant. The authorities attempted to express this concern in 1969 by modifying the financial structure of the statutory severance compensation scheme. In doing so they were still keeping at a distance from the individual employer and his redundancy decisions.

All this has meant a loss of direction. Individual firms have been left to get on with making people redundant whenever and however they thought fit. No criteria have been developed to reflect the community's wider interests which firms can take account of, even if they want to. At the same time, there is undeniable alarm among workpeople, and increasing disruption in British industry, about the spread of redundancies. A full six years after the establishment of the statutory scheme, the time is appropriate for a fundamental rethinking of redundancy policy. In making that analysis, a good deal can be learnt from ideas and experience in other countries as well as from what has happened in Britain since 1965. The ingredients of such a policy reassessment are now discussed.

As regards the substance (the question of procedure and machinery will be considered later), the first premise of existing policy which needs to be changed is the one about all redundancies being good. All recent experience in Britain (and in other developed industrial countries) points conclusively to the fact that older people find it exceedingly difficult to get new jobs. From that, two alternative and opposite policies can be pursued. One is to evolve policies which prevent redundancy among older people; the other to create systems which remove older people from the labour market. It is not impossible to reconcile these opposites. An over-all redundancy or continuity-of-employment programme can be devised with different kinds of provisions for three separate age brackets. From the time of a young person's entry to the labour market up to age 40 might be thought of as the period of mobility. Between 41 and 55 would be the period of redeployment. Thereafter, withdrawal from the labour force with a 'pre-pension' could become the principal alternative to employment. What has just been said bears close resemblance to patterns for dealing with continuity of employment being written into collective agreements between unions and employers in Germany.

To consider something of that kind would involve quite big

changes in Britain's present systems for handling redundancy. In place of the current discharge of community obligations solely through giving the redundant worker a lump-sum cash compensation and then leaving everything else to the market, employers and unions, as much as the public authorities, would need to join together in creating and administering a national manpower policy.

In the current statutory compensation scheme there is no scope for action concerning continuity of employment. Such continuity is especially important for older people. Recent evidence about labour markets in Western industrial countries clearly shows that older people find it much more difficult to get new jobs. But the evidence also suggests that where older people are not compelled (by redundancy) to give up jobs, they are well able to perform productive functions within an enterprise. Here the evidence is rather less comprehensive, but it also seems pretty certain that, with increasing age, manual workers in industry go through a number of transfers between jobs in the establishment's internal labour market. Older workers are frequently redeployed within establishments to jobs appropriate to the changing physical and mental characteristics connected with rising age. What effects internal redeployment of this type have on the cost structure of firms is not fully known. On the other hand internal redeployment clearly imposes the task of manpower planning on management. No matter how imprecise or rudimentary such planning is, it is still more bothersome for management than simply sacking the older worker.

In Britain two things have contributed to making this easy option more attractive. Since 1966 there has been considerable slack in the labour market and this has coincided with the advent of the compensation scheme. Consequently internal redeployment has been receiving less attention. Though this might make sense within the individual firm's own frame of reference, it is unacceptable to the community as a whole. This is not the same thing as saying that manpower should remain locked into a rigid pattern of employment. Rather, this line of reasoning suggests that mobility and job changes should be graded and subjected to a finer analysis. Changes of jobs within an enterprise, difficult though they can be for individuals, are undeniably less disrupting than total severance of employment in one place followed by re-employment in a quite different organization. Yet both kinds of job changes are essential if enterprises are to remain dynamic.

A logical and humane system for dealing with redundancies would set out to put the burden of big changes on the most mobile and adaptable age group, leaving the older workers to face less fundamental adaptations. Forced severance of employment would affect members of a firm's payroll in the age bracket with a top limit of forty or thereabouts. Unconstrained access to retraining should be available to such people and income maintenance during training should be at levels analogous to earnings in the jobs from which they are discharged. This over-all strategy is firmly embedded in the systems for handling redundancy collectively negotiated between unions and employers in Germany, as well as in the German public authorities' retraining and employment-service programmes.

Confining the biggest doses of change to the youngest segment of the working population will not enable the older groups to remain in unchanged jobs, pursuing unchanging vocations. A fully articulated manpower policy for Britain would need to concern itself with schemes for redeployment of people over 40 but below 55 years of age. In the first place, the preferred policy should be to enable this age bracket to have continuity of employment within the enterprise where they have worked for a number of years. And their redeployment, aided by training, would occur within the establishment itself. Part of that internal job-changing process would be a 'degressive' (see Chapter 12) income-maintenance guarantee. But manual workers in manufacturing industry are accustomed to their wages reaching a peak in their middle years and then declining. Guarantees of continuity of employment associated with a gentle decline in earnings would become the explicit norm for manual employees in manufacturing aged between 41 and 55.

This would be one part of the programme for the redeployment of older workers. And this is the right point at which to take account of the trend to declining employment in the goods-producing sectors of industrial countries. That long-term trend is in itself an imperative argument for outlining national policies for manpower. An intra-establishment redeployment programme for workpeople in their middle years would, in the long term, need to take account of declining opportunities in the manufacturing sector. Deliberate provision for inter-sectoral redeployment is necessary to deal with this aspect of changes in manpower demand.

A scheme for continuity of employment which can take in provision for shifts of manpower from the manufacturing to the services sector can be aligned with the adaptation of middle-aged manual employees from manufacturing to jobs in tertiary occupations. Here, too, there is need for much more retraining. Of equal importance is the role of the public authorities. State financed — but operated jointly with employers' and workpeople's representatives — public employment services would be the principal instrument for steering that category of manpower away from the manufacturing sector to service occupations. Schemes for income maintenance will have to be associated with shifting and adapting middle-aged employees. The analogy here is with the redeployment within firms that we have already considered. Workpeople aged 41–55, who move from manufacturing to the tertiary sector, will be faced with a reduction in income as market-determined wages are lower than in manufacturing. The drop in earnings arising from the change between sectors can be cushioned for a period by payment of degressive allowances of the type pioneered by the European Coal and Steel Community. Precedent for this is available in Britain in, for instance, redundancy arrangements operated by the National Coal Board.

In order to bring this about the public authorities will need to help through the employment services. Second, they will have to organize financial systems for the transitional income-maintenance arrangements. Finally, acting across the wider economic front, governments will have to go all out to encourage growth of the service sector. Such growth, in privately provided services, can be encouraged through taxation and monetary policies. More directly, governments can boost growth in service occupations by expanding public provision over the immense range of services for which the state takes responsibility in all Western industrial countries. Turning to the possibility of a programme for continuity of employment for workpeople over 55, the public authorities' functions become more important still.

The linking of systems for diffusion of redundancy with state schemes of retirement pensions is part of over-all policy programmes in France and Germany. In both countries, however, the scope for that kind of link does not appear until the individual is within five years of his retirement age. In what has been said so far here the upper age limit of the fully active working population has been put at 55 years. Implicit in this are two separate ideas. A longer-term objective in some industrial countries, among some interest groups, pursued with varying degrees of enthusiasm at different periods of time, is the accomplishment of a lower retiring age. In the kind of national programme for continuity of employment outlined in this chapter, there is clear scope for a third element to be superimposed on the two which have already been described. Given the existence of a public employment service sufficiently knowledgeable about the country's labour market, scope would exist for the deployment of younger early-retired people into part-time jobs, again principally in the service occupations. The two things would have to go together. Opening up of opportunities for part-time employment cannot be achieved, as has been shown by experience in Sweden, simply by expanding total demand for manpower. Use of part-time manpower requires a different habit of mind on the part of the employer, as much as new patterns of work organization. Expanding total demand for manpower contributes very little towards bringing about these changes. Officials of the public employment service, on the other hand, prodding and encouraging employers, can do something about the obstacles.

Programmes and institutions

The sum total of what has been said so far is that redundancies are part and parcel of the big changes affecting the use of human resources in industrially advanced countries. A rational and socially satisfactory system for dealing with redundancies requires explicit and continuing attention to the development of a total manpower policy. And, so far as Britain is concerned, there is a big gap that needs to be filled. For that purpose, as well as on the more mundane level of handling individual situations where redundancy is inevitable, new institutions and machinery for administration of policy are necessary. The French, as shown in Chapter 12, have established a network of Joint Employment Committees with terms of reference enabling them to move towards preparation of a national manpower policy. An intrinsic and profoundly important part of that structure is the tripartite association of unions, employers and the public authorities in the decision-taking process. Though the structure of institutions and the underlying philosophy is different in Germany, there too it is clearly felt that manpower decisions cannot be left to the employer alone.

Limited arrangements about redundancy

Leaving aside the big tasks of manpower policy, and the fact that the
proper context for handling redundancies is a national programme of
deployment of human resources, some points can be made about the
actual handling of redundancy situations in Britain. Neither the
public authorities nor workpeople's representatives in Britain have
rights and standing in relation to the employer, on occasions of
redundancy, comparable with the rights available to these parties in
France and Germany. Employers in Germany have, since 1969, had
a statutory obligation to inform the public employment service of
their intention to make changes leading to redundancy as long ahead
as 12 months before collective dismissal. The Federal Institute of
Labour has the right to make employers pay for retraining if they
fail to give the public employment service the required advance
notice. Officials of the French manpower services have statutory
authority to prohibit collective dismissals which employers have
notified as being in the pipeline. Britain's Department of Employment has no comparable powers when employers are contemplating
reductions.

In Germany, both by law and through agreements between
employers and unions, workpeople's representatives have rights in
regard to redundancy situations comparable to those available to
their public authorities. Similarly, on a statutory basis, and arising
from national agreements between employers and central trade-
union federations, rights of employee participation in the resolution
of redundancy situations are established in France. Increasingly
workpeople in Britain have been denying the employer a unilateral
right to extinguish the jobs of all or a part of his labour force solely
at his will. Despite some spectacular successes achieved by workpeople in preventing closure of enterprises through direct action,
there is no across-the-board system in Britain yet which obliges firms
to associate employee representatives in their decision making about
cutbacks in manpower.

A minimum programme of reform in the United Kingdom
involves setting these two things right immediately. The Department
of Employment needs powers to establish its presence as of right on
all occasions when redundancies affecting more than a minimum
number (say five as in Germany) of employees are envisaged.
Unions, either by promoting legislation, or through a centrally

negotiated agreement between themselves and employers, need to establish the right of participation by workpeople's representatives in management assessments of the need for redundancies, and the preparation of programmes for handling them if the necessity is established beyond question. In sum, the run up to a redundancy of any size, and its execution, has to be made into a tripartite operation. All of this needs to be done quickly. At the same time, a start has to be made on the bigger, more fundamental, manpower policy matters outlined earlier.

2 Extent of redundancies in Britain

Much of the trouble about redundancies in Britain is that no one knows for certain how many there are each year. Consequently, to the devastating threat of being without a job through no fault of one's own, is added the fear that comes from a risk of unknown dimensions. No estimate of the number of people suffering redundancy exists for the 1950s. There is not even sufficient precise information to allow a guess about the approximate size of the figure. Much can be read into this absence of information: one plausible view is that loss of employment through redundancy was not an occurrence of sufficient frequency to have caused official agencies, or academic observers, to apply themselves to its measurement. But such an inference would be valid only in part. By 1960 the Ministry of Labour had begun to take sufficient account of the impact of this phenomenon on industrial relations to start showing statistics of stoppages of work arising from disputes connected with redundancies. But in spite of occasional acute local difficulties it was not until well into the second half of the 1950s that redundancies began to take on the shape of a national issue.

Yet, as can be seen from Table 1, the first official guess gave a figure of 200,000 redundancies each year for 1958 – 61. There is no indication of how the NEDC arrived at this figure. But it is very likely that it was a rough approximation built from patchy information from newspaper reports, talks with employers and their organizations, and hints from the Ministry of Labour. Even so, that is the best available.

Table 1 Estimates of numbers of redundancies in Britain.

Source	Reference period	Number unpaid [1] (000s)	Total [2] (000s)	Civilian employees [3] (000s)	Total redundancies as percentage of civilian employees
NEDC [4]	1958–1961	...	200	21,879 [8]	0.91
Ministry of Labour [5]	1962	...	470 to 590	22,535	2.09 – 2.62
Department of Employment [6]	1968	500 to 750	764 to 1,014	22,639	3.37 – 4.48
OPCS [7]	1969	450	701	22,564	3.11

Notes and sources

(1) 'Unpaid' here means not entitled to receive payment under the Redundancy Payments Act 1965.
(2) All redundancies, i.e. 'unpaid' from previous column *plus* those receiving payment under provisions of 1965 Act.
(3) Total labour force *excluding* the self-employed, the armed forces and those registered as unemployed at employment exchanges.
(4) *Growth of the United Kingdom Economy to 1966*, NEDC, HMSO.
(5) Calculated from *Redundancy in Great Britain*, Ministry of Labour Gazette, February 1963.
(6) Report of the Working Group on Redundancy Payments Act, Department of Employment (cited in OPCS Survey), 1968.
(7) Office of Population Censuses and Surveys, Social Survey Division, *Effects of the Redundancy Payments Act*. HMSO, 1971.
(8) Average 1958–61.

1962 estimates

By 1962 the number of people redundant in Britain was between
470,000 and 590,000. These figures are calculated from a 1963
Ministry of Labour study. The empirical foundation is no more valid
than that for the much lower numbers estimated by the NEDC only
two years before the Ministry of Labour enquiry. Equally, as
approximations and only on that basis, they are no less good a guide
to the real situation than the earlier guess. Assuming that both sets
of figures have equal foundations of credibility, something very
striking results from a comparison. In the time between the two
reference periods there was quite a jump in redundancies as a
proportion of civilian employees. In 1962 this proportion had risen
to somewhere between two and three times the earlier figure.
Admittedly a redundancy ratio of a little over 2 to nearly 3 per cent
of all civilian employees is not fearsomely high. But a doubling, if
not a trebling, of this kind of traumatic experience in perhaps three
to four years could readily give rise to a great deal of alarm in any
community where the loss of employment is held in greater dread
than any other social deprivation.

Difficulties about making sensible estimates of the numbers
affected by redundancy have become a bit less acute in the years
since the Redundancy Payments Act. Once again, and appropriately,
the only useful source is the Department of Employment. Although
the information is better, there still has to be a fair amount of
guesswork. This is because in terms of the Act, information comes in
only about redundant people who qualify for cash benefits. As a
result, even though there are fairly accurate head counts to be got
from the information on payments of redundancy benefits, quite a
lot, indeed perhaps a sizable majority of redundant people do not
appear in this count. To get an estimate of how many people there
are of this kind, it becomes necessary to fall back on the kind of
method used by NEDC for their original approximation.

Quantities since 1966

For the years since 1966, there is a set of 'hard' figures about the
numbers paid compensation for dismissal arising from redundancy.
Because of the way these figures have been collected they are not a
reliable basis for fine judgement about total year-to-year changes, and

even less so for analyses covering shorter time spans. This is a minor shortcoming from the point of view of the attempt in this chapter to make an estimate of the over-all volume of redundancy and its variation in the course of the last fifteen years. For this purpose, it is necessary to add the number of people who, though redundant, are not counted as such because the payment-centred machinery of the Act takes no account of them. In any estimate of the total size of redundancies there will therefore be the 'hard' statistics which are a spin-off of the Act, and the considerably less reliable quantities based on 'informed judgement' about redundancies falling outside the scope of the statute.

As no authoritative year-by-year estimates can be attempted, there is a good deal to be gained from staying with just one source of information. The 1962 Ministry of Labour estimate has been considered earlier. The next piece of information available from that source comes from an internal Department of Employment study relating to 1968. The guess at that time of the number of people redundant, but ineligible for statutory financial compensation, was put at 500,000 to 750,000. Together with the 264,000 redundancies qualifying for statutory compensation that year, this gives a total of between 764,000 and 1,014,000 As a proportion of civilian employees this is 3.37 per cent and 4.48 per cent. In absolute terms, quite as much as in relation to the rate of growth from the original NEDC estimate, redundancy in 1968 was substantial. About 4 per cent of civilian employees in that year saw their jobs disappear through no fault of their own. The hazard of redundancy in 1968 appears to have been over four times greater than in the late 1950s.

Admittedly there is quite a lot of uncertainty about all these figures. And most of them would be unsuitable for any refined statistical analysis. Nevertheless they are usable as indicators of broad trends. There is confirmation of this from the findings of a survey[1] made by the Office of Population Censuses and Surveys carried out in 1969. From that data it was estimated that redundancies failing to qualify for payment under the Act were certainly not less then 450,000 and perhaps another 100,000 more. When turned into a percentage of civilian employees this is a range of 3 per cent to 3.5 per cent.

Pace of growth

Although the numbers qualifying for payment under provisions of
the Redundancy Payments Act do not show how many are affected
in total by redundancies, they are valuable in illustrating the pace at
which loss of employment from redundancies has been growing.

Table 2 sets out the available information. Redundancies have
gone up year by year, except in 1969, for the whole period since
statutory provision was made for payment of compensation. At the
same time, the number of people employed has been declining. But
here too, 1969 was exceptional in having a much more moderate
decline in total employees than any of the other years in this period.
For the present, leaving this unusual year on one side, in four out of
five years there were quite large increases in redundancy.

Table 2 Growth of redundancies which qualified for payment under
the 1965 Act.

	Number of individuals [1]	Civilian employees [2] (000s)	Redundancies as percentage of civilian employees	Index of redundancies as percentage of civilian employees (1966=100)
1966	138,845	23,209	0.60	100
1967	249,782	22,799	1.10	183
1968	264,491	22,639	1.17	195
1969	250,764	22,564	1.11	185
1970	275,563	22,391	1.23	205
1971	370,306	21,961	1.69	282

Notes and sources
(1)   Strictly, this is number of payments, but no individual would
       receive payment more than once in each year even if he was
       made redundant on more than one occasion.
(2)   Total labour force *excluding* the self-employed, the armed
       forces and those registered as unemployed at employment
       exchanges.

Most arresting in its impact is the growth of redundancies in 1967 compared with a year earlier. Redundancies as a percentage of civilian employees in 1967 were 83 per cent up on the preceding year. Immediately after this big rise, 1968 saw a quieter pace of growth of redundancies, with a rise of only 7 per cent. This abatement continued in 1969. Yet in that year the absolute volume of redundancies was, in fact, a bit higher than in 1967. After taking account of the decline in civilian employees over the two years, the apparent moderation of redundancies in 1969 can be seen in perspective. In this relatively calm year, redundancies were 85 per cent above the level of 1966. After that pause there was a marked resumption of the upward trend. Redundancies in 1970 rose 10 per cent above the preceding year, while 1971 saw a boom with a 38 per cent rise over the previous twelve months to a level almost three times that of 1966.

3 The British context

At least 750,000 people were dismissed because of redundancy during 1970 in Britain and it is quite possible that the number was as high as a million. Despite this margin of error, there is still doubt about the accuracy of these figures. Hard statistical information is just not available. Britain is not alone among Western European countries in this respect. What marks Britain out is the amount of discussion about redundancy that goes on in this country: in newspapers, in union conferences and among employers. But this apparently deeper preoccupation in Britain has not led either to effective policies or to the active assembling of precise and comprehensive information to give foundation for decision making.

Of the intensity of the concern in Britain about redundancy there can be no doubt. To an observer, from America,[1] the amount of publicity, and the extent of alarm, associated with the redundancy of even 20 or 30 workers in a relatively large firm, is sufficiently unfamiliar to make a striking impact. Curious though it might appear to people looking in from the outside, British focusing of attention on redundancy is wholly consistent with an underlying attitude to employment which displays two other prominent characteristics. One of these, once again noted with coldest clarity by an American observer,[2] is the over-manning of machines and particular operations in British industries. Related to this is the second feature of Britain's steady state industrial system — a slowness in adapting the structure of its industry to changing patterns of domestic and international demand.

What the reality is and what the image is a moot point. It is however undeniable that workpeople's organizations in Britain have traditionally, strongly set their faces against any actions by employers that might extinguish existing jobs. This approach found its most concrete expression in what used to be called the Amalgamated Engineering Union. A delegate Conference in 1957 instructed their Executive Council 'to conduct a national campaign against redundancy and unemployment and for the Right to Work'. That resolution contained a warning to 'the employers that this Union will move into action to safeguard the livelihood of our members and will demand the Right to Work, and that the necessary action will be taken to enforce our demands'. Although other British unions did not put their position with such rigour, the general view among organized workpeople, particularly at shop-floor level, was that collective bargaining pressure should be exerted to prevent the disappearance of existing jobs. No clear evidence is available about whether employers welcomed or chafed under this constraint on their scope to introduce new machinery which would be labour displacing or to organize work in a different way which would have the same outcome. Although the situation was not quite one of a fletcher spending all his life making arrows, or a blacksmith shoeing horses for two score years, there was general accord among observers of the British industrial scene that strong pressures held the distribution of manpower in a rigid industrial matrix, prevented flows of resources, both human and capital, from one cell to another, and obstructed contraction in some areas, compensated by expansion in others.

Inflexible manpower

Official pronouncements, articles in learned journals – and in less learned ones – tended to share this common theme of disquiet about the strength of resistance to industrial change. It would be quite wrong to think that all this began only in the 1960s. A Private Member's Bill put to the House of Commons in 1950 marks a useful base date.[3] Though only five clauses in length, that Bill in both substance and implication is remarkably illuminating. General though the feeling was in British industry that a worker once started on a job would normally go on doing the same thing for all his working life, this was based on nothing firmer than custom and practice. This structure of convention designed to provide employees with security, relying as it had to on unspoken understandings, put a premium on keeping things exactly as they were.

Paradoxically, but evidently wth sound judgement, the 1950 Security of Employment Bill attempted to create a stronger right for workpeople in their jobs. This was to be achieved by the employer drawing up a memorandum containing the material terms and conditions of his contract of service with his employees. There may seem, to someone unacquainted with industrial relations in Britain, more than a degree of strangeness about the fact that legislation was being proposed in 1950 (and in a Private Member's Bill, at that) to provide employees with some rights in relation to the people by whom they were employed. Yet this unpretentious little Bill was something quite radical: that employers should actually contract with members of their workforce the length of notice that would be given if it became necessary to terminate employment. While the Bill was wholly true to the time-honoured tradition of letting the parties in the collective bargaining process determine all questions of substance, it was nevertheless unconventional in saying that the employee should have in writing 'the manner in which the length of notice (of termination of employment) shall be related to the length of service or compensation paid in lieu thereof'. By getting this kind of thing written down – and the Bill had things to say about other items which would need to go into the written contract – the sponsors were trying to get people to take notice of the need for adequate guarantees of security to employees. They were also trying to establish a context for persuading workpeople that their interests could be protected in ways other than by their holding on to a particular job and attempting to fight off any change which looked like a threat to its existence.

Better though it was than nothing at all, that 1950 Bill pitched its proposals for workers' rights pretty much at a minimum. For one thing, as we saw earlier, the Bill aimed at setting up new procedures. Its sponsors were wary of stepping on the sacred ground of substantive items reserved only to trade unions and employers. Another aspect of the minimal approach was implicit rather than apparent. In tone and wording the Bill reflected the spirit of its time by an acceptance that decisions about these things were a prerogative of management alone. Although quite a lot was wrong with it, that Bill at least showed the concern of a group of people (who were later eminent in Conservative party affairs and in government) about the need to give workpeople support and confidence, so that their automatic response to change was not one of refusal and resistance.

In setting out to encourage this kind of change of approach, the authors of the Bill were not motivated by social considerations alone. Their wish to create a feeling of security among workpeople was as much, perhaps even to a predominant extent, a function of a quite widely held view that increases in industrial production and more rapid economic growth would be easier to get if workpeople were better protected against the arbitrariness of redundancy generated purely by market forces. One part of this view is clearly put in the cliché much used at that time 'security and change go together'. About this there was considerable agreement. Much less agreement existed about the kind of effective action that could be taken to realize it. The major part this uncertainty arose from a timidity about interfering with traditional systems. For, customarily, job security for manual workers in Britain has been a subject reserved for settlement through collective bargaining between employers and workpeople's representatives.

Collective agreements versus the law

Such reliance on the voluntary bargaining system between employer and organized employees has of course been the strongest and most highly prized characteristic of the British system of industrial relations. On the matter of job security, as on other issues that are settled through bargaining, this approach specifically implied the exclusion of third parties, no matter how benign their intentions, from the making of policies and application of practical measures. This embargo applied most particularly to statutory intervention by government. Employers and trade unions competed with each other in their abhorrence of governmental intervention in industry's own processes for regulating conditions of work and settling disputes. There are a variety of good reasons for thinking that Britain's collective bargaining system was, at least until the late 1950s, fairly effective in coping with the immediate and short-term relationships between employers and employees. In a decade which has earned the reputation of having 'over-full' employment, the issue of job security was not of sufficient importance to occupy busy trade union officials' time. In the time honoured trade union tradition, a nodding and winking arrangement had evolved. At bottom this consisted of a readiness on the part of union officials to give such support as they could to workpeople in individual establishments who wanted to oppose redundancy.

Labour turnover in Britain, as far back as 1950, was not very different from that in other Western European countries. There are problems about the concept and about the actual process of counting. Nevertheless the 'separation rate' in Britain was in the 30 – 40 range of every 100 manual employers in a twelve-month period. This separation rate is a sum of both voluntary and involuntary changing of jobs. So far as trade union officials considered job security in the 1950s, they excluded the possibility of statutory means of underpinning workers' rights. Quite apart from the general dislike of legal encroachment on 'free' collective bargaining, on this particular question trade unions had a more specific worry. In a rather simple-minded way they were apprehensive that the asymmetry in favour of the worker which appeared to exist in an unregulated labour market would disappear if the law was brought in. So long as jobs were plentiful, there was nothing to prevent workpeople from leaving one employer and going on to another if they wanted to. Among unions, there were real fears that despite its benefits, a contract of employment would also restrict the employee's freedom to change jobs. Concern about freedom that might be lost prevented trade unions from welcoming what might have been done through the law to increase their members' rights in their jobs. At the same time their own preoccupation with matters of the moment prevented them from giving full attention to job-security clauses in collectively negotiated agreements. Unlike their American counterparts, British unions generally neither sought nor achieved collective agreements containing plans for handling redundancies, and financial compensation provisions.

Employers and unions

One clear point emerges: there is little systematic information about arrangements between unions and employers in the 1950s concerning redundancy. But it is possible to piece something together. One reason for the lack of information is that such arrangements as were made tended, on the whole, to be local rather than national. For this there were both philosophical arguments and ones based on expediency. Without doubt the majority of employers in the private sector were not, at that time, prepared to regard questions of redundancy as a proper subject for negotiation with trade unions at either industry or national level. Broadly the approach was that this was part of management's business of managing, and the proper thing was to arrive at *ad hoc* arrangements with the particular group of workpeople affected by redundancy. Running through this view is a feeling that accords with the attitudes which permeate the Private Member's Bill of 1950. Preoccupied as they were with gaining improvements in wages, most union officials were apparently content to collude with employers in keeping the whole thing in low key.

What employers and journalists, not to mention the occasional Ministry of Labour committee of enquiry, described as restrictive practices and what, equally invariably, rank-and-file trade unionists spoke of as protective measures, had at their root a fear of redundancy. Indeed throughout the mid-1950s the chief point of controversy, and principal source of aggravation in British industrial relations, was not so much excessive wage increases as restrictive practices. The focal point for job demarcation and its mirror image, opposition to redundancy, was firmly at plant level, or in a sub-system within the plant. In the absence of systematic negotiated procedures between unions and employers for managing redundancy situations, it is wholly unsurprising that workpeople as individuals, and in their work groups, should have striven to reject this reality. In sum, neither employers nor trade unions were prepared to think constructively and plan a programme of action to deal with such situations.

Ministry of Labour efforts

Unspectacularly, but with great doggedness, the Ministry of Labour kept pushing the idea of the need for arrangements that might make redundancies more palatable. And untypically for that well-meaning Department, this persistence was as much a result of appreciation of economic need, as of concern about social values and smoother industrial relations. Although phrases like 'structural change' would never have passed the Ministry spokesmen's lips, officials were by the late 1950s beginning to worry about economic growth, and the manpower constraint on that desirable objective. Not only was the Ministry of Labour behaving out of character in taking account of such wide-ranging matters that it normally regarded as solely the concern of long-haired types elsewhere in Whitehall, but it had with great perspicacity worked out a connection between fears of redundancy, and the application of restrictive practices by workpeople.

Taking a deep breath, the Ministry of Labour plunged. 1961 saw the publication of a booklet, which for this traditionally reticent Department was of almost garrulous length in running to 37 pages of information, advice and exhortation about redundancies.[4] The Ministry set out to encourage industry to learn about provisions made by some employers. Two years later the Ministry of Labour updated the survey.[5] At the same time the Department attempted to collect information about the number of workers dismissed as redundant. All this activity was not in isolation. Ever since its foundation, in the early spring of 1962, the National Economic Development Council had become much concerned about ways of increasing labour mobility to help speedier contraction of employment where that seemed necessary, that in turn enabling expanding enterprises to get extra manpower. NEDC, more than any other single force, is entitled to claim credit for having recognized the key role of policies and administrative procedures for moving workpeople from one job to another, in any strategy for quickening changes in the structure of British industry.

In Chapter 2 an attempt was made by counting heads to show the dimension of redundancy as a policy issue. It is evident from that chapter that before statutory requirements were laid down in 1965, and to a substantial extent even after that, much estimating of numbers redundant is based on informed guesswork. NEDC's own guess in 1963[6] was 200,000 for the average number of workers who become redundant each year. That figure was of course hedged about with qualifications, and there is fairly persuasive evidence to support a higher figure. Relatively small though the NEDC figure for people being made redundant is, and despite its diplomatic abstention from making a forecast, the NEDC was of firm opinion that 'Redundancy has a far greater significance for economic growth than the actual number of workpeople directly affected by the contraction of particular firms or industries would suggest.' This disproportion of significance arises because 'The fear of redundancy acts as a brake on industrial expansion, whether it causes strikes, restrictions or resistance to change.' For the first time an official body had made the link between restrictive practices and workers' apprehensions about loss of employment explicit. On yet another score, NEDC voiced something that had been in the air for quite a time 'From the viewpoint of growth', that Council maintained, it was essential 'to see whether more cannot be done to assist mobility and to tackle the problems to which redundancy gives rise.'

Recognition of a problem is one thing, methods for its solution are another matter. Hence, in recommending what needed to be done about this problem area so clearly delineated by its own efforts, the NEDC had to content itself with outlining possible alternative courses of action.

4 Why pay redundant people?

In all Western industrialized countries there is a consensus on the proposition that workpeople should be given money when they are made redundant. Rules governing the amount to be paid, the method of payment and the entitlement to the money, differ from country to country. Equally there is considerable variety in the systems devised for making rules for handling redundancies in their general aspect and on the specific issue of cash payment. Effectively, only two systems have been employed for establishing procedure on redundancy questions. One is by negotiation of agreements through collective bargaining between organized workers and their employers. With Britain as the solitary exception, the preferred approach is through collective bargaining. Although some countries have statutes which affect the treatment of redundancy, nowhere is the core of redundancy arrangements determined wholly by legislation except in Britain. What is of interest is not the matter of statutory provision, as against collectively bargained arrangements for redundancy, but the overwhelming emphasis in British legislation on establishing a fund and setting out rules for payment from it to redundant workpeople.

Britain's statute made clear a principle which, though central to all western countries' arrangements, was until that time incompletely displayed. The British contribution of clarity arose not from any passion for teleological analysis, rather it was an unavoidable feature of the parliamentary processing of a statute. That debate, though it did spell out the emphasis on money payments, was far less conclusive in establishing the rationality of such action. But as it was a debate conducted nationally, and unparalleled by analogous discussion in other Western industrial countries, there is advantage in taking it as the point of departure for an analysis of the case for cash payment as the mainstay of the strategy for dealing with redundancy.[1]

European consensus

Three sets of considerations have played a part in bringing about the consensus in Western industrial countries that cash payments are desirable. In the first place there is the community's collective acceptance of its obligation, compounded from social, economic and moral considerations, to protect and sustain members facing exceptional difficulty. If this is characterized as society's obligation to the citizen, then the second set of considerations can be seen as a discharge by firms of their obligation to society. Finally the giving of sums of money by employers to redundant workpeople is a consequence of the relationship between the two groups, each dependent on the other for the operation and success of the enterprise. While in the first two sets of considerations there is an amalgam of social, moral and economic motivations, the case for cash payment arising from the direct employer-to-employee relationship has as its linch-pin arguments based largely on economic rationality.

Without exception industrial countries make provision for income maintenance of people who do not have work. Why communities do this is a complex and interesting question. Central in any explanation is the proposition that industrially advanced Western countries contain work-oriented societies. Since the mid-1930s it has also been a basic premise that governments must manage the economy in such a way as to provide job opportunities for all who wish to work. From a combination of these axioms arises a collective social obligation to the individual member of the community who is without work. Provision is therefore made, by law, to provide money for those who are prepared to work but unable to find it. There are differences between countries in the level of unemployment benefit, the manner of its payment and with regard to the systems used to raise funds to finance the schemes. Nevertheless, unemployment benefit or, for the individual who has had a long spell without work, some form of supplementary income maintenance from the state is universal practice in Western industrial countries. The common characteristic of grant of these forms of income maintenance by the community to the individual is the entitlement of the unemployed person to benefit, irrespective of the cause of his loss of employment. When unemployment occurs as a consequence of the termination of an individual's employment because of a contraction in the demand for labour, in a given firm or enterprise, that individual becomes eligible for unemployment benefit as a normal course of events.

Cash payments to redundant workers are sometimes regarded as an additional layer of income maintenance for the period of unemployment suffered by a redundant man while he is in search of a new job. From that approach cash paid out to redundant workers might be seen as a way of cushioning the discomfort of transitional unemployment. It is of course possible to argue that this justification for cash redundancy payments does not hold in cases where people are able to get new jobs immediately on termination of their previous employment, without an intervening period of unemployment. In Britain this frictionless redeployment took place with 17 – 25 per cent of redundant employees in 1969. In the discussion of the grounds for legislation on redundancy in Britain, the authors of the Bill were quite clear that they were not attempting to supplement the redundant man's income while he was unemployed and in search of a job.

Britain's legislation

Those who sponsored the British statute for redundancy payments stressed the compensatory purpose of associating cash benefits with job termination.[2] Redundancy pay was intended as compensation for loss of security, possible loss of earnings and fringe benefits, as well as the uncertainty associated with, and the anxiety produced by, a compulsory change of jobs. In the Labour Government's view, these losses would be suffered by the individual even if he were to get a job as soon as he was made redundant.

Although the discussion was not conducted in these terms, by implication an important general principle was being propounded. The individual worker was being conceded property rights in his job. Redundancy payments were being offered as something to be set off against the cost of loss of the job as property, and the appreciation of value of that property in terms of promotion prospects for the individual made redundant. Acceptance of this principle raises an important issue: if the worker has property rights in his job, does this constitute the right to a given job at a particular place with a specified enterprise?

Compensation for what?

Cash benefits for redundancy might therefore be seen as safe-guarding the individual's interest by the community's collective action. That action might aim at income maintenance above the level of normal unemployment benefit, or the provision of compensation to the man who has lost property rights in his job. In no sense, of course, are these purposes in conflict. Governmental action, or more general public support for associating schemes of cash payments with the occurrence of redundancy are based on a combination of these aims. Even where, as in Britain, there is explicit legal rejection of redundancy payments being regarded as an element of income maintenance during unemployment, events in the labour market since the 1965 Act lend credibility to the view that recipients of redundancy pay are making use of it to top up their normal unemployment benefit to bring their total income rather closer to the pay achieved while in employment. There is some controversy then as to what community objectives are sought through money payments being associated with redundancy situations. But that controversy is nothing to the difference of views which surrounds a third suggested community aim underlying this kind of provision. To a far greater extent than is the case with the other two objectives, it is a matter of theory and philosophy that cash redundancy benefits are repayment of money deducted by employers from workpeople's wages as a sort of compulsory saving. Inevitably the implications of this kind of proposition are profound but largely untestable by objective criteria. It follows that bodies such as the ILO take particular delight in debating this sort of issue. To the extent that it is at all plausible to argue that cash payments to redundant workers are in some way connected with compulsory saving imposed on all workers, there are, implicit in this, elements of subsidization and transfer payments.

Employers' obligations

The argument put forward so far contains a threefold classification.

One concerns the protection of the individual's rights by the community acting as custodian of generally held social and moral values. The second set of reasons for redundancy payments is embedded in the direct relationship of employer with worker. To separate this wholly from the collective concern of the entire community would be artificial and unrealistic. When a firm is making people redundant because its market is shrinking, it is unlikely to have a lot of spare cash to pay out to employees in recognition of their past services. Redundancies in expanding enterprises are another matter.

Yet curiously, within those limitations, a surprising number of employers in Britain had of their own accord decided to give cash compensation to redundant employees. Length of service has frequently been taken as both indication of loyalty, and the basis for calculation of the amount to be paid. There is probably an overlap here with the concept of compensation for the worker's property right to his job. The longer a person works at his job the more strong, some would maintain, becomes his right to it. In Britain this is recognized by the one piece of union formulated convention about redundancies, which is embodied in the phrase 'last in, first out'. Where, as in the United States, length of service is the chief criterion of promotion in many blue-collar occupations the strength of association between years put in and property rights is of course far greater. So while the employer might voluntarily wish to compensate those who had served him well for a number of years, but whose services he no longer needs, this wish is not independent of society's expectations about the appropriate course of action for him to take.

Views of the community

An interesting but probably unanswerable question concerns the relative weight of the pressures to which the employer responds in offering redundancy money. To say that his motives are not necessarily altruistic is not to suggest that all employers are capitalists, red in tooth and claw, indifferent to the sufferings of their employees. Most plausibly, many of the rules within which relationships between employers and employees are conducted can be seen as attempts on the part of management to fend off community disapproval based on a feeling that the rich and powerful should shoulder their obligations to the underdog.

What the community finds acceptable or repulsive is subject to change. It is now exceedingly difficult to tell why, for instance, when Lancashire cotton mills were being shut down during the 1952 recession, redundancy payments were infrequent and, when made, usually of the order of £1–£2 for each year of service.[3] At that time, despite the textile unions' protests, there was no public outcry. The fact that redundant managers in the industry were receiving 'golden handshakes' particularly points the community's apparent indifference to the impact of redundancy on manual workers. Within about six years things had changed so substantially that the statute promoted by the government to bring about a reorganization of the industry (Cotton Industry Act, 1959) made government grants of new capital to firms conditional on arrangements having been made for 'the payment of compensation in respect of loss of employment due to the elimination of the excess capacity'. That Act went on to require that 'bodies representing the interest of a majority of the persons employed' should have agreed to those arrangements 'so far as they relate to persons whose interests are represented by those bodies'.

That apart, another feature of the Cotton Industry Act relevant here was the requirement arising from the statute that the scheme for compensating Lancashire cotton workers should be financed by a levy on the whole of the cotton industry. There seem to be good grounds for thinking that the recognition by a firm of its obligations to its redundant workers is strongly influenced by the community's views about the social obligations of business enterprises. On top of this, British experience highlights the fact that, unless there is a good deal of prodding by the government as custodian of the whole community's interests, an industry (as distinct from individual firms) is neither willing nor apparently able to devise compensation schemes in common.

Sectional interests

In the third and final category of causes the discharge of obligations associated with redundancy is an interactive matter between those whom English law has described as 'master and servant'. Normally the bulk of rules governing this relationship are not formulated by statute in Western industrial countries. Their basis lies in negotiated agreements made through collective bargaining between organized groups of workpeople and their employers. In the main, these agreements are voluntary, dependent on the good faith of both parties for their performance. Around this core of voluntarily established agreements, there are statutory provisions imposing legal compulsion on firms and employees. These statutory requirements differ from country to country in quantity, and the intensity of their incidence on the voluntarily established agreements between employer and worker. In the terms of the propositions outlined in this chapter, agreements based on collective bargaining can be seen as particular expressions of narrower sectional interests. By contrast, statutory provisions regarding employee-and-employer relationships embody the general interest perceived by the community as a whole. On the issue of cash compensation for redundancy, there is a clear interface between the general/community interest and the sectional interest of workpeople, given form in agreements which they have collectively negotiated with employers.

From the worker's viewpoint, one object of the collectively bargained redundancy agreement is to restrain firms considering slimming their labour force to reduce costs. By ensuring that cash compensation for redundancy is as substantial as unions can make it workpeople are able to prevent firms from regarding the cutback of their payroll as being all gain and costless. This object, and the second aim of negotiated cash compensation for redundancy, is helped along by the size of the sums of money involved. That is to say, if individuals have to settle for the second best, amounting in this context to a loss of job, then it makes sense for them to get as much cash as they can out of it.

Community and sectional interests

At the interface between the community interest and the sectional objective of organized workpeople lies a conflict. So long as the community believes in continuing economic growth, constraints on that objective are undesirable and require removal. From this it follows that it is not in the community's interest that firms retain more people than are really needed. Anything, therefore, which puts a cost disincentive on a firm's ridding itself of surplus manpower thwarts the general interest. The other side is the cost of a multiplicity of individual losses. This may be heavy enough to cause action by workpeople to resist the introduction of new techniques or improved methods of production.

Unless the Government, acting for the community, takes some part in making arrangements for dealing with the displacement and redeployment of manpower which is inseparable from technological change, collectively bargained systems for coping with such situations are likely either to cause industrial disharmony, or to put up obstacles to the modifications of the structure of employment which is a necessary condition for economic growth. This is not to deny a role for direct employer-and-employee collective bargaining in making arrangements for cash compensation when jobs are terminated. What the available evidence appears to show is that neither collectively bargained arrangements on their own, nor statutory arrangements alone, can adequately take the strain and enable the necessary alterations to occur without disruption. In the countries in continental Europe both these elements have been present to a far greater extent than was the case in Britain until the 1965 statue.

Echo of 'surplus value'

Traditionally, collective bargaining of wages and conditions in industry in Western developed countries is part ritual and part rational. Claims from workers' organizations are supported by a mixed bag of arguments, some appealing to equity and social justice, others challenging basic capitalistic principles or using the strength of organized labour to damage the employer and his profitability. Much of this reasoning is inexplicit as well as unclear, and observers of the practice of collective bargaining have tended to be like J. S. Mill rather than Walter Bagehot in failing to distinguish between the 'dignified' and the 'efficient' parts of the process. It is as part of the theatrical nature of collective bargaining in industry, that some of the remaining arguments for cash compensation for redundancies must be seen.

Sometimes it is said that these sums of money are deferred wage payments. On this argument the occasion of redundancy (for reasons that are unclear) is a situation in which wages which were foregone become payable to the man who is about to lose his job. Such substance as there is in this justification of money compensation for redundancy comes from its faint echo of ideas of the class struggle and exploitation of labour. In the arena of collective bargaining this kind of genuflection towards the Marxist pantheon serves much the same purpose as was assigned to the monarchy in Bagehot's view of the way the Constitution works. While the idea of money paid to a redundant man being the restitution to him of part of the surplus value wrung out of his labour by his employer has a nice flourish, neither unions nor employers in Britain are inclined to pay any attention to it.

Still with the smack of the class struggle is the proposition that money paid out by firms to men whose jobs are terminated represents the workers' share in the increased value of the enterprise. Here the argument concedes nothing in its convolution to the medieval schoolmen. The rise in value of the enterprise (of which redundancy pay is the sacked worker's share) might be held to have arisen in two ways. Looking at events in the past, it might be argued that the capital accumulation represented by increased asset value which remains in the firm contains a contribution from the worker who is to be dismissed. To that historical — or future — wealth the worker is entitled to lay a claim.

Some of the arguments for cash compensation for redundancy set out in this chapter are clearly much weaker than others. Where the reasoning appears fanciful, or seems largely a product of wishful thinking, it is not entirely bereft of significance. For Britain it is true that reason, and rational systems for dealing with the contingency, are not outstanding features of redundancy situations. Before the enactment of the 1965 statute, all parties acted as though each occasion of redundancy was the first such event to appear. The fashion, and the norm, was an inversion of the Boy Scout motto to read 'Be unprepared'. A social anthropologist observing customs in British industry might have been tempted to say that advance preparation for dealing with redundancy was deliberately ruled out as a means of propitiating the gods, for fear that to make plans might draw their wrath.

5 Who pays, how much, and to whom in Britain

Having considered the framework of reasoning, such as it is, for redundancy payment, it is appropriate to ask these questions. This chapter will consider the answers that are possible for Britain, where far greater precision is possible about the events following the Redundancy Payments Act of 1965. But even the improved data is not sufficiently extensive or reliable to allow complex statistical manipulation. Between 1958 and 1963 the Ministry of Labour published three commentaries. The 1958 publication came as a result of talks that had been going on in the Minister of Labour's National Joint Advisory Council from 1956. Published under the then trendy title *Positive Employment Policies*[1] the 1958 document was wider in coverage than the two which followed it. *Positive Employment Policies* gave nearly one-fifth of its pages to the subject of redundancy and 'employee security', but the greater part dealt with things like job satisfaction, opportunities for advancement, and the grant of contracts of service to employees. By contrast, the two later publications were wholly taken up by discussion of the circumstances and treatment of redundancy.

To the Ministry of Labour, the 1958 report was a step towards giving wider publicity to the 'initiative of a number of leading British firms' who had developed and applied 'forward-looking employment policies providing full consideration' for workpeople likely to be affected by change. The pronouncements in *Positive Employment Policies*, taken together, provide a useful benchmark for measuring progress since 1958. It is, however, strongly paternalistic and allows for little worker participation in discussions. The tone is very much that management knows best and is the best judge of what needs to be done.

Best British practice

When dealing with cash compensation 'leading British firms' in 1958 repeatedly referred to 'ex gratia' payments. This amounted to wholesale denial of any role for collective bargaining in the determination of the amount of cash made available by the employer to workpeople whom he was making redundant. Firms were not paying out cash because they had been persuaded or coerced into making agreements with workpeople's representatives. If the influence of organized workpeople's pressure is ruled out in that fashion, the explanation for employers' behaviour must be elsewhere. It may be that the employer was responding to a combination of the community expectation of appropriate behaviour and his non-economic bonds with people who had served his enterprise.

The general points of principle about influences shaping the grant of cash compensation to redundant employees at the time *Positive Employment Policies* was published go quite a way to explain the nature of the payments and their size. In considering what follows it must be borne in mind that the examples of redundancy pay contained in *Positive Employment Policies* were not by any means typical of schemes applied by firms in 1958. What proportion of firms applied the best of practice is unknown. But a guess that perhaps 10 per cent led and the remaining 90 per cent were the led, is unlikely to be too wide of the mark. Leading the field among the practitioners of the best is a firm that offered redundancy compensation which would be judged very good even by the demanding standards of the 1970s. But then the fact that this firm was idiosyncratic is established not only by its willingness to pay any worker who was made redundant 'not less than three months' money in lieu of notice' as well as all pension benefits, but also, beyond this, by a general declaration of intent that the handling of redundancy would be 'the subject of full consultation with staff representatives'.

'Ex-gratia' payments

Prevailing best practice was more typically found within a range of which the lowest point was payment of two weeks' wages preceded by two weeks' notice. In the middle of the range of 'best' employers were those who arranged to pay something on top of two weeks' wages. A not uncommon way of topping up was to give another one weeks' pay to workers with 2 − 5 years service. The amount rose by steps reaching 12 weeks' pay for 40 years or more service. It was fairly common too for special provision to be made for employees who were 50 or more years of age. Special consideration for such workers was also built into the other kind of scheme, which offered flat rates as against wage-related payments. An example cited in *Positive Employment Policies* about this type of compensation quotes amounts of £2 per year of employment, when the total length of service was less than five years. Workers who had been employed 5 − 10 years were entitled to 10 shillings more, for each year that they had put in, than their less senior colleagues. The sum rose by 10 shillings for men who had had over ten years' service. For the individual who had been with the firm for 20 years or more, the compensation at £5.10s. was generous, by the then current standards, yielding lump-sum payments of £110 to £247.

It would be wrong to pretend that anything but the crudest of calculations are possible about the level and quantity of redundancy

Table 3 Average severance payments under 178 company policies in 1962, and statutory redundancy payments in 1970.

Number of com-pleted years of service at time of dismissal	3	5	10	15	20	25
1962 severance payment [1]	£15	£24	£47	£65	£89	£109
Range of payment in 1970 [2]	£20–£90	£20–£150	£100–£300	£200–£450	£300–£600	as for 20 years' service

Notes and sources
(1) Calculated from 'Redundancy in Great Britain', Table 5, Ministry of Labour Gazette, February 1963.
(2) Calculated for lowest and highest ages in each length of service group on basis of one week's pay = £20 for male manual workers (see the *Redundancy Payments Scheme,* Appendix C).

compensation in 1958 or thereabouts. But the point of real interest lies on what assessment can be made about the generality of the good compensation schemes of the late 1950s. Despite data limitations it is possible to make some guesses, and, in consequence, comparisons between the late 1950s and the early 1970s.

In 1959 all firms which exceeded the customary two weeks' pay considered the length of service of the man to be made redundant. Emphasis on long service was almost universal. It is highly likely that all men who had worked for over 20 years with a firm would have got the top rate of redundancy compensation. On the evidence of *Positive Employment Policies* firms with the most generous principles of compensation were likely to have paid around 12 weeks' pay: about £150. In 1970, on average, a man with 20 years' service received, under the provisions of the 1965 statute, anything from £300 to £600 depending on his age at the time of redundancy. These were the absolute maxima. The more normal scope of compensation is set out in Table 3.

Cash before and since 1965

This difference in the cash value of compensation for redundancy brought about by the 1965 Act is striking enough. And, although this kind of historical comparison is no measure of the adequacy of redundancy compensation current at any one time, it undeniably is an indicator of progress. Achieved progress is, in fact, much greater than is shown by a comparison concerned wholly with the amount of cash compensation some time before and subsequent to the Act. At least equally important is the universality of coverage brought about by legislation. It still remains worth saying that the kind of provisions examined so far, which existed in 1958, were strictly confined to a minority of firms with 'forward looking' employment policies. Consequently those workpeople who in 1959 got cash payments at a level of between one-quarter and one-half of the 1970 standards of compensation were indeed fortunate and very much a minority.

How was this compensation financed? All payment to redundant workers was a charge on the particular firm. Until the introduction of the statutory scheme there were no general arrangements for diffusing the cost over a base wider than its own income or revenue from the sale of capitalized assets. Considered in this light, it is quite remarkable that any employers committed themselves to paying out any redundancy compensation at all. From a solely economic viewpoint it makes very little sense for employers to pay people with whom their connection is coming to an end. Payment of higher basic wages, or any of a variety of incentive bonuses, to workpeople is practical good sense in so far as there is a connection between such expenditures and higher output and profitability. An employer could gain far more, when slimming his workforce, by giving 'redundancy compensation' to those workers he retained on the payroll than by spending that money on redundant workers. A smaller but much encouraged workforce would be worth the money.

A fair conclusion is that firms which paid redundancy compensation did not do this on the basis of any economic benefit/cost analysis. Nor was this reaction a response to sustained and powerful collective bargaining pressure by trade unions on behalf of organized workpeople. Had there been such pressure, there might have been a wider diffusion of compensation schemes for redundancy among more firms. While that must be a matter of conjecture, there can be no doubt at all that greater trade union involvement would have introduced something nearer to parity in status between employer and employee, and gone some distance towards removing the paternalistic odour from the arrangements that did exist. As firms do not appear, on this reasoning, to have been actuated by undiluted economic self-interest, or by collective bargaining pressures, their behaviour can be explained as a consequence of the acceptance of a sense of social or community obligations. Of course the government was ready to cheer, from the sidelines, any employer who was prepared to look ahead in order to make provision for schemes of redundancy, and to implement them with kindness and charity.

Basis of compensation

Yet what provision existed was unilaterally determined by employers. This was certainly overwhelmingly true up to 1958, and continued to remain applicable over a substantial field of redundancy arrangements between that date and the 1965 legislation. Though the actuality of employer-determined redundancy arrangements seems rather unpalatable from the perspective of more recent years, an impressive tribute to the grasp of issues embodied in those schemes lies in their wholesale incorporation into the Redundancy

Payments Act. In any provision for redundancy compensation there
is in the first place the issue of the basic unit of compensation. In
employer initiated schemes this unit was generally taken as a week's
pay for the worker concerned. Once the issue of the unit of
compensation is determined, it becomes necessary to settle, in some
fashion, the number of such units to be given to each one of the
people whose jobs are to be terminated. Although, for firms
concerned wholly with their own economic self-interest, there was
no evident justification for such action, employer initiated cash
compensation for severance usually tended to work out total
redundancy pay by multiplying a man's terminal weekly wage by his
number of years service. Occasionally a further degree of progression
was built in to enable men with longer service to end up with a bit
more cash than would result from that formula. Above and beyond
this, the redundancy package in the 1950s tended to include a bit
over the odds for older workers who were being discharged. This too
is further illustration of individual employers acting not solely from
economic motivations. No satisfactory scientific explanation has
been offered for these actions of a minority of firms when there was
no compulsion on them to do so.

Quite a lot happened between the publication of *Positive
Employment Policies* in 1958 and the appearance of its successor,
Security and Change, in 1961. In January of that year the Minister
of Labour's National Joint Advisory Council (NJAC) set up a
working party to find out more about what was happening in
industry about redundancy arrangements, and to see what could be
done to help things along. That working party got on with its project
in almost indecent haste, and by July had a report ready which was
the basis of the publication *Security and Change*,[2] which was quite
strikingly different from its predecessor in what it had to say and in
its presentation of information and views. For one thing, *Security
and Change* discussed redundancy not only as an event that
occasionally occurred in industry, but as a phenomenon requiring
detailed analysis with a view to arriving at underlying principles.
What is more, the authors were even prepared to make statements
about desirable norms of behaviour based on their view of the
general principles common to all redundancy situations.

Security and Change also contained a much more professional
attitude to turning up available information. Laudable though this
increased technical competence is, it creates something of a problem

Table 4 Percentage distribution of firms of various sizes[1] by characteristics of their arrangements for redundancy in 1959 and 1962.

Characteristics of company policies	Below 500		500–999		1,000–1,999		2,000–4,999		5,000–9,999		10,000 and above		Total number of firms	
	1959	1962	1959	1962	1959	1962	1959	1962	1959	1962	1959	1962	1959	1962
1 week's notice: no severance pay	67	52	58	34	41	33	37	22	24	38	19	13	106	121
Extra[2] notice: but no severance pay	13	20	18	16	21	21	8	12	19	9	14	8	37	58
No extra notice; but severance pay	18	15	18	34	25	27	31	44	29	38	57	45	63	122
Extra notice and severance pay	2	12	7	15	12	18	23	22	29	16	10	35	30	70
Total number of firms	45	65	45	73	56	84	48	77	21	32	21	40	236	371

Notes and sources

(1) By total number of employees.
(2) This means anything more than 1 week's notice.

Derived from *Security and Change* (Appendix Table C), Ministry of Labour 1961; and 'Redundancy in Great Britain' (Table 3) Ministry of Labour Gazette, February 1963.

for the analysis attempted here. For the 1961 Ministry of Labour study is based on 236 cases, information on which was 'drawn from knowledge of current practices acquired by the Industrial Relations Officers of the Ministry of Labour in the course of their ordinary duties'. Now *Positive Employment Policies* too was a product of information from that same source. Yet the contrast between the two publications is so great that either the Ministry of Labour's Industrial Relations Officers had suddenly had an information explosion on questions of redundancy while they were 'in the course of their ordinary duties', or there must have been a spate of redundancy agreements in industry since the compilation of material for *Positive Employment Policies.*

Security and change

That is one worry. Another is the temptation to use the figures given in the 1961 publication to draw conclusions as though the statistics provided a valid basis for generalizations about what was happening in the economy as a whole. But something can be learnt from the figures, especially if they are set against the statistical information provided by the last of this set of commentaries on redundancy prepared by the Ministry of Labour in 1963.

Table 4 shows the varying characteristics of arrangements made by firms for dealing with redundancy, and a comparison is attempted between the situations in 1959 and three years later. Moreover the table sets out information that can be used to compare the performance of firms grouped by size, as established in terms of the numbers on their payrolls. The characteristics used to classify redundancy arrangements in Table 4 move through a scale. At one end are firms who gave only the minimum of one week's notice and no cash compensation whatsoever. At the other end are the good performers, offering both extra notice and redundancy pay. Making the not unreasonable assumption that the picture given in Table 4 is not simply a statistical illusion of improvement produced as a result of better data collection by Ministry of Labour officials, valuable information can be extracted. In the three years over which the observations were taken, redundancy policies became much more widespread throughout industry by somewhere between 50 to 60 per cent on the 1959 figures.[3]

In 1959 nearly 7 out of 10 firms with less than 500 employees had no provision for doing anything for redundant workpeople beyond one week's notice of dismissal. Now, although the Ministry of Labour did not claim to have anything like a representative sample in its enquiry of firms falling in this size group (or indeed for the others) what is undeniable is that these cases contained some of the best provisions existing in British industry. From that it is quite reasonable to conclude that so far as a generality of firms employing less than 500 people is concerned, cash compensation for redundancy would not have been forthcoming from anything more than, say, 10 per cent of employers in this category. Total employment in firms of this size in 1958 was 3.5 million, and some 90 per cent of these workers were unprotected against redundancy. In reality, that is probably an overestimate of the number enjoying some severance compensation. For, even among the best performers, only 20 per cent made provision for cash compensation, and the bulk of firms where workers (17.8 per cent) would have been entitled to cash would not have got more than one week's notice.

Changes between 1959 and 1962

In 1962 quite sharp changes had occurred within the same category of firms. Over 32 per cent of these employers had decided to give their workpeople more than one week's notice. Most striking among the developments in the three years was the jump in the proportion – from 2 per cent to 12 per cent of these small firms – with redundancy arrangements including both money compensation, and extended periods of notice. This rate of improvement in the availability of the best package for the redundant worker in the smallest firms was nearly matched by alterations of arrangements brought in by employers with payrolls of 10,000 and above. Curiously, although 57 per cent of large firms had arrangements in 1959 for giving cash compensation, only 10 per cent were prepared to pay cash while at the same time offering extended notice of discharge. By 1962 the latter figure had gone up to 35 per cent.

Returning to over-all coverage, and again on the basis of the Ministry of Labour enquiries, an attempt can be made to estimate the number of employees in the private sector covered by redundancy arrangements entitling them to cash compensation. In 1959 a total of 1,105,000 employees in the private sector were known to the Ministry of Labour to be covered by redundancy arrangements of some kind. Of these 668,000, nearly 61 per cent, were covered by provisions which allowed them cash compensation. In 1962 that figure had risen to 74 per cent. 1,161,060 employees out of a total of 1,569,000 covered by redundancy policies were eligible for cash compensation. That, on its own, sounds like a reasonable performance. Yet at a time when about 1.2 million workpeople enjoyed some guarantee of a cash cushion against redundancy, employment in the manufacturing industries alone stood at nearly 9 million. Admittedly a proportion of manufacturing employment was in the public sector, and the cash compensation coverage of redundancy schemes so far discussed relates solely to private firms. But the proportion of manufacturing employment falling within the public sector in 1962 was sufficiently small to be ignored, without damage to this argument. Looked at in that perspective, the availability of cash compensation on redundancy was confined to only about 13 per cent of people working in the manufacturing industries in 1962. This is much more modest than the proportions which came out of the Ministry of Labour's figures.

Rules about sackings

Although coverage of the total number at hazard was still quite small in 1962, the three years from 1959 had seen a good deal of progress in that diffusion of redundancy policies had been going ahead fairly rapidly. And that, in turn, led to more workpeople becoming eligible to some form of cash compensation. Though available information is neither comprehensive nor very detailed, there is enough of it to indicate that the quantitative change was not accompanied by positive developments regarding other provisions for redundancy. Firms' rule-making about things to be done when workpeople would need to be made redundant was, in 1958, almost without exception a subject for unilateral management decision. The 1963 Ministry of Labour enquiry indicates that formal, signed, redundancy agreements between workpeople's representatives and management existed in only 5 per cent of the arrangements known to Whitehall by that time. No more than 18 out of 371 redundancy arrangements had been the subject of any kind of collective bargaining, though employees' representatives had been offered opportunities for consultation in about 40 per cent of the total arrangements existing in private industry.

One conclusion to be drawn is that workpeople's organizations were almost totally indifferent to making arrangements for redundancy. The point has been made that trade unions, certainly at national level, were largely uninterested in the making of redundancy arrangements. How strong this lack of interest was becomes evident from the fact that, even when employers in the private sector were willing to work out some method of giving redundancy compensation, these plans or intentions were not negotiated by representatives of workpeople's organizations. What is more, while individual employers had been getting on with introducing redundancy policies and the habit had been spreading more widely in industry, there was no corresponding shift of interest on the trade union side.

One result was that all redundancy arrangements existing in 1962 were established solely by management fiat, and more than four out of ten of them had no scope for expression of any worker views whatsoever. A possible conclusion is that trade unions tried to get a voice in this process but were denied it by management's obduracy. Given the growth of trade union strength in that period, this is implausible. Set against the Ministry of Labour's conclusions regarding procedures adopted by firms establishing redundancy policies that the pattern in 1962 was 'roughly the same as it was three years ago', the whole notion loses credibility. If the British trade unions had tried to involve themselves between 1959 and 1962, even the staunchest believer in the impotence of trade unions would confess himself bewildered by their ineptitude.

Employers' decisions

No matter how paternalistic their approach, employers who voluntarily set out to establish schemes of cash compensation for redundancy, were acting outside a solely economic set of considerations. Difficult enough as this was for firms, the pressures against fixing anything beyond a minimal scale of cash compensation were clearly substantial.

The level of cash compensation was indeed quite low. Some estimates are possible for 1962. One way of illustrating the change brought about by the Redundancy Payments Act is to take the amount of compensation which a man with 20 years of service received under that statute, and to compare it with the benefit that a similar length of service would have attracted in 1962. Among the voluntary/unilateral redundancy schemes existing in 1962 were 28 that allowed the possibility of cash compensation ranging from £151 to £200 for such employees. In other words, some 8 per cent of firms with redundancy arrangements offered the possibility of a week's pay for each year of service. The key difference in cash compensation for redundancy between the periods separated by the year of legislation of the Redundancy Payments Act lies, of course, in the differing extent of coverage. Before the Act, for the man who had worked 20 years or more with one employer to be eligible for a week's redundancy pay for each year of service would have required great good fortune. Such a man would have had to be among the total of 87,000 who were on the payroll of the 7 per cent of firms with this level of generosity in their severance pay policy. By comparison, in 1969 almost 53,000 people got 20 and more weeks' severance pay.

Incidence of costs

When, in 1961, the Ministry of Labour first tried its hand at something approaching a professional job of investigating what was happening about severance pay in British industry, the best that it could do with regard to the cost structure of schemes was to say 'little is known of how firms finance these payments, other than out of current revenue'. That statement contains some ambiguity. But, translating the St James's Square phraseology, it is possible to arrive at what is meant. So far as enquiries by the Ministry's officials could establish, there were no arrangements for redundancy schemes analogous to those sometimes operated in industry for pensions or sickness, where both employer and employee contributed voluntarily to a fund. Firms which had pension or sickness schemes of this kind customarily established them as an adjunct to the normal process of collective bargaining for wages and conditions. The Ministry of Labour's Industrial Relations Officers were fairly certain that neither employers nor trade unions had approached each other to work out agreements for setting up redundancy compensation funds to be financed by a formula requiring contributions from worker and employer.

Funds for cash compensation clearly had to be found wholly from the resources of individual firms. What then was the cost of redundancy payments in 1959? Any attempt at working out the cost involves a lot of guessing, and the results can only be rough approximations. National Economic Development Council estimates (see Chapter 2) put total annual job losses through redundancy at 200,000 for the period 1958 − 61. It is known, from the 1961 Ministry of Labour enquiry, that 74 per cent of employees of those firms which had redundancy policies were eligible for some severance payment. If all the 200,000 redundancies had occurred in firms with redundancy policies, the number receiving cash compensation could have been as high as 148,000. But that clearly is a serious over-estimate, for the arrangements for redundancy compensation unearthed by Ministry of Labour officials existed solely in the 'forward looking' enterprises.

Once again, an attempt can be made to sketch what could have been happening. For this, it is as well to examine the two official enquiries together, and regard the product of calculations as covering a range of possibilities that may have applied in 1959 as well as 1962. On our estimates firms in the private sector which had redundancy policies in 1959 gave some severance coverage to a total payroll of 1,105,000. Of those, 60 per cent were included in policies containing cash compensation clauses. The manufacturing industries then employed about 8.4 million people. If the total number of workpeople known to be eligible for cash compensation at redundancy is put as a proportion of total employment in all manufacturing industries, the result is 8 per cent. NEDC's estimate of annual redundancies was 200,000. Eight per cent of that is 16,000, and some indication of the total receiving cash redundancy compensation.

The basic figures on which this arithmetic is based are not particularly sound. Additionally the logic of the relationships implied in the calculation is open to question. On the latter point it is not true, for instance, that private-sector employment was identical to total employment in all manufacturing industries taken together. Plenty of other methodological objections can be raised. But as the steps of the reasoning employed here are reasonably clearly set out, without any concealed assumptions, alternative methods might be devised to take the argument further. In 1962 about 13 per cent of all private-sector redundancies were likely to have attracted cash compensation, a total of 26,200 people. Putting all the pieces together then, it looks as if, in the period 1959 to

1962, the number of workpeople who received severance payments each year was about 16,000 – 26,000.

Public sector and cotton textiles

There are two further factors to be taken into account. In the first place there is the specific issue of redundancies in the cotton textile industry associated with the Cotton Industry Act of 1959. If full account could be taken of cash payments made to workers displaced in that industry, the annual totals of people receiving severance pay for the three years to 1962 would be higher than suggested by the previous calculations. A similar consequence flows from the second factor that has been excluded so far. In the period being considered, there were industry-wide redundancy agreements between unions and the public-sector industries of coalmining, gas, electricity, transport as well as atomic energy. In principle it should be possible to make quite precise estimates of numbers of public-sector employees given cash compensation. In fact, and for no impressively convincing reasons, information from these industries is difficult to come by. However, taking everything together, the people in receipt of such compensation probably numbered about 30,000 in 1962.

On the fairly plausible assumption that people with 20 years' continuous employment with one firm were no more frequently made redundant in 1959 – 62 than during 1969 (for which detailed figures are available), some 23 per cent of 200,000 were likely to have been eligible for the maximum cash compensation. But notional eligibility is one thing, getting the cash quite another. Of firms with redundancy policies that had provisions for giving money on termination of employment, only 15 per cent went to the top figure of compensation. At best, therefore, some 7,000 redundant workers in each of the years from 1959 to 1962 would have stood a chance of receiving 20 weeks' pay at a cost of £1,400,000 (taking a week's pay as about £10 for the average worker). That is one layer of the cost of the schemes which were in operation before statutory provision was made in 1965. This piecing together of bits of information can be taken further. The grand total of redundant workers receiving cash benefits was somewhere in the region of 30,000 during the years covered by the Ministry of Labour enquiry. Exclusion of those likely to have been in line for maximum compensation leaves an annual 23,000. For the bulk of these cash compensation was given in terms of relatively few weeks of pay and, although there was a progression connected with the length of service, the effect of this was not big. Probably about 70 per cent got 2 – 3 weeks' pay, the remainder receiving 4 weeks' pay as compensation, giving total amounts of £480,000 and £280,000. Adding on the cost of paying benefits to the long-service people raises the total sum involved to about £2 million. Something approaching one-seventh of this was probably paid by the public sector, and the over-all burden of redundancy payment carried by private industry is likely to have amounted to about £1.8 million.

6 Cash flows from the 1965 Act

Redundancies generate drama, mostly tragedy. The effects of the 1965 Act in Britain were well in keeping with that tradition. It is especially difficult to play down the drama in relation to the change in money expenditure on severance payments in the two periods separated by the 1965 statute. On a basis of crude estimate it appears that not much more than £2 million a year was being paid out by employers to redundant workpeople in the five or so years preceding the severance-payment legislation. Yet in the first full year of implementation of the Act, the amount of money paid out was more than £26 million. Making generous allowance for any possible undervaluation in the £2 million figure for the earlier period, it is still probable that the increase after legislation was at least fivefold.

Figure 1 shows the growth of expenditure since the provisions of the Act have been applied. Table 16 (Appendix) sets out the figures in full.

In 1966 about £26 million was paid out. There was a 90 per cent rise in 1967, taking the total payment to £50 million. It is only the contrast with that explosive rate of growth that makes the 23 per cent rise in 1968 appear modest. Moreover 1969 saw practically no increase at all. That stability was quite temporary. A 17 per cent rise in 1970 was followed by an increase of nearly 49 per cent in 1971 to £108,238,000.

Comparison with ITB grants

In the six years ending 1971, total expenditure arising from the Act amounted to nearly £381 million, or an annual average of £63.5 million. Perspective on these quantities is important and one can

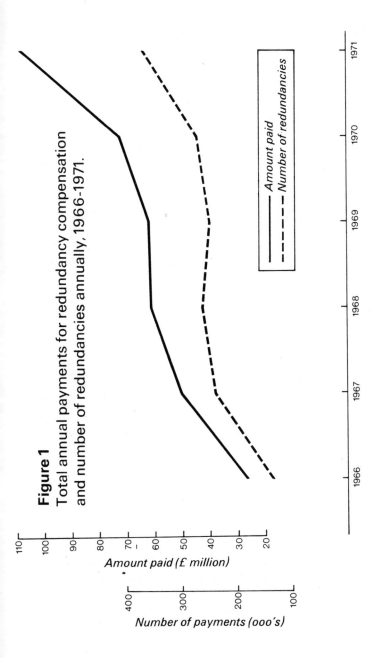

Figure 1
Total annual payments for redundancy compensation and number of redundancies annually, 1966-1971.

compare expenditure on severance payments to other Whitehall generated manpower programmes. In 1968 the Department of Employment was costing the Exchequer £52 million. That figure covers the entire package of manpower programmes and the DE's industrial peace-keeping activities; severance payments alone took £62 million. This disparity has been growing because the total amount paid out for redundancy has risen much more sharply than the DE's expenditure on other labour market activities.[1]

Another obvious basis of comparison is the money being spent on training in industry through the Industrial Training Boards. Gross levy yield from ITB operations since 1968 has been £130 – £170 million. Of this, the net transfer element which constitutes direct financial incentive to firms to increase and improve their training has been about £60 – £70 million. There can be argument about this, but it is not unreasonable to compare that incentive element of the outcome of the operations of the Industrial Training Act with the money going to severance payments. It is an arresting thought that the actual amount changing hands through the activities of the ITBs has been at most some £7 million more annually than the amount being paid to individuals whose jobs have come to an end through no fault of their own.[2]

Raising the money

Except when the employer is insolvent, he pays the redundant workers. How much depends on length of service, income while in employment, and age bracket. The employer is then able to get a lot of it back from the Redundancy Fund established by the 1965 statute. Money for the Fund is raised through contributions paid by employers. These contributions are collected by the Department of Health and Social Security together with the normal National Insurance contributions payable by employers (and workers). Thus the Fund's receipts are derived solely from employers who pay a fixed sum each week for each employee working a minimum 21 hours. Contribution for male employees is higher than for women, in the ratio of two to one. Unlike the graduated element in National Insurance contributions, employer payment to the Redundancy Fund is not related to the level of pay of individual employees. Quantities by source of origin of funds are set out in Table 5.

Money given by employers from their own coffers rose from

Table 5 Sources of funds for severance payments generated in Britain by the Redundancy Payments Act 1965 (£000s; and Index 1969=100).

	1966[1]	1967	1968	1969	1970	1971
Cash flow to redundant workers from their employers	6,606	12,492	15,460	23,307	33,585	51,149
Index (1969=100)	28	54	66	100	144	219
Payments from Redundancy Fund[2]	18,482	35,382	43,789	34,992	33,620	51,149
Index (1969=100)	53	101	125	100	96	146
Special payments from Fund[3]	1,504	2,339	2,588	3,587	5,336	5,940
Index (1969=100)	42	65	72	100	148	165
Total cash flow in severance payments	26,592	50,213	61,837	61,886	72,541	108,238
Index (1969=100)	43	81	100	100	117	175

Notes and sources
(1) For period 6 December 1965 to 31 December 1966.
(2) Rebates received by employers from the Redundancy Fund.
(3) These payments (Section 32 of 1965 Act) are to redundant employees whose employers have not been able to carry out their severance-pay obligations (usually on grounds of insolvency).
Department of Employment Gazettes, various issues.

nearly £7 million in 1966 to about £15 million in the space of two
years. Payments from the Redundancy Fund were at a higher level,
but their rate of growth matched the rate of growth of cash flow
from employers. At this point, it is necessary to take a look at the
provisions governing the distribution of costs of severance payments
of the 1965 statute until they were amended four years later. Before
1969 money had to be found to reimburse employers two-thirds of
their outlay on severance payments for workers in the lower age
bracket (40 years and under). A curious basis of reasoning underlay
the requirement that the Fund would give a bigger slice of
reimbursement for employers' costs of severance payments for
workpeople who were more than 40 years of age. What prompted
that provision is described and analysed in Chapter 8. The important
thing here is that employer outlays in redundancy compensation for
older workers attracted reimbursement at a rate of about seven-
ninths of the cost incurred.

From Table 5, it is easier to work things out by looking at the
events of 1966–68 separately from those occurring since 1969. For
each year to 1969 cash flow from the Redundancy Fund to
employers with redundancies was very nearly three times the value
of severance payments borne by the employers. Seen in another
way, an employer handing over the statutory severance pay in this
period had to dip into his own pocket for about 35 per cent of the
total amount.

Insolvency payments

It follows that, most of the time, two channels of money flow
converge to make up the compensation. If an employer becomes
insolvent, the worker does not lose his right to severance pay, and
the money for this comes entirely from the Fund (see item 'Special
payments from Fund', Table 5). One thing to notice is that this is
the only set of circumstances in which the redundant worker has
direct experience of people and organizations, other than his own
employer, connected with the statutory severance-pay arrangements
by contact with the DE's local office.

More from individual employers

A big change came three years from the start of the scheme. The first two rows in Table 5 show quite clearly the effect of what was done. There was a new parity between the Fund and the employer liquidating a redundancy. Starting with the first full financial year after the amending legislation[3] the Fund's contribution to the severance payment package was reduced. For three years after the start of the scheme the Fund carried the bigger share of the cost of redundancies, with the smaller share borne by individual employers. That principle of joint financing remained unchanged. Previously the Fund had reimbursed the employer at two rates. The choice between the rates was determined by the age of the man or woman to whom severance payment was made. There were only two rates simply because the lump-sum calculation was made by drawing a line above age 40. Anyone who had years of service after that age became entitled to one and a half week's pay for each year. The cost of that higher rate of compensation was split 78 per cent to the Fund, and 22 per cent to the employer. For people aged 40 and below, the split was 67 per cent to the Fund, with the employer paying the remaining 33 per cent. It all became much simpler after the amending legislation. The Fund simply matched the employer £ for £ for the whole of the compensation bill for redundant employees, irrespective of their age.

Criteria for calculating the cash compensation for redundant workers remained unchanged. The above 41 age group remained entitled to one and a half week's pay for each year of service. The cost displacement from the Fund to the employer was not related to one particular age category. But for reasons explored later the transfer of the weight of incidence on to the employer was higher for the older than the younger beneficiaries. Issues raised by the amending legislation in 1969 were more than mere detail about the financing of the scheme.

Drain on the Fund

One, and very probably the central, reason for reorganizing the finances of the scheme was that the Fund kept running out of cash. True, a good deal was said about changes in the method of financing helping to prevent things which were undesirable as a matter of philosophy and principle. This was chiefly to do with fears that the original formula of cost sharing between employer and the Fund was providing an incentive for older people to be made redundant. This is a complex and fundamental question, and it is considered more fully in Chapter 7. What remains undeniable is that, except for the period immediately following the 1969 changes, the Fund was persistently in deficit. There is little ground for surprise that this should have happened. When the original contributions were fixed at 2d for each female employee and 5d for each male, no one had anything but the vaguest idea of how much money the Fund would need to pay out, because there were no reliable figures of the then current level of, or future projections for, involuntary job severances.

Within twelve months of the start of the scheme the Fund was £1 million in the red.

In common with practically every previous incumbent of that post, the Minister of Labour at that time was strong on integrity. When he explained that it would be wrong to clear the deficit by letting the Fund borrow from the Treasury, Parliament did not question this. It was, in the official view, essential to increase revenue to the Redundancy Fund to clear the deficit. With the increase he was seeking, the Minister was confident that not only would the Fund be back in the black, but it would also be able to build up reserves. Far from the deficit being wiped off, the Minister had to get authority to increase the Fund's borrowing limit by 50 per cent to £12 million, no more than eight months after his confident statement. That was just as well, for the year 1967 ended with the Redundancy Fund owing the Treasury £7 million.

Borrowing for the Fund

Meanwhile the people at the Department of Employment and Productivity were doing very well at learning by doing. They had got to the point where they could recognize, at a fairly early stage, when a deficit was brewing. And 1968 was full of activity. In April the borrowing limit was raised to £15 million. But very soon after that DEP officials were sure that that ceiling would not accommodate the deficit to come, and in August the limit was raised to £20 million. For good measure, Statutory Instrument 1968/1264, laid before Parliament in August 1968, ordered 'in respect of any contribution week beginning on or after 2 September 1968 Section 27 (2) of the Redundancy Payments Act 1965 shall have effect as if for the sums therein specified there were substituted respectively the sum of one shilling and three pence in the case of a man and of sevenpence in the case of a woman'.

Between the assurance in 1966 that doubling of the contributions to the Fund would expunge the deficit as well as allowing something to be put to reserves, and SI 1968/1264, which hoisted contributions to 1/3d for men (and 7d for women), much had altered. It did not, for instance, matter greatly that the Minister of Labour's hopeful predictions had turned out to be hopelessly wrong. Not only had that minister disappeared from the scene, his ministry too had changed to the spanking new Department of Employment and Productivity, with nothing less than a First Secretary of State at its head. Given the rules of the game, no politician would seriously expect the new First Secretary to have any recollection of the things said by her predecessor. In any case it was just as well that both contributions and the borrowing limit were raised, for despite the increased revenue (in the last four months of the year) 1968 was a record year for the Redundancy Fund — the deficit was £16 million, easily more than twice the previous year's amount.

Why were the sums wrong?

But still, it was all getting rather embarrassing. Why did Whitehall keep undershooting in its estimates of likely outgoings from the Fund? Right at the start, there was not much information to go on. But getting the sums wrong to the extent of £16 million three full years after the scheme started is the kind of arithmetic usually attributed only to the avionics industry. The debate on the Act 'to reduce the rebates payable under Section 30 of the Redundancy Payments Act 1965' was addressed in part to that question. Explanations offered on behalf of the DEP had a dejected air about them.[4] Prediction, it was argued, of the demands on the Fund was bound to be approximate. There were a lot of variables. Neither the age, the length of service nor the take-home pay of people likely to have their jobs terminated could be worked out with any accuracy in advance of the event. Having said that, the junior minister argued that the chief cause of the high expenditure was not so much a rise in the number of payments, but a growth of their average size. This was clearly something new, as it did not appear in the explanation offered three years earlier by the Minister of Labour, who by striking contrast based his case on the quantity of claims having turned out to be nearly 25 per cent greater than had been thought likely. So here, perhaps, a change of some significance had occurred.

Starting from the proposition that the root of the Fund's troubles lay in the rising average size rather than the over-all quantity of payments, the Government could see continuing difficulties in prospect. One factor in the growing size of the average redundancy lump-sum compensation was the rise in pay since the start of the scheme. Then again, in the Government's view, the amounts paid were boosted by the changing age composition of those whose jobs were being terminated. All of that could be, or might not be, valid. But there was no denying that the £16 million owed to the National Loans Fund had to be paid back somehow. Unless something pretty drastic was done there was not much hope of the Redundancy Fund having enough income to pay off that debt.

A 200 per cent (250 per cent for women) increase in contributions within the span of three years is drastic by any standards. There had until then been surprisingly little fuss from the employers about increases in contributions to the Fund but that could not be expected to go on indefinitely. It was decided in Whitehall to go for a reduction in outflow from the fund by means of a cutback of the rebate.

Size and composition of redundancies

Can anything sensible be said about the size and composition of redundancies reflected in the cash flows discussed so far? Is, in other words, the nature of the beast fully recognized? And of course, there is the less important question about whether or not explanations offered by ministers were well founded and consistent taken over the life span of the scheme. It will be necessary to return to the aggregate figures in Table 5 to point to more recent developments. That will help in appraising the success of the 1969 measures. One aim was to alter the age distribution of redundancy. Whether the underlying aim was to reduce the load carried by the Redundancy Fund, or there were wider, more socially significant considerations, is not immediately material.

Indexes of redundancies by age groups are given at Table 9 (in Chapter 7). More information on redundancies analysed by age can be found in Table 10 and Table 20 (Appendix). The one thing clearly shown by Table 9 is the absence of any marked changes in the distribution by age of the people whose jobs were being terminated because of redundancy. Take, for instance, the 50 – 59 age group. For 1966, as a whole, redundant men of that age represented 26.1 per cent of the total male redundancies paid for under the statutory scheme. In the year that followed, that group's share fell to 25.3 per cent. Twelve months later the situation was practically unchanged (at 25.4 per cent), and the 1969 proportion was identical with the previous year. There was a 0.1 per cent rise for 1970, but a more substantial change in 1971 brought the proportion down to 24.5 per cent. If the figures are taken quarter by quarter, the range of fluctuation becomes a little greater. The index for the 40 – 49 age group did not rise either (see Figure 3). Only for the oldest, the 60 – 64 age group, was the index above expectation.

The over-40s

None of this is strong enough (see fuller analysis in Chapter 7) to bear out the proposition that in the second and third years of the scheme a mutation had occurred, producing more redundancies among older workpeople. Before the 1969 changes, what mattered most to the cost structure of the scheme were the totals on each side of the dividing age of 41 years. Table 9 (and related tables in Chapter 7) attempts the most usable age-group distribution that the data allows. Starting from the point that anyone over 41 belongs to the older, and, from the point of view of the fund, more costly category of redundancies, the important thing to do is to establish the change in the proportions of the costly and the less costly groups. (Because of the data, the closest possible approach to that categorization is to take 40 as the dividing age.) In 1966, 67 per cent of all redundancies occurred among people who were 40 years and more in age. In 1968, when the Government was claiming that the incidence of redundancy among older people was going up, the proportion of redundancies suffered by the over-40s had risen to 68 per cent. That a change from 67 per cent to 68 per cent is a rise cannot be denied. Yet, it is hardly enough of a change to provide the foundation for the view that the uneven and discriminatory incidence of redundancies among older people needed to attract greater concern in 1968 than in the preceding two years of the working of the statutory scheme.

It seems, from the analysis so far, that there was little basis for the assertion in 1969 that developments over the previous four years had been such as to arouse special concern about protecting the older age groups against redundancy. That is not, of course, to say that the ratio of older to younger workers, broadly unchanged though it was, was therefore a reasonable and acceptable one. If the official argument had been that the number in the over-41 category was too large, and the financial arrangements of the scheme needed to be changed to reduce that figure, that would have made good sense. Quite big economic and social policy questions are raised by that issue as is shown by the discussion of German views in Chapter 13. But the argument that the scheme was having a discriminatory and differential impact on the older age group, and more particularly, that the intensity of this difference was growing, is not sustained by the evidence except for the 60 – 64 group. A great deal was said about the undesirability of the older worker taking the main brunt of redundancies. For instance, on behalf of the Government, it was argued that the higher level of benefit to which the individual in the over-41 category is entitled, induces him to volunteer for redundancy whenever the opportunity becomes available.

Protection for older workers

In proposing amendment of the system of financing in 1969, the Government spokesman strongly argued that it was undesirable to allow, if not encourage, the older group to behave in that way. For it is more difficult to find a suitable job for the older man than for his younger colleague. Moreover the older man accepts training less readily. But with the financial arrangements as originally written into the scheme, an employer with the need to reduce his work force had, it was argued, no reason to reject the older worker's offer of voluntary inclusion among those who had to be dismissed. While the individual was attracted, on this argument, by the extra money, the employer suffered no loss. The cost of the extra payment for the older worker came entirely from the Fund, and everyone was apparently maximizing his satisfaction. Though the point was never actually expressed in official views, there was a presumption that employers usually found it quite useful to reduce the age of their labour force. There is no direct evidence about that, but even at best the employer, so it was suggested, had nothing to lose if the older workers on his payroll wanted to take their redundancy pay and go.

At issue was the object of reducing the older worker's propensity to accept redundancy. One logical way of doing that was to make it less worthwhile for that worker to accept redundancy. That could have been done by reducing or eliminating the difference in the level of redundancy compensation received by people who fell on different sides of the age dividing line. The CBI did indeed propose that the age limit for the higher compensation level should be put up by 10 years so that only those aged 51 (and over) would have an entitlement to it. That of course would not have contributed to preventing the older workers bearing the brunt of redundancies. But it would have protected the Fund, and reduced the cost to industry of the statutory redundancy scheme.

Shifting the cost

What the Government proposed was, on the face of it, exceedingly ingenious. Instead of operating a levy and rebate arrangement, under which at best the employer was thought to be indifferent about whether the older or the younger members of his labour force were to be made redundant, the modified pattern of financing was intended to build in a disincentive to the dismissal of older workers. Thus the higher levels of benefit to which people over 41 were entitled were preserved. In turn, their propensity to volunteer for redundancy remained unchanged. But the employer was expected to give up his neutral posture, and think twice before terminating the older worker's employment. Instead of the older redundant worker's higher benefit level being costless to the employer directly involved, it became a significant addition to his total redundancy bill. Now, whatever the truth and the merit of the official reasoning that the change in the financial structure of the scheme had as one of its principal objects the deceleration of redundancies in the older age group, that claim at least establishes a basis for assessing the success of the measure in hitting its target.

Calculated costs to employers of redundancies in four age groups are given in Table 17 (Appendix). A high degree of actuarial or statistical accuracy cannot be claimed for these figures. They do, nevertheless, indicate the pattern and are estimates only because the figures published by the DE are of arithmetical averages of redundancy compensation derived by dividing the total number of payments into the aggregate cash flow from both the Fund and employer. There is no official information about the volume of compensation by age of recipient. The method of estimation is given in the notes to Table 17. Until 1969 the employer paid only 22 per cent of the lump-sum conpensation for years of service over 41 years of age, while workpeople aged 41 and below, took 33 per cent of their lump sum compensation from their employer.

With the Redundancy Rebates Act the Fund and employer took equal shares of the cash compensation, irrespective of the age of the redundant worker. The calculated information is set out for four separate age groups in Table 17 (Appendix). The principle of what is to be discussed now applies equally to men and women. Yet, almost without exception, even when they have service of equal length, the men receive higher compensation. That difference arises simply from the direct connection between men and women's normal pay and the level of the statutory redundancy compensation, and the fact that women generally receive lower pay than men.

Amounts of compensation

On our calculations (see Table 18, Appendix), at 1968 pay levels the average lump sum paid for the youngest (aged 40 and under) redundancies was £113.40 for men. The sum given in compensation to the 41 – 50 group was £249.60. For the next group (51 – 60) the cash payment on average worked out at £387.20; and the oldest and longest-serving people (61 – 64 years of age) averaged £429.30. Within that range of total payments, the cost to the particular employer involved in the redundancy varied from £37.80 to £95.40, (see Table 17, Appendix). The cost, in other words, was paid 33 per cent by the employer for the younger redundancies, and 22 per cent for the older ones; the rest was paid by the Fund.

Turning to the changes brought about by the 1969 amendment to the financing of the scheme, it is best to keep off the statistics for that particular year, because of the complications caused by the application of the old set of rules for one part of the year, and the new set for the other part. On 1970 wage levels, the new distribution of burden sharing between the Fund and the employer produces considerable differences from the quantities and ratios of the earlier periods. Total payment to the average redundant worker 40 years of age and under rose by some £16 over the 1968 level to £129.00. For other age groups too the amount of compensation rose by percentages not very different from that applying to the lowest age category. In terms of the actual sums of money, however, the increases for the older age groups were substantially different from the £16 for people of 40 and under. That change in compensation for the different age categories between 1968 and 1970 was solely the result of rises in pay. But the object, it will be recalled, of the 1969 measure was to put an extra load on the employer with a redundancy to deal with.

The employers' share

The first thing to note is that even with the original financial arrangements, except in very specific and limited circumstances, making the older employee redundant was not less costly for the employer than the termination of employment of a younger worker. On average, the under-41 age group were likely to have had 6 years' service with their current employer, as against the 11, 15, and 18 years which were the averages for the other three age groups. So the probability was quite high that the older the man, the longer he would have been with his employer, and the greater the sum of money that would become due to him on termination of his employment. Even allowing for the fact that the employer got 78 per cent rebate for pay related to the individual's years of work after the age of 41, the actual cash cost falling upon the employer could have been anything between 47 and 156 per cent higher for employees above 41 than for redundancies in the lower age group.

On this basis at a minimum, there was something of a misconception in the reasoning put forward in 1969 when the argument was deployed for changing the basis of finance of the redundancy scheme. It is already evident that, far from the employer being unaffected by the age category of the employee who was to be made redundant, under the original provisions of the scheme, the average employee in the 41 – 50 age group cost him 47 per cent more in redundancy pay than one in the lowest age group. An employee in the 51 – 60 bracket cost the employer 128 per cent more in redundancy pay than a man under 40 would have done. For the oldest age group, the rise in the employer's cost is even more striking. To make the average 61 – 64 year old worker redundant cost the employer well over two-and-a-half times more than for a worker of 40 or less. True, the actual money difference between

£37.80 and £86, or even £95.40 is not enormous. Neither is it chicken feed, especially if the redundancy is a sizable one and hundreds of people are involved.

Ostensibly the purpose of the change in the cost split was to make the employer less ready to make the older employees the prime choice when the labour force had to be reduced. And, as we saw earlier, the official view was that this change would come about if employers found it more expensive to dismiss older workers than their younger colleagues. From the figures looked at so far, it is quite clear that right from the start of the scheme, the cost to the employer has been greater the higher the age of the worker made redundant. By cutting back the rebate from 78 per cent to 50 per cent the intention was to widen the cost differential even further and this was achieved by the 1969 measure. Had that been the sole objective the relative costliness of redundancies in the older group could have been made considerably greater. For if that 50 per cent rebate for the older group had been yoked to the original 67 per cent repayment by the Fund for severance payments to the 40 and below category, then the financial disincentive to making the older group redundant would have become still more substantial.

In the event, the Redundancy Rebates Act reduced the payment from the Fund not only for the older age group, but for the lower end of the age range too. This lends support to the view that off-loading the burden from the Fund to the employer implicated in a redundancy was as much motivated by the wish to protect the Fund, as by the more explicitly stated objective of protecting the interest of the more vulnerable older worker. A big cost displacement did nevertheless come about from the new burden-sharing arrangements. Where previously a redundancy in the 41 – 50 age group was only 47 per cent dearer to the employer than in the youngest age group, with the new provisions the difference was nearly 121 per cent. Moving up the age scale to the 51 – 60 group, the new cost differential was about 245 per cent by contrast with the original difference of 128 per cent. For the oldest of the age brackets the cost displacement effect was larger still. In 1970 the cost to the individual employer of a redundancy in 61 – 64 group was very nearly three times the amount he would need to pay in severance compensation to an employee aged 40 or less.

Aggregate costs

All this is based on rough estimates. After acknowledging that, the evidence is still powerful in suggesting that if employers had been over keen to make older employees the victims of redundancy, their reasons for doing so could not have been based solely on considerations of financial gain or loss. And if employers were originally holding on to younger workers even though it was dearer to dismiss the older employees, a further widening of the cost disadvantage might not be enough to shift the balance in favour of retaining the older employee. That is one criticism that can be made of manipulating financial costs to influence the categories of manpower entering the stream of redundancies. There is another, equally big, criticism to be made about that kind of reasoning. This time it is a question of coming at it from the aggregate, or over-all cost viewpoint.

In 1968 the Department of Employment and Productivity made a detailed large-scale survey of the total labour costs of employers in Great Britain for the whole of manufacturing industry. Other sectors were also comprehensively covered with the exception of agriculture, forestry and fishing, the distributive trades, and the professional and scientific services. Information was collected from employers under nine categories of labour costs. Provision for a redundancy was one of the items. Some of the others, apart from wages and salaries, were: costs of vocational training; payment in kind; contributions for the selective employment tax; and the costs of establishing funds for private social-welfare payments. Assessment of the validity of information obtained from the survey can be made on the following criteria. Of the firms approached in manufacturing industry, 86 per cent returned usable information. An identical response rate was obtained from informants in the non-manufacturing sector. In all about 46 per cent of those employed in manufacturing and non-manufacturing activities were covered by the survey.

There is quite a lot of new and interesting information about costs of redundancy which can be got from the 1968 survey. Estimates can be made from it about expenditure on provision for redundancy outside the statutory scheme. For the present, the most interesting thing is the use that can be made of the survey to illuminate the discussion about providing a cost disincentive to

Table 6 Labour costs, wages and salaries and cost of provision for redundancy by employers in 1968.

Industry group	Average labour cost per employee[1] (£s)	Average wage and salary per employee[2] (£s)	Average provision for redundancy per employee[3] (£s)	Employees in employment[4] (000s)	Total labour costs (£000s)	Total wages and salaries (£000s)	Total provision for redundancy (£000s)
Manufacturing industries	1132.9	1034.5	4.0	8613.1	9,757,781	8,910,252	34,452
Mining and quarrying	1256.9	1040.7	12.4	485.9	610,728	505,676	6,025
Construction	1359.6	1192.5	3.2	1505.8	2,047,286	1,795,667	4,819
Gas, electricity and water	1296.0	1129.5	4.7	412.5	534,600	465,919	1,939
Transport and communication	1304.6	1144.2	7.1	1584.1	2,066,617	1,812,527	11,247
Insurance and banking	1424.5	1078.3	2.1	665.0	947,293	717,070	1,397

Notes and sources

(1) Department of Employment Gazette; August 1970; Labour costs in Great Britain 1968; Table 1; average annual expenditure per employee by industry.
(2) As above.
(3) As above; the net cost i.e. statutory contributions made under the 1965 Act plus statutory and voluntary payments to employees less rebates under the Act.
    British Labour Statistics, Historical Abstract; Table 135;
(4) Some industry groups were not included in the 1968 labour costs survey; for example distributive trades and professional and scientific services, agriculture, forestry and fishing. The non-industrial civil service has also been excluded from the calculations.

employers who might otherwise choose to make older workers redundant in preference to their younger employees.

In Table 6 the survey findings for industry groups have been combined with the size of their payroll, and from that, the volume of provision for redundancy made by employers in 1968 has been calculated. For all the sectors of activity covered in the survey taken together, the total volume of funds for financing redundancies was £59,879,000 (see also Table 7).

That figure does not give the full expenditure on redundancy by employers in the whole economy. Earlier on, in Table 5, we saw that the total cash flow in severance payments in 1968 was £61,837,000. This figure too does not give a full account of the financial costs of redundancy in 1968. Here the incompleteness arises from the absence of information about voluntary cash flows that were taking place outside the statutory framework of the 1965 Act. The estimate from the labour cost survey made by the Department of Employment and Productivity, on the other hand, suffers from the

Table 7 Estimates of costs of redundancy payments in 1968 (£000s).

Voluntary and statutory expenditure on redundancy by principal industry sectors [1]	59,879
All employers' contributions to Redundancy Fund under statutory scheme [2]	39,274
All employers' payments to redundant workers under statutory scheme [3]	15,460
Total statutory charge upon employers	54,734
Voluntary expenditure on redundancy by employers	5,145

Notes and sources
(1)   All industries except agriculture, forestry and fishing, distributive trades, and professional and scientific services.
(2)   Derived from Redundancy Fund annual accounts.
(3)   Calculated from information provided by Department of Employment.

weakness that it has neither statutory nor voluntary cost information for several sectors of activity. In Table 7 parts of the two sets
of information are brought together.

The second row gives the sum of money contributed, under
statutory requirement, by all employers. The coverage of the 1965
Act is comprehensive: all employees except those in share fishing, in
the docks, and the non-industrial employees of the Crown, come
within its ambit. The third row in Table 7 also has the same wide
coverage. This figure represents the irrecoverable sum of money paid
out by employers who had redundancies in 1968. Row four shows
the total statutory charge upon all employers' wage bills taken
together, and that amounts to £54,734,000. Yet, by reference to
Table 5, it is clear that the total statute-generated flow (excluding
special payments from the Fund) is £59,249,000. Reconciling these
two figures is not difficult. In fact, the statutory scheme in 1968 was
paying out more than it was receiving from employers' contributions. The deficit was being made up by borrowing from the
National Loans Fund.

Outflows from the Fund

That shortfall of income to expenditure still does not give the
complete picture of the financial transactions arising from the
statutory redundancy payment scheme. The point to be firmly
borne in mind is that, in principle, the scheme is self-financing. All
payments made within the statutory redundancy compensation
system have to be financed by employers. There have been lags in
closing the gap between the principle of the scheme and real events.
Just as the gap between the outgoing of £59.3 million and the
income of £54.7 million, in 1968, was covered by loans from the
exchequer, an additional £2.6 million given in compensation to
workers whose own employers had defaulted on their statutory
obligation also had to be borrowed from the National Loans Fund.
In 1968, the statutory scheme was in debt to the government to the
extent of £7.2 million.

We know (see Table 5) that in 1968 there was a total cash flow in
statutory redundancy payments of £61.8 million. From Table 7 we
have a possible voluntary expenditure of £5.1 million by employers
on compensating people who had been made redundant in 1968.
Assuming for the moment that it is a fairly plausible figure, it is

possible to add it to the total statutory cash flow, and to arrive at the figure of £66.9 million as the grand total of cash spent in severance compensation in the course of 1968. It is almost certain that this figure is not too far off the mark. Some uncertainty, of course, attaches to the £5.1 million voluntary expenditure, because the figures come from two sources with two differing ranges of coverage. What this amounts to is that the top row of Table 7 gives the total voluntary and statutory charge, not for *all* industry groups, but for the principal ones. But the second row of the table gives the value of the levy raised from all industry groups, including the ones which were omitted when the figure for the top row was being calculated. There is, that is to say, an underestimation of the cost voluntarily incurred by employers, in the economy as a whole, in providing something over the statutorily established severance payments to employees.

There are good reasons for believing that the extent of under-estimating is not big. For one thing, neither agriculture nor distributive trades (with one or two chain stores as striking exceptions) are particularly distinguished by their concern for the well-being of their employees. It is unlikely that they would have spent enough in voluntary redundancy schemes to make any difference to the total estimated here.

Professional and scientific services, the other excluded category, is a different case. All the available evidence points to a much higher proportionate rate of compensation for white collar employees than for manual workers. Although there has been a recent growth in re-dundancies among professional and scientific personnel, this is not likely to have been sufficient to make a really sizeable difference to employers' costs in voluntary redundancy compensation. Moreover the actual rise is considerably less than might be thought from the amount of attention this kind of redundancy tends to get from the media. More specifically, regarding the cost estimate for 1968, 'executive' redundancies still lay in the future.

That is one side of the argument for the view that employers' non-statutory costs for redundancy pay in 1968 are not underestimated in Table 7. Another strand of this argument concerns the fact that the really big spenders, when it comes to giving compensation over the legal minimum, were the National Coal Board and British Rail. More recently, the docks have joined this category. Once again, this does not affect the estimates in the table, as the scheme in the docks did not get into full swing until 1969. Quite evidently, some of this reasoning suggests that employers' voluntary spending on redundancy compensation might have been higher than estimated in the table, and against that, other parts of the argument suggest the opposite view. On balance, it is quite safe to return to the conclusion that the figure of £5.1 million fairly indicates the extra-statutory severance compensation paid by firms to redundant employees.

Effect of new formula on labour costs

Table 8 looks at employers' contributions to the statutory redundancy payments scheme in terms of the cost-sharing formula as it was before the 1969 change and as it was affected by that modification.

Once again, it should be noted that the labour costs, as well as the wages and salaries given, understate volume of expenditure on these items in the whole economy. And that is because certain, minor, industry groups were omitted from the Department of Employment and Productivity survey. It follows that the employers' share of the statutory redundancy payment, when put as a proportion of total labour costs/total wages and salaries, gives a resulting percentage which is an overstatement. With that background, the figures in Table 8 are illuminating.

What is at issue, is the balance between the cash that the employer has to pay out of his own coffers, and the amount that he receives from the Redundancy Fund for compensating workpeople whose jobs are being terminated. Before the change brought in by the 1969 Act, the direct employer payment, in the aggregate, amounted to 0.097 per cent of total labour costs in the group of industries included in Table 8. Or, as a proportion of total wages and salaries, the employers' direct share of the statutory redundancy payment stood at 0.109 per cent. In 1969 there was a shifting of a bigger share of the cost away from the Redundancy Fund, and on to the individual employers making workpeople redundant. Consequently, if the cost-sharing formula established in 1969 is applied to the 1968 data, there is a rise in the employers' share of about £14 million for that year – an increase of something approaching 92 per cent. At first sight, that appears as a pretty impressive piece of burden shifting. A quick look at Table 8 shows that even with this altered cost distribution, employers' non-recoverable costs on

Table 8 Employers' total costs as affected by 1969 changes of method of financing the Statutory Redundancy Payments (SRP) Scheme.

Total labour costs in 1968 (£000s) [1]	15,964,304
Total wages and salaries in 1968 (£000s) [1]	14,207,110
Employers' actual share of SRP in 1968 (£000s) [2]	15,460
Employers' actual share as percentage of	
(a) total labour costs	0.097
(b) total wages and salaries	0.109
Employers', estimated, share of SRP in 1968 applying reduced (1969) level of rebates (£000s) [3]	29,625
Employers', estimated, share assuming reduced rebates as percentage of	
(a) total labour costs	0.186
(b) total wages and salaries	0.209

Notes and sources

(1)   See Table 6.

(2)   Calculated from Department of Employment figures.

(3)   Estimates were calculated by assuming that the reduced level of rebates of 50 per cent was applied in 1968. The employer would have paid half of the cash flow of the statutory scheme in that year (see Table 5).

severance payments rose to only 0.186 per cent of labour costs, and
0.209 per cent of wages and salaries.

Something quite important is established by all this rattling of
quantities. Since 1969 sums of money which individual employers
have to pay out to workpeople whose employment they are
terminating could, in some cases, be a substantial burden on
particular firms. But for all employers taken together (in the not
untypical year 1968) the extent of the shift of costs lay between
0.097 and 0.186 per cent of their total wage costs. Furthermore,
because of the exclusion of certain industry sectors from the
computation of the total wage costs, even these proportions are
higher than was the case in reality. The policy makers were aiming to
bring about a shift in the behaviour of employers by applying a
financial deterrent. The weight of this deterrent can be judged from
Table 8. Under the new cost-sharing dispensation, the cost incidence
on employers rose to a full one-tenth of 1 per cent (and something
on top of that), but still remained short of one-fifth of 1 per cent.
Whether this degree of change is sufficient to cause a shift of
behaviour among employers in general is very doubtful.

A matter of redistribution

What general principles are illustrated by the detailed analysis of
information attempted here? The basic foundation of the financing
system for the British redundancy payments scheme can be, and is,
frequently overlooked. Though administered by Whitehall, the 1969
statutory scheme is financed wholly by what amounts to a levy or
impost on, and only on, those who employ other people. Although,
since 1966, the Department of Employment has handled £381
million of redundancy money, not a single penny of it has come
from general taxation. Even the cost incurred by the Department of
Health and Social Security in raising the levy, as well as the
administrative costs of the Department of Employment and Productivity (not to mention the Paymaster General, the Department of
the Environment, HM Stationery Office, Treasury and several other
Departments who had small pickings) were paid for by the people
falling within the levy base – that is to say, all employers who come
within the scope of the statute.

All costs of redundancy compensation in Britain are costs to
industry alone. It is the employer *qua* employer who is bearing the

financial cost of compensating workers whose jobs are terminated through no fault of their own. In this and other respects, there is a good deal of similarity between the methods of finance of the statutory redundancy scheme, and of the industrial training system established by legislation in 1964.

Legislation about training in 1964 established the Industrial Training Boards and authorized them to raise levies from firms falling within their industrial catchment area.[5] Industrial Training Boards (ITBs) are by statute composed of employers, trade unionists and people representative of education and training. Final administrative and financial responsibility is in the hands of the Secretary of State for Employment, who ultimately decides the membership of the ITBs. Once established, the ITBs are charged to raise money from their industries to be used as an incentive for increasing the quantity and raising the quality of training among the firms that come 'within their scope'. Each ITB has until 1972, had the right to decide the level of the levy it will raise from its constituents. On grounds of constitutional propriety, and because final responsibility lies with him, the Minister has a final say about the levy proposed by each ITB. Effectively, this is a long-stop function, which enables him to exercise a check on ITB money-raising activities. In actual fact, the Department of Employment has had the ITBs on loose reins. For all practical purposes, the Boards have been free up to 1972 to determine how much money they would collect by levying their member firms.

Analogy with ITBs

The 1969 Act made raising the money for boosting training a decentralized and participative activity for industry. In structure and spirit the operation was distanced from Whitehall. It was a complex machine that the 1964 Act established for training in Britain. This complexity, of which the mechanism for raising levies and paying back grants was a central element, arose from the government's wish to stir up interest within industry about the amount and the quality of training. Over-simplified, the idea was to achieve impact on training in British industry by working on firms' cost calculations. This financial impact on employers (at least until the modification in 1969) was not a significant aspect of the Redundancy Payments Act. Equally fundamental as a measure of the difference between the two statute-based systems is the much simpler, Whitehall-based system of raising money for the finance of the redundancy scheme. No 'Redundancy Boards' with representatives from industry and trade unions were established. The administrative structure of the Department of Employment was simply enlarged, particularly in its Accountant General's Department. Cash for the scheme is collected by the Department of Health and Social Security and handed over to the Department of Employment's Accountant General. From there on, the whole thing is a simple mechanism for transfer payments.

With the ITB scheme all employers, except those specifically excluded, (usually because they are small) have to pay the levy. All but the most exceptional ITBs have applied the levy as a percentage of employers' wages bills. Amounts have varied from Board to Board in any given year, and no one Board has retained the same rate of levy throughout its existence. Once the ITBs have got the money in, their chief object has been to hand back, as much of it as possible, to the firms from whom it has come. In principle, and by and large in practice, all firms which pay levy get back some of the money from their Board. No two ITBs can be accused of resembling each other in their policies and working methods. Nevertheless they all set out to give grants to their constituents who had contributed.

Although no one is quite sure about this, taking all the years of the ITBs' operations together, it is probable that something like £50 – £70 million has been transferred annually from one set of firms to another as a direct result of the working of the levy and grant schemes. How much of an incentive to more, and higher quality, training is provided by the ITB system as a whole, and specifically by the financial stimulus, is still surrounded by conjecture and controversy. About one thing there is reasonable certainty. Over the six years (1966 – 71) for which information is available about the statutory redundancy payments scheme, the ITB mechanism had produced a total cash transfer of somewhere between £300 and £420 million. Of course, the gross cash flows over the six-year period were much larger. In all probability, the sums involved were not less than £780 million, possibly rising to nearly £900 million.

For an external agency to be able to get firms to change course, because by doing so they will reduce costs, is a pretty big undertaking. Something approaching £900 million over six years as the measure of the financial pressure on firms to increase training does probably rank as a big effort. By contrast the juggling of the cost-sharing formula in the redundancy scheme as a way of affecting employer behaviour is bound to seem puny. With the statutory redundancy scheme, although all pay the levy, only those employers who have redundancies find themselves at the receiving end of cash flows from the central Redundancy Fund. And then, as we have seen, the employer gets back only a part of his costs. Here the analogy with ITB finance is good. Within the statutory training arrangements, even firms which succeed in attracting grants of a higher value than their levy payment are still not fully compensated for the costs they incur in training. Total training costs, that is to say, are made up of the firm's actual training costs and the sum of money it pays in levy to its training board. The best that it can do is to get all its levy back in grant and a bit extra to put towards its actual cost of training.

Net costs

Something similar, at least in principle, also happens to the statutory severance cash flows. To begin with, the firm with the redundancies has itself to pay the full compensation to which its workers are eligible. At the same time, the employer will have paid the 'redundancy levy' during that, and preceding, years. Against that gross cost of the redundancy, the employer receives a 'grant' from the Redundancy Fund. The exact net split between the employer and the fund depends in the first place on how much the employer has paid in levy over the years. Secondly, there is the employer's propensity to have redundancies. If an individual employer has repeated bouts of redundancy, the 'grants' he gets from the Fund have less and less of his own contributions in them. Increasingly the particular firm is siphoning off the money contributed by other employers whose redundancies, and claims on the Fund, are smaller or non-existent. That leads on to the final factor determining the split of the cost of compensating redundant employees. This has to do with the incidence and distribution of redundancies among firms. We saw earlier that in the ITB levy and grant scheme pratically all firms in the network got some part of their levy returned to them in the shape of grant. This is simply because it was the exceptional enterprise that did no training at all.

True, there has been a growth in the volume and spread of redundancies during the lifetime of the statutory scheme. Even so, it is still the exception rather than the rule for enterprises to have redundancies. While, in the industrial training context, practically every firm shares a piece of the action, redundancies are still sporadic and extremely unevenly distributed among employers in the British economy. Consequently the element of transfer payments in the statutory redundancy compensation scheme is much higher than within the ITB system. Firms which do not have redundancies are subsidising those that do. The 1969 rejigging of the cost-sharing formula was a straight imposition of a constraint on the transfer payment and subsidy element of the scheme. Firms with redundancies, after 1969, were compelled to find a bigger share of their redundant workpeople's cash compensation from their own resources than was previously the case. Costs of compensation were concentrated more at the point of redundancy and less diffused over industry as a whole. By doing this, Westminster and Whitehall were able to eliminate, at least for a period, the embarrassment of charges of poor management associated with the Fund being perennially in the red.

7 People and payments

Enactment of the 1965 statute on redundancy payments not only made it obligatory upon employers to make severance payments, it also, for the first time, opened up a vein of information about the characteristics of redundancies. Consistent with tradition and history, this information comes as a spin-off from the Department of Employment's work in administering the scheme. Typically, and in keeping with normal Whitehall custom, no arrangements were made to gather information to help in observing how the Act's provisions were working out in practice. And, of course, no one did anything about setting up a monitoring system designed to establish whether the aims sought were in fact being attained. Directly traceable to these causes is the staggering fact that six years – and £381 million – after Parliament carried the legislation, no one knows exactly how many people lose their jobs each year in the British economy. For about those eligible to benefit from the Act, the Department of Employment can provide information only of the number of *payments* made, as distinct from data about the number of *people* becoming redundant and entitled to severance pay.

As the administrative structure for implementing the statute is geared to assessing entitlement and making payments, there can be no cause for surprise that no direct information about the *people* involved in the process has been sought or made available in a systematic way. That makes sense if the soundness of the basic premise is accepted without challenge. If more than merely handing over money to redundant workers was in the minds of the people who brought in the legislation, then the present information flow from the statutory scheme is not good enough. At this stage, it is fair to ask 'more information for what?'. For a start, more information is necessary to make it possible to decide whether anything useful is being gained from the dismissal of large numbers of people. When the Act was being prepared, one big justification was that it would break down workpeople's resistance to change. As a result, there would be freer flows of manpower in response to signals from the market indicating where such resources could be most profitably employed – gains to the whole economy as well as the individual. Then again, solely from the individual's viewpoint, good information about the dimensions of the hazard of redundancy could help to bring about the positive approach to change that the sponsors of the Redundancy Payments Act were out to encourage.

Payments equal people

The main body of information available from the Department of Employment concerns how many individual *payments* have been made and the total sums paid out. These data are published once a quarter in the DE Gazette. Additionally, information is given about the average value of payments obtained by dividing the quarterly total of cash outflow into the number of payments made in that three-month period. For the greater part, the figuring that has been done in previous chapters is based on this source of information. Strictly speaking, those figures are inaccurate. It has been necessary to assume that each payment is equal to a redundancy. But this is not entirely true because there are occasions when people who have received severance pay appeal to the Tribunals for increases in compensation. Though the error arising from this double counting is quite small and does not invalidate anything that has been considered so far, it remains a shortcoming. Of far greater importance is the missing information about people who are excluded from benefit under the provision of the 1965 Act. There is no certainty about this, but some evidence is accumulating to indicate that quite a few people are being caught up in a second redundancy within less than two years of their first forced termination of employment.[1] If that happens, they are debarred from benefit within the statutory severance payments scheme.

Something over a quarter of male manual workers and well over one-third of the women employed in all industries and services taken together in 1968 had had less than two years of service with their employer (see Tables 21, 22, Appendix). That is a rough indication of the extent of exclusions from entitlement to redundancy compensation from the statutory scheme. It is only a rough indication of the over-all situation because fewer white collar employees suffer this exclusion as less of them have below two years of service. Another element of the roughness of the estimate lies in the very uneven distribution between industries of people with this short period of service. Only about 10 per cent of the workpeople in mining and quarrying had less than two years service, as against 43 per cent in construction. In the transport and communication group, under 6 per cent of manual employees in British Rail come within this category. By contrast, and predictably, in road haulage contracting, almost 38 per cent of the workpeople did not quality for the statutory redundancy benefit. But all male workers, with the solitary exception of those in the building trade, were much better off than the women. Taking Order XXVI of the Standard Industrial Classification, rather more than 47 per cent of women who worked in cinemas, theatres, radio, in sport and 'other recreations', as well as in a wide variety of miscellaneous services, were ineligible for redundancy compensation if they were sacked, as they had not worked with their employer for the minimum qualifying period.

Excluded categories

Nor are these the only excluded categories. Young people at work during their sixteenth and seventeenth years of age, who have their employment terminated before they become eighteen, have no entitlement to severance compensation. No adequate method exists for estimating how many such people there are each year.

Quite how much uncertainty there is about the total quantity of redundancies in Britain is confirmed by one independent source of information. Mention was made earlier of a survey, commissioned by the Department of Employment, undertaken by the Office of Population Censuses and Surveys (OPCS) about the effects of the Redundancy Payments Act. The OPCS tried to find out the number of 'unpaid redundant'. Curiously, the survey results on this point are strikingly vague. In the section of the OPCS report concerning this issue, reference is made to an unpublished Department of Employment internal study of this category of redundancy. The best that the OPCS is able to do is conclude 'that on any reasonably inclusive definition of unpaid redundancies the Department of Employment estimate of a minimum of 500,000 cases per year' is consistent with information from its own sample survey of employees. While all this indicates limitations in both the Department of Employment statistics, and in the OPCS survey, it is also confirmation of the difficulties involved in making broader use of such survey work as has been done in Britain on redundancy.

There is much more involved in this inadequate collection and supply of information than mere frustration for disgruntled researchers. It can be argued that the insufficient allocation of resources to data collection prevents not just the process of evaluation, but also has an adverse effect on the operational objectives of the 1965 Act. This is the background of an attempt here to analyse and interpret such information as is available. Crude though it is in many respects, the justification is simply that at the end of it there is likely to be a little more information about the events in the labour market since the introduction of the statutory severance payments scheme.

Quarterly analysis of redundancies

Practically all the quantitative information about redundancy payments available from the Department of Employment is set out in Table 20 (Appendix). That table covers 1966 – 71. Figures are available for each quarter of each year, and there are of course annual totals. It is possible to give information separately for men and women, and the table does that.

In Figure 2 total redundancies (for men and women taken together) are graphed quarter by quarter. In the presentation so far, as well as here, the number of payments is taken to equal the number of redundancies though this is not entirely true. As the two pieces of information are closely tied together, Figure 2 graphs the quarterly cash flow in severance compensation as well as the number of redundancies. Figure 1 (in chapter 6) contains the same information on an annual basis for 1966 – 71.

It is essential to remember that these figures relate only to those redundant people who are within the net of the statutory scheme. As emphasized, many redundancies excluded from statutory benefit remain in the background and unrepresented in the quantities to be considered here. In terms of the annual totals, in 1967 there were over 100,000 redundant workers more than in 1966, the first full

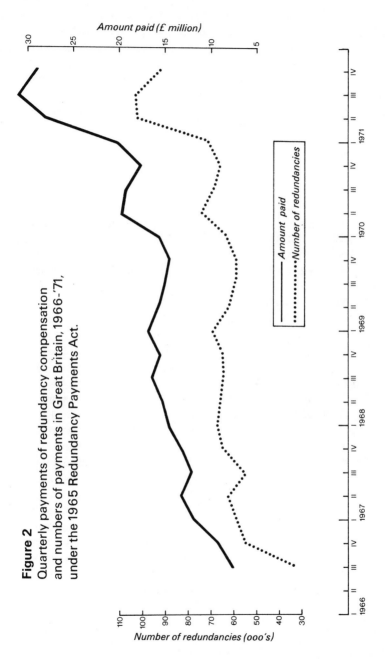

Figure 2
Quarterly payments of redundancy compensation and numbers of payments in Great Britain, 1966-'71, under the 1965 Redundancy Payments Act.

year of the scheme. That year-on-year rise of 72 per cent is by far the biggest in the six-year period ending in 1971. Indeed, the annual rate of redundancies for the next two years remained close to that of 1967. While there was a rise of 6 per cent in 1968, 1969 redundancies were down by the same 6 per cent to the 1967 level. The ups and downs over these three years can be summed up by saying 1968 had about 15,000 more redundancies than the year that preceded and followed.

Rising volume

There was a bigger change in 1970. Redundancies then were running at about 12 per cent above the 1969 (and 1967) level. There was a big jump in 1971, which had a redundancy rate 37 per cent higher than that of the preceding twelve months. Still more strikingly, 1971 redundancies were running at something over two-and-a-half times the rate prevailing five years back, in 1966. Clearly there has been a big rise in redundancies during 1971, while during 1967 – 70 there has been a remarkable constancy. Another aspect of those figures is that there is no persuasive evidence of an upward trend in the volume of redundancies. Totals for each year (Table 20, Appendix, and Figure 1) indicate this quite clearly, and Figure 2, which plots the number of redundancies quarter by quarter, makes the picture clearer still.

Another test of the change of the intensity of the incidence of redundancy in the whole economy is to take the annual totals and put them as percentages of the total population at risk. Annual totals of redundancy we can take from Table 20 (Appendix). The other figure, to provide the over-all population within which redundancies are taking place, can be chosen from a variety of series published by the Department of Employment. Probably the best is that for "employees in employment". On that basis in 1966 there were six redundancies for every thousand at work. There was a rise to eleven for every thousand in 1967, and that figure remained unchanged for the next two years. In 1970 it went up to 12 for every thousand employees. And, of course, 1971 saw a big rise to 17 redundancies for every thousand people who were at work.

Proportions by age group

What has been said so far is about as far as can be got by direct
reference to information about redundancies available from the
Department of Employment. From now on, this chapter sets out to
bring together data from a variety of other statistical material
published by that Department. A lot of what now follows is
impressionistic and conjectural. But this approach is the only
feasible one and is justified because it helps to fill out the picture
and to make events more comprehensible. This is all the more
important because not much is known about the detail of the
aggregate characteristics of redundancies since the statutory scheme
has been at work. Worse still, a great many misapprehensions exist
about what is going on.

One illustration of this, about the notion that there is an upward
trend in the level of redundancies, has already been discussed. Our
estimates of what has been happening since 1966, at different times
in each year and for people in different age groups, are to be found
in Table 9.

There are a variety of ways of approaching the issues. As good a
starting point as any is to begin with the question as to whether
those who become redundant have characteristics in common that
distinguish them from the general working population. Things which
might set redundant people apart could be to do with age, sex, the
industry in which they are employed and the occupations they
pursue, especially in terms of the level of skills that they have to
practise. As the question of the age of people who are made
redundant crops up quite often, it is worth while to take this as the
initial focus of the analysis.

One thing is immediately apparent from Table 10. More older
people become redundant than would be the case if redundancies
were uniformly distributed over the four age classes. Taking 1966 as
the benchmark, a little over 45 per cent of men in the labour market
were under forty years of age. In terms of that age class's share of
employment a uniform distribution of redundancies would have
meant that 45 per cent of the redundant men, in that year, would
have had to be below the age of forty. Yet, in actual fact, only 33
per cent of all the redundant workpeople were under 40 years of
age. And in this youngest age group both men and women shared
this disproportionate security against redundancy. But moving up on

Table 9 Redundancies in each age group as percentage of total male and female redundancies and indexes (1966=100) of redundancies[1] by age group[2] for men and women; and male redundancies as percentage of all redundancies.

MEN

Years and Quarters	Under 40 years %	index	40–49 years %	index	50–59 years %	index	60–64 years %	index
1966 I	32.6	97.9	23.5	104.9	27.1	103.8	16.8	92.3
II	30.3	91.0	22.1	98.7	27.4	105.0	20.2	111.0
III	31.6	94.9	22.0	98.3	26.7	102.3	19.7	108.2
IV	36.4	109.3	22.4	100.0	24.6	94.3	16.6	91.2
Quarterly average	33.3	100.0	22.4	100.0	26.1	100.0	18.2	100.0
1967 I	34.0	102.1	22.7	101.4	25.6	98.1	17.7	97.3
II	34.2	102.7	22.9	102.2	25.1	96.2	17.7	97.3
III	32.9	98.8	22.9	102.2	25.6	98.1	18.6	102.2
IV	31.7	95.2	22.7	101.3	24.8	95.0	20.8	114.3
Quarterly average	33.2	99.7	22.8	101.8	25.3	96.9	18.8	103.3
1968 I	33.4	100.3	22.9	102.2	25.1	96.2	18.6	102.2
II	32.7	98.2	23.3	104.0	25.5	97.7	18.8	103.3
III	29.9	89.8	22.3	99.6	25.3	96.9	22.5	123.6
IV	31.9	95.8	23.1	103.1	25.7	98.5	19.2	105.5
Quarterly average	31.9	95.8	22.9	102.2	25.4	97.3	19.8	108.8
1969 I	31.8	95.5	22.1	98.7	25.1	96.2	21.0	115.4
II	32.0	96.1	22.7	101.3	25.2	96.6	20.1	110.4
III	31.0	93.1	22.8	101.8	25.6	98.1	20.5	112.6
IV	32.7	98.2	23.0	102.7	25.5	97.7	18.7	102.8
Quarterly average	31.9	95.8	22.6	100.9	25.4	97.3	20.1	110.4
1970 I	33.1	99.4	22.5	100.5	25.6	98.1	18.7	102.8
II	33.2	99.7	23.1	103.1	25.4	97.3	18.3	100.6
III	32.1	96.4	22.3	99.6	25.6	98.1	19.9	109.3
IV	33.4	100.3	22.6	100.9	25.2	96.6	18.8	103.3
Quarterly average	33.0	99.1	22.7	101.3	25.5	97.7	18.9	103.9
1971 I	34.3	103.0	21.7	96.9	25.1	96.2	18.9	103.9
II	36.2	108.7	21.8	97.3	24.3	93.1	17.7	97.3
III	33.8	101.5	21.9	97.8	24.5	93.9	19.8	108.8
IV	34.7	104.2	21.4	95.5	24.2	92.7	19.7	108.2
Quarterly average	34.8	104.5	21.7	96.9	24.5	93.9	19.0	104.4

WOMEN

Years and Quarters		Under 40 years		40–49 years		50–59 years		Male redundancies as % of total redundancies
		%	index	%	index	%	index	
1966	I	35.1	102.0	29.6	97.7	35.3	100.0	76.9
	II	35.1	102.0	29.9	98.7	34.9	98.9	77.1
	III	33.3	96.8	31.4	103.6	35.2	99.7	77.3
	IV	34.3	99.7	30.1	99.3	35.6	100.8	78.3
Quarterly average		34.4	100.0	30.3	100.0	35.3	100.0	77.6
1967	I	35.0	101.7	30.4	100.3	34.6	98.0	79.7
	II	34.5	100.3	31.6	104.3	33.9	96.0	78.4
	III	34.5	100.3	31.3	103.3	34.3	97.2	79.0
	IV	33.0	95.9	31.6	104.3	35.3	100.0	80.8
Quarterly average		34.3	99.7	31.2	103.0	34.5	97.7	79.5
1968	I	33.8	98.3	31.4	103.6	34.8	98.6	80.6
	II	34.6	100.6	31.3	103.3	34.0	96.3	81.1
	III	33.5	97.4	33.0	108.9	33.5	94.9	81.9
	IV	33.0	95.9	32.6	107.6	34.3	97.2	84.3
Quarterly average		33.8	98.3	32.1	105.9	34.2	96.9	82.0
1969	I	34.1	99.1	32.3	106.6	33.6	95.2	81.4
	II	35.1	102.0	31.5	104.0	33.4	94.6	81.3
	III	32.7	95.1	32.0	105.6	35.3	100.0	79.9
	IV	33.1	96.2	32.7	107.9	34.3	97.2	80.4
Quarterly average		33.7	98.0	32.1	105.9	34.1	96.6	80.8
1970	I	32.8	95.3	33.0	108.9	34.2	96.9	80.4
	II	33.1	96.2	31.8	105.0	35.1	99.4	79.0
	III	33.5	97.4	31.5	104.0	35.0	99.2	78.4
	IV	35.1	102.0	30.7	101.3	34.2	96.9	78.4
Quarterly average		33.6	97.7	31.7	104.6	34.6	98.0	79.0
1971	I	35.7	103.8	29.5	97.4	34.8	98.6	79.1
	II	37.6	109.3	29.2	96.4	33.2	94.1	79.6
	III	35.6	103.5	29.5	97.4	34.8	98.6	79.6
	IV	36.1	104.9	29.2	96.4	34.7	98.3	81.1
Quarterly average		36.2	105.2	29.4	97.0	34.4	97.5	79.9

Notes and sources
(1)   The redundancies figure is the number of redundancy payments made under the 1965 scheme.
(2)   Employees under the age of 18 years and over 64 years (59 for women) are not eligible for statutory redundancy payments under the 1965 scheme. Calculated from information made available by the Department of Employment.

Table 10 Redundancies (SRP) and employees in the labour market; each age group as percentage of all redundancies and all employees.

		Under 40 years		40–49 years		50–59 years		60–64 years	
		Men	Women	Men	Women	Men	Women	Men	Women
1966	*SRP redundancies* [1]	33.3	34.4	22.4	30.3	26.1	35.3	18.2	—
	Employees in labour market [2]	45.2	44.8	20.0	20.9	19.2	19.1	7.7	—
1967	*SRP redundancies*	33.2	34.3	22.8	31.2	25.3	34.5	18.8	—
	Employees in labour market	45.5	45.2	20.2	21.2	19.0	19.0	7.9	—
1968	*SRP redundancies*	31.9	33.8	22.9	32.1	25.4	34.2	19.8	—
	Employees in labour market	45.7	45.1	20.8	21.8	18.6	19.0	8.0	—
1969	*SRP redundancies*	31.9	33.7	22.6	32.1	25.4	34.1	20.1	—
	Employees in labour market	45.2	45.4	21.1	22.3	18.4	18.4	8.2	—
1970	*SRP redundancies*	33.0	33.6	22.7	31.7	25.5	34.6	18.9	—
	Employees in labour market	45.3	45.2	20.8	21.9	18.6	18.9	8.2	—
1971	*SRP redundancies*	34.8	36.2	21.7	29.4	24.5	34.4	19.0	—
	Employees in labour market	45.4	45.0	20.3	21.7	19.1	19.4	8.3	—

Notes and sources

(1) Those eligible for redundancy payments under the statutory scheme.

(2) Total in labour market — i.e. those in employment plus registered unemployed.

Calculated from Table 5 and Department of Employment Gazette, September 1971, and June 1972.

the age classes a sex based difference in the incidence of redundancies appears on top of the disadvantage connected with the loss of relative youthfulness. In the 40 – 49 age category there is a closing of the gap for men. In 1966, 20 per cent of all males in the labour market were this age, and about 22 per cent of all male redundancies were from within this age group. This contrasts quite sharply with the fact that although of all women at work, some 21 per cent were in the 40 – 49 age group, some 30 per cent of redundancies were carried by this category of women.

Greater impact on older people

This discriminatory differential in the impact of redundancy on women is maintained for the 50 – 59 age class. Women of this age formed only 19 per cent of total female employment in 1966, but over 35 per cent of all redundancies among women were drawn from this age bracket. The older the man or woman, the greater the propensity to redundancy. And women are worse affected.

There is an important point at issue. Right from the start of the statutory severance payments scheme, the redundancy rate was higher for the two oldest age groups in the working population. Some of the laboriousness in the earlier part of this exposition can be removed by use of the term 'redundancy rate'. For instance in 1967 the redundancy rate for men below the age of 40 was practically unchanged (at 33.2 per cent) from that of the preceding year – the redundancy rate being the share of total redundancies in a given year falling to each of the four age categories.

These observations about the incidence of redundancy so far have been focused on the pattern as it was in 1966. As soon as the pattern is considered over the five-year period, a remarkable constancy is evident. A lot of economic scene-shifting was going on during these years. In the early part of the period the economy was being squeezed, and towards the end efforts were being made to reflate it. A change of administration had taken place in Westminster, and the new men were pledged to a different style of government. Sterling had been devalued. For practically the first time in most people's memory, Britain had a large balance of payments surplus. Meanwhile, in factories, coal mines, in the railways and the docks the redundancies kept happening. What is more, year in, year out, from 1966 to 1970 the redundancy rate of men under 40 years of age stayed put at 32 – 33 per cent.

For the oldest group 1969 was a bad year. Their redundancy rate rose to 20 per cent. Yet, the extent of this change must be measured by reference to 1966, when the corresponding rate was fractionally above 18 per cent. And this is the largest variation in the redundancy rate over the five-year period for any of the age classes. Most important of all is the fact that despite a thumping great cost displacement produced by new legislation, the situation in 1970 did not materially differ from that of 1968. What is important to establish at this stage, is that the pattern of redundancy, for both age and sex distribution, remains substantially unaltered from the start of the operation of the statutory scheme to the most recent date for which information exists.

Who should get more?

How redundancies are shared out among the different age groups is important for a variety of reasons. Indeed, once the principle of compensation for compulsory termination of employment is established, the question of the kind of person that is to be made redundant becomes of absolutely central importance. How much of a key issue this is was amply demonstrated by the people who drafted the statute for the scheme launched in 1965. Compensation derived from that Act is calculated on two criteria. Length of service, by number of years of employment with the firm, is an obvious criterion that just had to be taken into account. Building in the preferential element of compensation for years of work accrued over the age of 41 was less obviously justifiable.

This preferential treatment of older workers arose from implicit considerations, which were not analysed in any detail before the introduction of the scheme, and have not been explored any more fully since then. What accounts for this biasing of the statutory scheme in favour of older people? Quite evidently most of the things said in reply to the question 'Why pay redundant people?' raised in an earlier chapter come into play in response to the question being asked here. But that is no more than to establish the case for redundancy compensation, not quite the same thing as saying that people in different age categories should get compensation at differing rates solely on the criterion of the difference in their ages.

It is, of course, easy to say that the case is self-evident for biasing the provision of financial compensation towards the older groups among workers facing redundancies. But self-evident truths are sometimes a cloak covering intellectual laziness. The apparent grounds for a different level of severance pay for older redundant workers are pretty straightforward. They have more interests vested in the job that is disappearing. These are both economic and non-economic interests. All case studies of redundancies in Britain have in common the finding that older employees lose more by way of pension rights and minor, but significant, fringe benefits than their younger colleagues.

Moreover, though there is no clear evidence, it is highly plausible that older workers find it more difficult to build up new entitlements to these privileges in the jobs that they get after they have become redundant. Again, though the information is not good on this, there appears to be another big economic loss. Especially the semi-skilled manual worker (and possibly the wholly unskilled too) suffers from a loss of something that is probably best described as 'know-how'. Sometimes this characteristic is described as a 'specific' skill in the sense that it exists only in relation to a particular place of work and a given production technique. Unlike the skills of the time-served craftsman, specific skills are not transferable from one work situation to another. A nominally semi-skilled or even unskilled man with long years of service in a particular workplace might well have been doing jobs requiring a good deal of knowledge and experience though confined to a limited range of activity. Redundancy for such men brings big losses from reversion to the skill class to which they nominally belong.

Losses from job losses

That kind of decay in the individual's position produces two kinds of economic loss. For a start, there is a deterioration in his level of earnings. But it does not stop there. Work on the human ageing process has shown that the older (and here the over-40s rank among the older group) person is slower at acquiring new skills. Consequently, not only is there a cut-back in the earnings of the older redundant person when he finds new employment, but it is also more than likely that it will take him longer to climb back to his previous manual facility than would be the case for someone younger.

Tied up with this is the non-economic deprivation of decline in status. And there are a great many other intangible costs that fall more heavily on the older individual. But reverting to the purely economic aspect, there is another specific difficulty faced by the older man. His job prospects in the labour market are less good than those of someone ten years younger also put out of work by the same redundancy. On a variety of counts then, the older worker appears to be losing more when he is made redundant than the younger man in the same predicament. On top of all that the older man's job search is lengthier and more uncertain of success.

While these are a sample of the arguments that can be used for giving older workers special and preferential treatment, they do not establish the validity of the case for that preference to be expressed through higher financial compensation. A perfectly respectable case can be made out to show that the compensation differential in favour of older workers may have the effect simply of making them the principal target of employers engaged in slimming their labour force. Especially in the light of the disadvantages awaiting older people after redundancy, the higher financial compensation might, in fact, be doing that group of workers more harm than good. Before following through the implications of this, it would be useful to eliminate one possible source of confusion.

These disadvantages for older workers that could be associated with the preferential rate of financial compensation paid to them are significant only on occasions when there is scope for choice by the employer about which workers should be given their cards.

What is being considered here is the justification for the approach adopted in the 1965 Act to give higher compensation for years of service put in after 41 years of age. This present discussion is not about whether more of the older group of employees have been at the receiving end of redundancies year by year since the start of the statutory scheme. What is being attempted at this stage is a consideration of the rationale for having this two-tier system of redundancy benefit. Furthermore, another immediate purpose of this analysis is to arrive at a view about whether this two-tier structure of benefit might have had an immediate impact on employees and employers alike in the difficult process of deciding whose jobs would be terminated and who would be retained.

First in, last out

The distinction between total closure and a payroll reduction needs firmly to be borne in mind in connection with the remainder of this piece of analysis. Throughout the late 1950s and in the early years of the 1960s, British trade unions had very little policy about redundancies. But when the thing could no longer be put off, and full-time trade union officials as well as workplace employee representatives were compelled to negotiate specific redundancies, they tended to unite under the banner 'first in, last out'. Although describing that trade union approach as a policy is glorifying it beyond its deserts, at least it had a rationality. The purpose was plain. Employees who had worked longest with a firm had the greatest amount of interests vested in that particular job. It was highly probable that longer service would correlate with age. By insisting on the brunt of redundancies being borne by workpeople who were new (relatively) entrants to a firm's labour force, organised workpeople were protecting as best they could, older employees from the rigours and losses of redundancy. In another good down to earth way, this approach made sense. If the younger members of an enterprise's workforce lost their jobs, they could more readily get others.

Where the 1965 Act changed the scene was in its offer of cash compensation as an apparent substitute for the security that workpeople, especially the older ones, had previously attempted to establish by their insistence on the 'first in, last out', principle.

It is simple and attractive to take the view that all the emphasis before the Act was on job protection and that the focus shifted afterwards to getting out with as much cash compensation as possible. A horde of apparently good reasons can be cited to sustain that view. Impressionistic, but powerful, evidence exists from case studies of particular redundancy situations to show that though employers generally accepted the idea of sacking the newest members of their labour force, this was not to their liking.

Increasingly, throughout the 1950s, speed and physical agility were edging out experience and knowledge as the principal determinants of productivity among semi-skilled and unskilled manual workers. On strict cost and productivity considerations, employers stood to gain from keeping the younger employees. For the employer, there was only one real economic advantage in the 'first

in, last out' principle. The actual cash cost of redundancy compensation to the firm was lower if the worker dismissed had little
service. Difficult though it is to say anything precise about this, it
would be wrong to ignore the fact that some non-economic altruistic
influences were probably present too.

Employers' attitudes

What employers really did when faced with a choice between ties of
loyalty and a more productive labour force is anybody's guess. All
that can be said is that the 1950s were not a time of abrasive
management. A good deal of the benign paternalism of traditional
British management still stalked the land. Mergers and take-overs
were not yet household words. Multi-national companies (currently
particularly prone to cutting back on manpower) had still to make
their mark, and no one except geologists had even heard of the term
conglomerate. In fact there is some evidence to show that there was
greater resistance in Britain to manpower shedding at times of low
demand than in the United States. Ties of loyalty, making for
retention of the longer-serving employee when redundancy could
not be put off, is wholly consistent with that kind of stable state in
industrial relations.

Not enough is known about the age distribution of over-all
redundancies in Britain in the years preceding the 1965 Act to allow
the kind of guessing done on other issues in this study. What we do
know is that, no sooner did the statutory scheme begin to operate,
than evidence started to pile up to show that the redundancy rate
among the over-forties was higher than for the younger age group.
That happened, for all practical purposes, instantaneously with the
launch of the statutory scheme. Two quite diametrically opposed
explanations can be offered with equal plausibility for this phenomenon. One explanation is simply that nothing at all had changed. The
age distribution, that is to say, of the over-all redundant population
in Britain in the years immediately before 1966 was in fact such that
the incidence of compulsory termination of employment was higher
among the older people in employment than their younger fellow-
workers. Such an explanation would suggest a straight continuation
of earlier patterns in the constancy of the shares in total redundancies of the different age groups during the lifetime of the
statutory scheme. Taking that reasoning, the financial provisions of

the 1965 Act, and the differing cost to the employer of selecting redundant people from the different age groups, were all neutral in impact. In this respect, at least, everything remained the same after the Act.

But it is possible to argue that the Act brought about major transformation. On this reasoning, before the 1965 Act came in, workers fought and largely won their redundancy battles in that they were able to force employers to retain older employees, while placing the main burden of redundancy on those under 40. Alternatively employers deeply conscious of their obligations to their workpeople refrained voluntarily from putting out into the cold those long serving employees who they knew would find the labour market harsh and unaccommodating. Consequently, redundancies were higher among those who could best cope with them: workpeople in the below-40 age group.

Then came the Redundancy Payments Act. And everything changed. Far from workpeople and their representatives asserting the sanctity of the principle 'first in, last out', the men with long service volunteered in swarms to be made redundant whenever occasion offered. Added to this, the employers too (instantaneously abrasive of behaviour) seized on every opportunity to reduce the age of their work force, salving aches of tattered loyalties with thoughts of princely sums in compensation to erstwhile employees with many years of dedicated service. Taking all this together, it would not be surprising if the pattern of incidence of redundancies swung right round and produced a disproportionate rise in the redundancy rate among all those people to whom the statutory scheme gave preferential financial compensation. Where the truth lies between these two explanations is anyone's guess.

8 Are older workers at greater risk?

Whether or not the 1965 Act caused a radical change in the age distribution of people whom firms were making redundant is an open question. Without a laborious and lengthy combing of records, nothing can be established one way or the other. Such a project is expensive in time and effort, and the outcome unlikely to be conclusive. This study analyses redundancies by age group from the time that the statutory scheme came into operation. The pattern of age distribution from 1966 onwards will now be examined to identify changes which have been taking place and to try to draw conclusions from them.

All the figures examined now again relate solely to redundancies among people eligible to cash compensation under regulations established by the 1965 Act. To get some idea of events over the years, it is necessary to bring together the figures about those who actually received benefit under the statutory scheme and the total population of workers 'eligible' for severance compensation as a consequence of the 1965 Act.

The heading 'Civilian employees' in Table 11 represents the estimated total of the working population in Great Britain eligible for benefit under the statutory severance payment scheme. Using those figures, and the known quantities of payments made under the scheme, the percentage distribution by age groups has been calculated. That information is the central point of interest in Table 11.

The first full year of activity under the statutory scheme was 1966 and can be used as the base year for comparing developments that followed. But, to begin with, the picture of events in that year, as given by Table 11, while confirming some of the things that

111

Table 11   Redundancies (SRP)[1] by age groups as percentage of eligible[2] civilian employees[3] in corresponding age groups.

Year	Men/women	Under 40		40–49		50–59		60–64	
		Civilian employees (000s)	Redundancies as percentage of employees	Civilian employees (000s)	Redundancies as percentage of employees	Civilian employees (000s)	Redundancies as percentage of employees	Civilian employees (000s)	Redundancies as percentage of employees
1966	Men	5,870	0.62	2,948	0.83	2,826	1.01	1,101	1.80
	Women	3,120	0.35	1,796	0.53	1,641	0.68	—	—
1967	Men	5,807	1.10	2,913	1.51	2,740	1.77	1,097	3.29
	Women	3,159	0.54	1,799	0.86	1,609	1.06	—	—
1968	Men	5,788	1.16	2,946	1.63	2,645	2.02	1,091	3.82
	Women	3,210	0.49	1,850	0.80	1,614	0.98	—	—
1969	Men	5,751	1.08	2,974	1.48	2,566	1.92	1,095	3.58
	Women	3,287	0.48	1,915	0.78	1,575	1.00	—	—
1970	Men	5,711	1.24	2,888	1.68	2,584	2.11	1,082	3.74
	Women	3,313	0.58	1,884	0.96	1,618	1.22	—	—

Notes and sources

(1)   Those eligible for redundancy payments under the statutory scheme.

(2)   Employees below 20 and over 65 years of age are excluded from benefit under the 1965 Act.

(3)   Figures for number of employees in Great Britain by age group are published annually in June in the DE Gazette. Figures for numbers registered as unemployed by age are published twice yearly in the Gazette, referring to January and July figures. These were averaged to obtain a yearly figure and that figure for numbers unemployed was subtracted from the number of employees in each age group. This gives estimates for employees in employment in each age group and eligible for payment (if they have the required length of service).

have already been said, shows up starkly the differential and discriminatory incidence of redundancy on the different age categories. Total eligible redundancies among men under 40 in 1966, as a proportion of civilian employees in that age group, amounted to 0.62 per cent. The corresponding figure in the 40 – 49 group was 0.83 per cent, rather more than one-third as much again as for the youngest age group.

As if that were not bad enough, redundancies in the 50 – 59 age group were equivalent to 1.01 per cent of civilian employees of that age. Although people in their 50s were nearly 63 per cent more at risk of redundancy than men under 40, this disparity pales into insignificance when placed against the difference between the oldest and the youngest of the eligible age categories. For the under-40s and the 60 – 64 age groups, the contrast is between 0.62 per cent and 1.80 per cent. In other words, of every thousand men below the age of 40 who were eligible for statutory redundancy payments, about six actually faced that contingency and received benefits. For the over 60s this figure rises to eighteen.

Year-by-year variations

So much for the deployment of the incidence of redundancy in the opening year of the scheme. And the conclusion from that is plain. A question of some interest is whether the whole span of years from 1966 bears the same profile of incidence of redundancies as that first post-statute year. The first thing to note is that there has been a rise in the volume of redundancy for all age groups during the five years for which information is given in Table 11. Now, two questions have to be answered. In the first place, how is this apparent growth in redundancy in the quinquennium to be squared with what has been said about the relative stability from year to year of total redundancies? And did the growth in the rate of redundancy between 1966 and 1970 occur in such a way as to change the incidence of termination of employment for the different age groups?

Attention has already been drawn to the fact that the only really large rises in the absolute volume of redundancies came in 1967 (and 1971). Putting 1966 on one side, the difference between the year with the lowest redundancies and that which had the highest was a matter of 29,000. Meanwhile, the number of civilian employees was declining. That fall in the number of people within the scope of the statutory scheme was taking place year by year in three of the four age categories. The 40 – 49 age group was unusual in breaking the pattern by having an increase in one year – 1969.

Now, although the change in the actual volume of redundancies from year to year was not very large, measured against a declining total of civilian employees the percentage rise over the years becomes bigger. Bearing in mind this tendency to over-inflate, arising from the method of measurement, the changes between 1967 and 1969 were modest (see Table 11). For the oldest (60 – 64) group, the redundancy rate in 1969 was about 0.29 per cent more than in 1967. In fact the 1968 rate of redundancy for this age group had been some 0.53 per cent up on the preceding year. In other words, if the first year of the working of the Act is excluded, there is no big and pronounced upward *trend* in the rate of redundancies, even among the very oldest category of civilian employees.

Looking down the percentage column for the under-40 age group in Table 11, it is evident that the fluctuation between 1967 and 1969 is quite gentle. The year 1968 saw a 0.06 per cent rise over the previous twelve months. After a fall of about 0.08 per cent on the preceding year, the 1969 rate of redundancy was down to below the 1967 level, for this group. In both the 40 – 49 and 50 – 59 age brackets too, this up and down movement is clearly apparent.

What does all this add up to? There is a gentle upward trend for each of the four age categories, but we must now consider whether older people covered by the statutory scheme were increasingly at a greater risk of redundancy with each succeeding year of operation of the system established by the Redundancy Payments Act. In any of the years the older age brackets had a higher rate of redundancy than was the case with the younger people, but we are concerned to discover if there is a general deterioration of the position of the older groups.

Worsening of older workers' position?

The period we consider is 1967 – 1969. One thing is immediately apparent. The position of the 60 – 64 age group was getting worse. In 1967 the ratio of the redundancy rates of the youngest to the oldest category was 1:2.9. In 1968 and 1969 it was 1:3.3: in each of the three years considered, the position of the oldest group deteriorated very slightly to that of the under 40s.

For the 50 – 59 group the situation was not very different; the ratio of redundancy rates of the youngest and this age group was 1:1.6 in 1967. In 1968 this went up to 1:1.7, and to 1:1.8 in 1969.

Nearest in age to the people with the lowest risk of redundancy come the 40 – 49s. Here, there seems to have been no change at all. In 1967, 1968 and 1969 the ratio of redundancy rates of the under-40s to this group stood at 1:1.4.

Impact on women

Older women, just like older men, are at greater risk of redundancy. The oldest category of women consists of the 50 – 59 group (women become entitled to state pension when they reach 60 years of age). And that category of women was exposed in 1966 to very nearly double the risk of redundancy faced by women who were under 40. By 1969 the older women had become marginally more disadvantaged. But the pace at which older women grew more exposed to redundancy than their younger counterparts was slower than for older men.

More interestingly, the pattern of redundancies among women, in total as well as by the different age groups, is quite different from that of their male counterparts if the first year of the statutory scheme is put on one side. In our reference period, women in each of the age groups (including the over-50s) had a lower rate of redundancy in the last year than at the start of the period. This was caused not so much by a decline in actual redundancies among women (though that did in fact happen to a minor extent), but was a result of the fact that the number of women in the workforce was rising during those years. Female redundancies, as proportions of women civilian employees in each age group, were at a lower rate, partly because the numerator was a little smaller in each case, but the greater part of the change is traceable to the increase in the size of the denominator, year by year, and for each age category.

A central reason for taking a close look at the age distribution of redundancy lies in the different labour market prospects for people in the various age brackets. One of the few certainties of information about manpower, is that people over 40 in Western industrial communities are facing growing difficulty in finding employment. This has been clearly happening most substantially, since the mid-1960s, but the changes underlying this set in at the start of that decade. Within that context, the working of the Redundancy Payments Act, in its implications for the age distribution of those whose jobs are terminated, is both significant and deserving of attention. Allied to this is the change of policy introduced in 1969, for running of the statutory severance payments scheme.

A new level of rebates

In January 1969, the House of Commons carried the Redundancy Rebates Bill. The opposition did not divide the House. The only votes cast against the Bill were those of the five Liberals. The Conservatives did not go along with the Labour administration with much enthusiasm. Absence of opposition was based on the fact that 'without this Bill', the scheme would be 'bankrupt by March', and the Government 'would not have anything to put in its place'.[1] Central to the measure was a reduction of cash flow from the Redundancy Fund. In Chapter 5 the misfortunes of the Fund were examined in some detail.

The Government had a choice to make. It could have raised the level of the levy on employers yet again, in order to build up the resources of the Fund. The decision to do something different was taken ostensibly because repetition of the old formula would have left 'unchanged the undesirable concentration of redundancy amongst older workers'.[2] The alternative was to 'share the cost of redundancy between employers as a whole and the individual employers' who were involved in a redundancies 'at the same time reducing the incentive to some employers to sack older workers'. All of this was to be achieved through a neat and simple change in the formula for sharing the cost of the lump-sum compensation between the individual employer directly concerned and the Fund to which the whole of industry had contributed.

Indexes for each age group

Taking the average of the four quarters in 1966 as 100, indexes have been made for each age group showing the quarter-by-quarter changes in their share of total redundancies. Now if it were true that the system of higher rebate payment to employers for compensation paid to older workers was in fact encouraging firms to hold on to their manpower below the age of 40, while providing an incentive to the discharge of the older groups, then it would be reasonable to expect to find evidence of a steadily increasing proportion of redundancies in all but the youngest age categories.

For disentangling the truth of this proposition, it is possible to turn to the indexes in Table 9. Figure 3 gives the same information in the form of a graph.

Undeniably the average of the four quarters in 1968 gives a redundancy figure among men in their 60s which is 8.8 per cent higher than the corresponding 1966 level, but the biggest boost to the 1968 average is given by the exceptionally high level of the index in the third quarter of that year. In the year that followed, redundancies among the oldest age group seemed well established at a high level for the first nine months. Moreover in 1969 there was no single large lump, as in the third quarter of the preceding year, which could be held accountable for having hoisted the quarterly average to an exceptionally high level.

Is that, then, conclusive evidence that there was a disastrously accelerating incidence of redundancy among people particularly badly placed to withstand the rigours of that upheaval? The changes in quantities might easily be read in that fashion. And that is particularly tempting to do, if there is a predisposition to show that governmental action taken in 1969 was not only well founded but also successful. For, in the final quarter of that year, the index for the 60 − 64 age group was down to a level last achieved as long ago as in the first three months of 1968.

Such a view would almost certainly be wrong. For one thing, the middle six months of the very first year of the operation of the Act had seen levels of redundancy among the oldest group that were not much short of the level of the corresponding two middle quarters in 1969. Though the later year was different from the earlier one in that 1966 has two separate three-month periods with a low level of redundancies for people over 60, and 1969 only had a fall in the index in the last quarter, this does not detract from the proposition that a high incidence of job losses in the oldest age group was neither a new nor a particularly powerfully growing phenomenon.

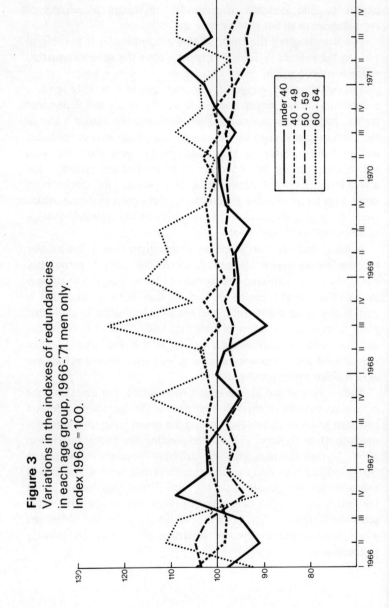

Figure 3
Variations in the indexes of redundancies
in each age group, 1966-'71 men only.
Index 1966 = 100.

under 40
40 - 49
50 - 59
60 - 64

Particular closures

If this begins to sound like a case of 'lies, damn lies and statistics', then it is time to bring in some external information which may help to clear up some of the conflict. The period spanned by the second half of 1968 and the first nine months of 1969 was pretty special. It was the time of the massive GEC-AEI redundancies, when a substantial proportion of redundancies arose from the complete shutdown of plants. There is evidence to suggest that in that kind of situation the average age of people being made redundant is higher than when employers are merely cutting back their payroll.[3]

It has, for instance, been shown that the workpeople affected by the AEI factory closure in Woolwich werĕ older than redundancies in general. This is something of a paradox. Arguments have already been rehearsed about how firms tend to pick off their oldest employees when cutting back on manpower. Yet one of the factors contributing to the above-average age of redundancies associated with total shut-down of plants is thought to be the inclination of younger people to go away while job opportunities in the local labour market still exist. Older employees stay put for as long as they can, either in the hope of an eleventh-hour reprieve, or in the expectation of generous severance compensation, or simply from fear and inertia.

Increased incidence of redundancies among people in the 60 – 64 age group between 1968 third quarter and 1969 third quarter was then, at least in part, a result of the nature of the particular redundancies that were taking place in that period. Furthermore there were well over 20,000 compulsory terminations of employment in coalmining over roughly the same period. Here the evidence is pretty good that the miner tends to be older than the average casualty of redundancies in other industries.[4] All of this is enough to cast grave doubts on the plausibility of taking the higher levels of the index for redundancies among the over 60s during one quarter of 1968 and nine months of 1969 as indicative of a long-term trend. Before 1968 (see Figure 3), there was of course no consistently upward trend in redundancies among this age group. Furthermore – more will need to be said about this – the curve fluctuates in a haphazard way in the period since the final quarter of 1969.

Such small tendency as there arguably might have been for more over-60s to become redundant, was by no means the case for people between 50 and 59. This divergence in the rate of incidence of redundancy between the two oldest age categories is both odd and significant. If there is credibility in the view that the older people were more exposed to redundancy because of the cost-sharing formula operated until 1969, then it would follow that the 50 – 59 group would have exposure to redundancies at a not dissimilar rate. So far as the levy and grant system for sharing the cost of redundancy between individual employer and the Fund goes, the impact for both age groups was the same. If the employer was more disposed to pick someone for redundancy because the Fund would meet 78 per cent of the compensation bill, the over-50 group would be equally eligible.

Higher risk for over-60s

Government spokesmen claimed, as justification for altering the financing system of the statutory scheme, their extreme concern to protect the older worker. Our information shows that this could have been true only in the most limited sense. It was argued earlier that for the oldest group of employees (60–64) it is just about possible to present a picture of an increasingly disadvantaged category. As soon as attention is turned to the group immediately preceding the oldest age bracket, the data cease to lend any sort of plausibility to the case put forward by the administration in 1969.

Paradoxically the level of redundancy among people in their 50s has been lower, since the inception of the scheme, than in the 40 – 49 age bracket. The fluctuation of the index over the years for the 40 – 49 category has been about the same as the variations of the index for people in their 50s. But for the 40 – 49 group the index has stayed at a higher level than that of any age group except the very oldest one. Once again the explanation for this is certainly not to be found in the split of the cost of redundancies between the individual employer and the Fund. If employers in the aggregate really were going all out to soak the Fund, the logical thing from their viewpoint would have been to achieve more redundancies in the 50 – 59 group than among those who were in their 40s. What the data indicate is that either firms were not aiming to achieve this, or failed dismally to do so.

Results of new cost-sharing formula

One outstanding feature of the statistics of redundancies analysed by age groups is their extraordinary incoherence. How it was possible for the Administration to have used that data to justify its stance with regard to the need for changes in the burden sharing of the costs of redundancies is baffling. Fortunately the Government stated plainly the outcome it expected from the redistribution of the financial burden between the individual employer directly concerned with a particular redundancy and the Fund. That new rebate structure of the statutory scheme became effective from the second quarter of 1969. Information is therefore available about the operation of the new financial formula for 10 quarters. That might be compared with the run of 13 quarters for which information exists about the working of the original cost-sharing formula.

Probably the simplest way of grasping the information about the third period before the Redundancy Rebates Act 1969 came into force, and the period since then, is in diagrammatic form. Figure 3 shows the variations in the indexes of redundancies for each group. The average of the four 1966 quarters is taken as the base (1966=100). Quarterly movements for each age group are plotted against that base line. Apart from the third quarter of 1968, the movements for each age bracket are remarkably uniform. Moreover the pattern of variations displayed by the last ten observations plotted on the figure (third quarter of 1969 to the fourth quarter of 1971) are surprisingly close to the shapes of the initial ten observations running from the first quarter of 1966 to the second quarter of 1968. The two segments are not of course identical. But the difference in the shape of the curves is quite small.

That, no matter how one looks at it, is extremely odd. There is no denying that the 1969 amendment in the Redundancy Payments Act brought substantially increased cost on employers involved. But this big new financial impost appears to have had no significant effect at all. Right from the start of the scheme the people over 60 were more at risk than any other group. And that risk remained unabated even after the switch round of costs.

When proposing that change, the Government claimed that it would make the older worker less exposed to redundancy. But redundancies in the 60 — 64 age bracket in the time since the third quarter of 1969 are much the same as before the money flows were altered. For that comparison, as well as what now follows, it is necessary to leave 1968 on one side, since it was a year with unusual and specific characteristics.

On the evidence of the data for 1971, it might be argued that a downward movement had set in for the 50 – 59 and 40 – 49 age brackets. On top of this, the rise in the index of redundancies for the under-40s, in this period, could be called in evidence of a change of focus on the choice of victims of redundancy. But how good are those arguments? In the fourth quarter of 1966, for instance, the index for the youngest group of redundancies was higher than the highest point that it reached in 1971. In other words, it is much too soon to conclude that the upswing in redundancies in this age group is caused by the new cost structure. Moreover as that altered distribution of costs came into operation in March 1969, it does not seem terribly plausible that it took anything up to eighteen months for its impact to seep through to firms that were supposedly so clever at ringing the changes on the Fund's finances to extract for themselves the maximum possible cost advantage.

The groups between 40 and 59

Explanation is needed for the downturn in the indexes for the two age groups falling between 40 and 59. That movement downwards is most marked from the first quarter of 1971. Here too, these most recent levels are not unprecedented. The index for people in their 50s, from 1966 fourth quarter to the fourth quarter of the following year, moved about not very differently from the most recent observations. Admittedly the pattern of redundancies among those aged between 40 and 49 in the most recent period has no previous parallel. But here the maximum downward movement in the index is marginally over 3 points.

Is it reasonable to attempt to evaluate the results of a policy introduced in 1969 on the basis of only two-and-a-half years actual experience? The answer to that has to be a fairly firm 'Yes'. For the evidence that was thought to provide the basis for that change, itself related to a time span of not much greater length. Any assessment, even if it chooses to leave judgement in abeyance about the effects on the 40 to 59 age categories, has no option but to conclude that the most vulnerable, the oldest, were not benefited by the new financial arrangements. For a policy founded on the expressed

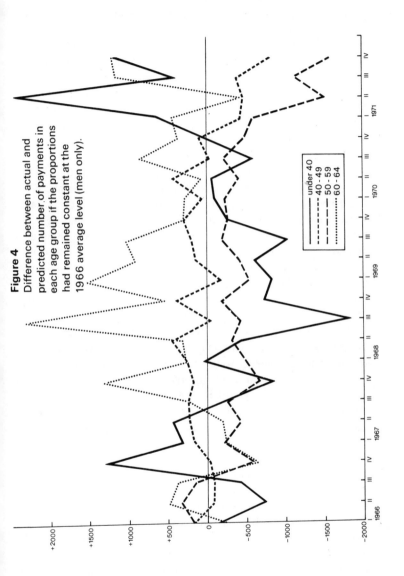

Figure 4
Difference between actual and
predicted number of payments in
each age group if the proportions
had remained constant at the
1966 average level (men only).

under 40
40 - 49
50 - 59
60 - 64

intention of doing something about the most disadvantaged, this outcome has to be counted as failure.

A lot more is involved here than the inability of a particular statute to lead to the results that Whitehall had in mind. The arguments put forward for the change in the financing structure of the 1965 statute, the intentions embodied in the 1969 amendment, as well as the outcome of the working of the scheme since that date, all point conclusively to an administrative muddle, traceable to a failure of the information systems available to the administrators running this pioneering venture. Above all, it indicates a confusion of thought about the purposes of the scheme.

Each criticism needs to be examined more fully, and this is done elsewhere in this study. For the present let us attempt to establish the validity of the Administration's ostensible case for making a fundamental reorganization of the financial basis of the scheme within three years of its inception. One method of considering if the incidence of redundancies among the older people was rising at a rate sufficiently alarming to cause the government to change course is to estimate how many people in each age category would have become redundant, quarter by quarter, during the ensuing years, if the level of redundancy had not deviated from the original 1966 level.

To answer the question 'Were the higher age groups more disadvantaged with the passing of the years?' estimates of the size of redundancies have been made for each group. These estimates and quantities result from applying the 1966 relationship between numbers in each age group to the total volume of redundancies during subsequent years. Results of that calculation for men are at Table 23 (Appendix). The information is also displayed in Figure 4.

Deviations from 1966 pattern

If the actual redundancies in each age group had kept to the 1966 ratio, one to another, in subsequent time periods, then the redundancies counted by the Department of Employment would be identical to the estimated quantities given at Table 23 (Appendix). Put in terms of Figure 4, all the curves for each age group would have coincided with the zero line that runs horizontally through the diagram. Figure 4 enables assessment of the relative deterioration, over time, in the condition of the people in the higher age group relative to employees less than 40. Observations plotted on the upper part of the diagram, above the horizontal zero line, indicate those three-monthly periods when the actual redundancies, in any of the four age groups, exceeded the number which would have resulted if the ratios of redundancies as between the different age groups had remained as they were in 1966. Likewise those parts of the curves which lie below the zero line show the extent to which redundancies fell short of the size for each age group which would have resulted if the 1966 ratios had continued to hold.

Each of the curves in Figure 4 show a good deal of movement. Moreover some of the swings from quarter to quarter appear pretty big. But in terms of actual number of bodies involved, the deviations from the quantities implied by the 1966 ratios are quite small. Starting with the lowest age bracket first, 21 of the 24 quarterly observations (88 per cent) are within the range of plus or minus 1,000 of the quantity which would have been derived from the 1966 ratio of redundancies among the under 40s to the total volume of redundancies.

There were only three occasions when the actual volume differed from the calculated figure by more than 1,000. One such deviation came at the start of the period. In the final quarter of 1966 there were 1,300 more redundancies in the youngest age group than would have been the case if the relationship based on the twelve-month period had held for the fourth quarter of the year. During July – September 1968 the actual volume of redundancies among people aged less than 40 years was about 1,800 lower than would have been the case if the base-year ratio had remained unchanged. Finally, in the spring of 1971, there were 2,400 more redundancies than would have resulted from the 1966 ratio. For most of the time, among this youngest part of the working population, redundancies were fewer than the quantities which would have been expected from the 1966 pattern of distribution.

Just as the actual volume of redundancies in the youngest age category was, for most of the time, lower than it should have been in terms of the 1966 relationship with other age groups, the opposite was true for the highest age category. Yet, for the 60 – 64 group, just as much as for those in the youngest age bracket, the difference in volume was largely within the plus or minus 1,000 band. Over 79 per cent of the observations indicate deviations of less than 1,000 from the 1966 norm of redundancies in the over-60 age group. Moreover no less than 14 of the 24 quarterly periods (about 58 per cent) showed redundancies in the 60 – 64 group which were less than 500 on either side of the quantity derivable from the 1966 ratio. And even that is not the end of the story. The deviation of the volume of redundancy among the over-60s, from the 1966 quantity, was well within 500, in 8 of the 13 quarters which preceded the changeover in the system of finance of the severance payments scheme.

Some peculiarities

In the summer of 1968 something rather odd appears to have happened. Actual redundancies among the 60 – 64 age group in those three months were well over 2,000 more than the 1966 ratio. At the same time, compulsory severance of employment of the under-40 category fell sharply (by 1,800) below that group's share on the 1966 basis. Why this happened cannot be explained with absolute certainty. One plausible explanation has to do with the characteristics of the particular redundancy situations emerging in that period. But that reasoning is not entirely satisfactory. While it appears that there is a bigger weighting of older people in redundancies caused by total closure of establishments than when jobs are lost because of a need for slimming down a given labour force, applied to the third quarter of 1968, this only explains the abnormal rise in the number of people aged over 60. It is not a sufficient explanation for the sharp downswing which occurred at the same time in redundancies in the under-40 age bracket.

Clearly the third quarter of 1968 was exceptional. And this unusual increase in the redundancies among the over-60s was made the basis of the Whitehall brief about the rising degree of disadvantage to which the oldest age category was being subjected. Quite possibly that may have been the consequence of poor interpretation of available information.

The argument for questioning the view about the worsening position of the over-60 age group has already been subjected to close scrutiny. Figure 4 and Table 23 (Appendix) also shows that the two age categories which fall between 40 and 60 had a small variation in the volume of redundancies calculated on the 1966 base ratio. One interesting characteristic of both the middle age groups, which is difficult to interpret, lies in their direction of deviation from the initial pattern. For the 40 – 49 group the curve is above the zero horizontal line for 12 of the 16 observations up to 1970. In absolute volume, this deviation from the size of redundancies for this age bracket from the 1966 base is not at all big. Up to the end of 1970 the 'excess' redundancies for this group were well under 300 except in the spring of 1968, the winter of that year, and in the second quarter of 1970. During 1971 the curve plunged below the zero horizontal line.

This means that the share of total redundancies falling upon employees between the ages of 40 and 49 has mostly remained at 200 – 300 above what it was in the initial year of the scheme. There was no upward trend, and the change in the rebate structure brought in from March 1969 has had no effect on the size of deviations or on the trend.

The phenomenon is interesting and it would be useful to be able to think up an explanatory hypothesis. More interesting still is the curve plotting the rate of redundancies in the 50 – 59 group. On the logic that the employer was more disposed to dismiss the older rather than the younger worker at times of redundancy, it is to be expected that there would be more redundancy among people in their 50s.

In fact, nothing of the kind happened. The initial share of redundancies taken by the 50 – 59 group in 1966 was higher than this group's share of total redundancies at any subsequent period. In terms of the diagram, the curve for this second-oldest category of employees remained consistently below the 1966-based zero horizontal line. Here, too, the deviation in terms of volume, though larger than for the 40 – 49 group, was not big. Again, there was no trend either upwards or downwards. This was true before the 1969 change of rebates, just as much as after.

Validity of case for altering rebate

In order to consider the validity of the case for altering the level of rebate paid out from the Fund, it is necessary to look at the statistics in Table 23 (Appendix) and the diagram, in two separate sections. If it was indeed the subsidy that was making employers choose the older for redundancy ahead of their younger colleagues, then the cutback in the rebate associated with the older employees should have had some effect. However the data establishes that there is no real foundation for the view that, as the statutory scheme continued to operate, the older groups continued to become *more* disadvantaged between 1966 and 1969. Moreover the information assembled and analysed earlier and in this chapter is sufficient to cast considerable doubt on the view that the change in the rebate structure has made any material difference to the share-out of redundancies among the different age groups. Were it not for the sharp movements in the share of each of the age groups in the second half of 1971, that conclusion could have been put even more firmly. Such movements have occurred before; moveover the events in the last six months of 1971 do nothing to support the view that the change in the cost-sharing formula is producing the benign result forecast by the Government.

The data and argument in this chapter have not been simple. Moreover the argument has swung backwards and forwards over time. Additionally some of the information and the argument has been repeated in attempts to clarify the underlying issues.

Let us now consider concepts. One idea firmly entrenched in the Redundancy Payments Act is the computation of higher severance compensation for the years of service put in after a worker has reached the age of 41. The reasoning underlying this is either extremely obvious or exceedingly opaque. In any case it has never been fully articulated, and there is conceptual uncertainty about what the scheme sets out to do.

The second conceptual muddle concerns the cost of that extra benefit. If we accept a fairly straightforward case for giving older people more compensation, there seems no logical connection between that and the financing of this extra benefit by the generality of firms (through the Fund). Why should the employer making people redundant be relieved of the burden of the higher compensation which each one of his employees with years of service beyond the age of 41 is entitled to receive? Why indeed? Then there is a third conceptual weakness. Was the higher benefit for the older people designed to make them more footloose, while the younger people with lower compensation entitlement remained entrenched? And, finally, what theoretical model of employer behaviour was visualized as likely in response to the levy and rebate characteristics of the method of finance established by the 1965 Act?

Some interpretations

That there was little clarity about these questions is made evident by the confusion of reason and argument surrounding the 1969 amending legislation. Consider, for instance, the change in the principle of subsidization from the Fund for the higher compensation paid to older redundant workers. Central to the original thought underlying this formula of cost distribution was the principle of a shared community aim as well as a common responsibility. The aim was a largely economic one: firms should have as unconstrained an opportunity as possible to decide on the age distribution of their labour force. It was this which led to the idea of the subsidy, from all firms collectively, to the individual enterprise which was paying higher compensation in order to lower the age structure of its labour force.

It is conceivable, but unlikely, that employers would prefer to put the brunt of redundancies upon their older workers simply on the grounds of their age. Perhaps employers inexplicity but deliberately set out to cut back on the less productive of their payroll. In a wide range of manual jobs in the production, particularly manufacturing, industries high labour productivity requires ability to keep up a long succession of short bursts of activity. This ability declines with increasing age. Consequently employers in the secondary sector of industry, given an unconstrained choice about a strategy for raising productivity, would opt for a young labour force. At what precise age the dividing line comes is not universally agreed, but the age of 40 probably marks the division.

In the course of the six years of the statutory scheme, redundancies among individuals under 40 have consistently been lower than the share of that age group in employment in the labour market. The disproportion in the 40 – 49 group has been a lot less, and to the relative disadvantage of that group in relation to its share in the total employee population. And, of course, the rate of redundancy among the over-50s has been enormously out of keeping with their share of jobs in the labour market. What is involved here is not a matter of a year-to-year deterioration of the position of the older workers. It is simply that they remain at continuous and more-or-less constant disadvantage in relation to younger people as regards redundancy. Between 1966 and 1971, then, year by year a big (but not rising) layer of older people have been getting the sack. Consequently the economic objective of getting a more productive labour force is being attained.

A social loss?

But at what cost? In 1971 nearly 54 per cent of men who had been without work for more than a year were over 55 years of age. In 1966, 1 per cent of the over-40s were unemployed for more than eight weeks. By 1971 this proportion had risen to 3 per cent.[5] There is no way of determining whether the shedding of older manpower would have occurred, and occurred at the same rate, if there had been no Redundancy Payments Act. The one expressed purpose of that Act was to achieve easier redeployment of manpower, and to break up the current pattern of employment of manpower resources and enable new flows to occur in keeping with structural and technological change. Underlying that was the assumption that the total demand for manpower in the whole economy would not slacken. Moreover that analysis assumed homogeneity of manpower. Each unit of labour was assumed to be substitutable for another.

In the event the assumption that full employment would absorb all available labour, has turned out to be false. And by their hiring-and-firing policy employers have demonstrated the falsity of the homogeneity assumption. The aspect of that latter point of greatest concern to this discussion is the employer preference for a young workforce at the cost of more redundancies for the older age groups. That the statutory scheme encouraged this cannot be established with certainty. But the 1969 modification of the grant/subsidy element was based on the belief that the scheme was encouraging employers to make more people over 40 redundant.

If we suppose that the subsidization from the Fund of the higher level of compensation for years of service above age 41 had indeed led to employers taking the decision to reduce the less effective, older elements in their labour force, should that not have been counted as a successful attainment of the economic objectives contained in the legislation? To what extent could the attempt to counteract the alleged cause of this economically beneficial develop- ment be held to be justified by the kind of cavalier reasoning set out by the government spokesman when the amending legislation was being discussed in 1969? Was this a situation where specific and tangible economic objectives were at cross purposes with profoundly important, but less evidently concrete needs of the community?

These are especially important questions because the view which led to the building in of better compensation for the older worker, as a part of the 1965 Act, was founded on the idea of community responsibility to the individual who would be at hazard because of a more open and flexible pattern of working life. The older individual's greater compensation for the heavier loss suffered by him was not seen as an obligation on his immediate employer. The benefits of a more effective labour force with a higher average productivity were seen as accruing to the whole community. Subsidies from the Fund were therefore a method whereby industry as a whole shared in the higher cost of ensuring a socially desirable objective without burdening the individual employer with those wider costs. Had that been done, there would have been a brake on movement towards the economic objective. Yet the cutback on the subsidy for the higher compensation for the older redundant employee, introduced in 1969, would have done precisely that, if it had altered employers' attitudes to reducing the average age of their workforce.

Neutrality of the cost formula

In reality, the evidence does not support the proposition that the swing of the balance of costs on to the employer and away from the Fund has significantly altered the incidence of redundancy among the older age groups. Once again, although there is no knock-down way of proving this, a reasonably well-founded conclusion from this analysis is that the rate of redundancy for the older age groups could have been just as high if the cost of the extra benefit paid to them had been shared, in the same way as for compensating employees of under 41.

Moreover there can be very serious doubt about the awareness of employers of the cash costs of redundancy. In Chapter 6 it was shown that, as a proportion of all firms' total labour costs, expenditure on provision for redundancy amounted to 0.097 per cent before 1969, and 0.186 per cent after that date. When redundancies are the consequence of complete closures, the different costs of compensating workpeople in the older and the younger age brackets have no relevance. Differential costs matter only when a firm is reducing its labour force.

A firm needs to make detailed and fairly complex calculations to evaluate the cost difference of a given quantity of redundancies composed of alternative combinations of its employees drawn from the older and the younger age categories. The data give no indication that firms would have sufficient financial incentive to embark on such exercises systematically. In fact there is nothing more than an *a priori* view to back the proposition that the cash flows generated by the 1965 Act (and as modified in 1969) have had any measurable influence on the age composition of people selected for redundancy.

By this test, however, the Act cannot be judged to have failed. The people who brought in this statute had not thought deeply about what effect it would have on the age distribution of employees selected by firms for redundancy. From their point of view there had been no need to go too deeply into this, because they assumed that manpower was homogenous and no one person or category of persons would be more at risk of redundancy than any other, though they did recognize that employers could be reluctant to hire older workers if the heavier costs of making them redundant fell on the individual firm.

The idea of using shifts in cost burden, from the general to the particular employer, as a method of affecting the age balance of people made redundant, was thought up three years after the Act had come into operation. That idea did not work, but then it remains questionable whether or not the main objective at that stage was the protection of the older, more vulnerable, group against a higher rate of redundancy. More likely the chief objective was to stop the rapid outflow of cash from the central Fund. Initially, however, there was unqualified clarity about the purpose of the original legislation. It was intended to erode workpeople's resistance to technical change and the consequential need to change jobs.

9 Opposition to redundancies

Central to the thinking behind the Redundancy Payments Act of 1965 was the view that big changes in the prevailing pattern of manpower utilisation in Britain were needed to enable quicker and uninterrupted economic growth. As the main growth promoting agent of that time, the National Economic Development Council (NEDC) was deeply persuaded of the need for policy and administrative measures to shake up the existing pattern of manpower use, and for the creation of greater flexibility in the labour market.

Industrialists, as much as NEDC, were alarmed by signs that appeared at that time to indicate a likely labour supply constraint on the otherwise achievable rate of growth of output. Worry about the speed of introduction of new technology was the other side of that same coin. It was not so much a shortfall in total labour supply which seemed likely to prevent growth of output at higher levels than had been the case in the recent past. More, the issue was one of redistributing the available manpower. This meant allowing new production processes to reduce employment in some industries and occupations, while enabling that displaced manpower to provide the necessary labour input in other areas of activity where growth would be held back in the absence of such manpower inflows.

A key issue on which employers, trade unions and the para-Whitehall planning machinery were all agreed was the need to create a system of transfer of manpower which would overcome workpeople's fear that unemployment was the inevitable result of a job being lost. No one had much doubt about the practical consequences of this understandable apprehensiveness displayed by workpeople. Most people concerned with policy making were of the mind that introduction of new technology and methods in large areas of British industry was proceeding too slowly for comfort. That moderation of pace on the part of management was attributed by many to managerial reluctance to embark on changes in their enterprises which would place them in conflict with their employees. All of this can be put much more sharply. Workpeople, and their collective organizations, were the real impediment to the modernization of British industry. This is because their attitude was one of 'what we have, we hold'. And managers were too scared of disputes with their employees, or insufficiently tough minded, to do things that would deprive men of their established livelihood when the individuals concerned had done nothing to deserve that kind of treatment.

All of these views were based on the piecing together of information about the mood and feeling in industry. And, indeed, there could be no other method for arriving at an evaluation of the situation. On the trade union side, official pronouncements on the issue lent strength to the view that workpeople's organizations were hostile to changes which threatened existing jobs and the pattern of employment of their members. But that too was a qualitative index of mood and opinion, and not a scientific measure of whether the analysis was factually well founded. One quantitative indicator which was available, and could be used for a little more detached analysis, was the Ministry of Labour information on stoppages of work in industry arising from industrial disputes. But statistics about strikes and their causes are notoriously difficult to interpret, and all sorts of caveats have to be made about their coverage and reliability.

Stoppages of work

Statistics of stoppages of work on a national basis have been given in annual articles in the Ministry's Gazette from 1914 onwards. From 1957 regional breakdowns were produced and occasionally in the earlier years, there was an analysis of the causes of stoppages. Since 1960 this has become a regular feature. In the analysis of disputes by cause of origin, stoppages are classified under eight categories. The nearest any of these comes to providing an indicator usable for the purpose discussed is in the classification of stoppages under the general heading of 'disputes concerning the employment or discharge of workers (including redundancy questions)'.

In the published figures there is no separate treatment of disputes arising solely from conflict about redundancy. However the Department of Employment and Productivity prepared a special series in connection with the OPCS study of the effects of the Redundancy Payments Act. An incomplete but still useful discussion is possible on the basis of those figures about the extent of conflict in British industry arising from compulsory severance of employment. Because of what has already been said about the characteristics of the statistics on stoppages, it is sensible to stick to a fairly simple analysis.

Was there less conflict leading to disputes and interruptions of work after the 1965 Act than in the five years which preceded it? As 1966 was the first full year of operation of the scheme, and information on a comparable basis exists up to 1970, there are two five-year periods for which data on either side of 1965 are available. Table 12 sets out the relevant figures.

The column of total days lost through stoppages of work shows the random movements from year to year. At least, that was true until 1967. From then on, there is a strong upward trend. The second column gives the number of days lost as a result of redundancy disputes. An immediately striking characteristic of these quantities is the sharp fluctuations from year to year brought out for the first five-year period, by contrasting 1962 with 1963. While in 1962 something over half a million working days were lost because of redundancy disputes, in the following twelve months the number of days lost from this cause had shrunk to 41,000.

Establishing any coherent pattern is difficult when the variations from year to year are so very big. One way round this difficulty is to work out an arithmetical annual average for one set of years and then compare that to the annual average for another period. A powerful objection to that approach lies in the distorting effect that a single year with an exceptionally high incidence of lost days can have on the annual average. For the period 1960 – 64, this distorting effect is produced by 1962. Taking that figure as it stands, days lost because of redundancy disputes on an average annual basis between 1960 and 1964 were about 182,000. Almost magically this figure shrinks to about 99,000 if the exceptionally big loss in 1962 is replaced by the average of the days lost in the other four years of that quinquennium.

Table 12 Working days lost through stoppages of work caused by redundancy disputes, 1960–1970[1].

Year	Total days lost from all causes (000s)[2]	Days lost from redundancy disputes (000s)[3]	Redundancy loss as per cent of total loss	Index of loss from redundancy disputes, 1965=100	Index of redundancy loss as per cent of total loss, 1965=100
1960	3,049	105.4	3.5	174	167
1961	3,038	147.8	4.9	244	233
1962	5,778	514.5	8.9	848	424
1963	1,997	41.2	2.1	68	100
1964	2,030	101.2	5.0	167	238
1965	2,932	60.7	2.1	100	100
1966	2,395	107.2	4.5	177	214
1967	2,783	31.7	1.1	52	52
1968	4,719	56.4	1.2	93	57
1969	6,925	102.6	1.5	169	71
1970	10,908	254.2	2.3	419	110

Notes and sources
(1) All figures relate to Great Britain.
(2) Department of Employment Gazette, May each year.
(3) Obtained from the Department of Employment: this is a sub-category of the set of causes given in the DE statistics, published as 'Disputes concerning the employment or discharge of workers (including redundancy questions)'.

Stoppages before and since 1965

If all that smacks a little of pedantic nit-picking, its justification must lie in the fact that an analysis of these figures can be put on display as evidence that a substantial gain has been obtained, so far as industrial disputes are concerned, via the 1965 Act.[1] Taking a straight average of days lost through redundancy disputes in the period preceding the Act, and contrasting that with the annual average for the five years which followed 1965, gives 182,000 days lost in the bad old days, as against a 40 per cent reduction under the salve of statutory severance provisions.

This immensely comforting scene becomes overcast if we remove the abnormally high 1962 figures. The loss of days caused by redundancy disputes in the period after the introduction of the severance payments scheme becomes nearly 12 per cent higher than it was in the years preceding the Act. On that evidence, at best, the verdict on the efficacy of the Act as a defuser of redundancy-generated industrial conflict has to be non-proven.

Working on averaged values for a period before the Act and for a comparable span of years after legislation leads to inconclusive results about the effect of the statutory scheme as a means of winning workpeople's co-operation in redundancy. Yet the people who brought in this scheme apparently remained confident that statutory severance compensation was helping to win employee consent to job changes which, though uncomfortable for the individual, were necessary and beneficial for the community.

As this idea is so central to the case for spending big sums of money on redundancy compensation, there can be no question of the need to see how far, and to what degree of thoroughness the outcome can be tested as a measure of the achievement of that goal. Finding out whether people's views have changed is difficult enough. To try to trace the cause of that change, or establish the connection between it and a particular given factor, makes the whole thing doubly complicated and unreliable. For these reasons the information about stoppages of work on redundancy disputes is the most telling indicator available about whether or not the 1965 Act has helped in overcoming workpeople's hostility to redundancy. Although there are shortcomings in using the stoppages data for making an evaluation of this kind, they do give a rough picture.

A simple analysis

What follows now is a presentation of the known facts about stoppages caused by redundancy disputes. Several different presentations are attempted in order to explore a variety of possible interpretations. For assessing the gravity of any stoppage of work in industry, three separable but related criteria are available. Possibly the most useful criterion from the broader economic viewpoint is the number of days of work that are not done as a consequence of a dispute.

This indicator is most frequently used when commentators make statements about the parlous state of Britain's industrial relations. Another criterion of turbulence in employer and employee relations is the number of occasions when work stops because of a dispute. Some people have argued with great passion that the real burden that breaks British industry's back is not so much the loss of a large number of working days, as the fact that there are a lot of stoppages each with a small number of days lost. These, it is said, are costly beyond price in disruption of production schedules, dislocation of delivery dates and the creation of disharmony between management and employees. The third and final way of counting the cost of an industrial stoppage is by making a tally of the number of workers involved in disputes.

Stoppages of work caused by redundancy disputes can be analysed and interpreted on each of those criteria. The earlier discussion about redundancy-generated stoppages in 1960 – 64, and for the years after the Act, was based on the annual average of 'days lost' in each period. Table 12 is wholly concerned with this loss from stoppages of work about redundancy disputes. Apart from the absolute volume that table contains figures of days lost from redundancy disputes, expressed as proportions of total days lost in disputes arising from all causes. In the final column the variation of those proportions from year to year is indicated in an index, with 1965 as the base year. The penultimate column also contains an index, again with 1965 as the base year, and this shows year-to-year variations in the actual quantity of working days lost through redundancy disputes.

Redundancy-based disputes

Mention has already been made of the sharp changes from year to year in the quantity of days lost as a consequence of redundancy disputes. Taking 1965 as the mid-point, there is nothing remarkably different in the later as distinct from the earlier period (except for the uniquely big loss in 1962). As the year-to-year changes are so odd and unpredictable, it is best to look at the indexes. But before doing that, something is to be gained from considering the redundancy-generated loss of working days as a percentage of the total loss of working days from all causes. Here, for 1960 — 64 the share of redundancy-generated loss varies between 2.1 per cent and 8.9 per cent, or, if 1962 is put on one side, between 2.1 per cent and 5.0 per cent. Things appear to have changed quite a lot in 1966 — 70, during which period the scheme was fully operational. In that five-year period the lowest share that redundancy-generated loss of working days took was 1.1 per cent, and the highest peak 4.5 per cent. But here too the events become clearer with the aid of the indexes.

Moving to the indexes, but still staying with days lost through redundancy disputes as a proportion of total loss of working days, the final column of Table 12 and Figure 5 give a useful push to the argument. And it does begin to look as though there were clear differences between the earlier and the later periods.

At no time between 1960 and 1964 did the index of 'redundancy loss as percent of total loss' fall below 100. Even leaving 1962 aside, it went as high as 238. Nothing of that order appeared in the five years after 1965. Indeed, for three of the five years of the operation of the scheme, the index stood at between 52.4 and 71.4. But 1966, admittedly only the first full operational year of the new scheme, was not at all good, with the index standing not much below what it was in 1961, and quite a lot higher than in 1960. Worse still, 1970 (the most recent year for which figures are available) showed a sharp rise, and though that level still was a lot lower than in four of the five years preceding the Act, it introduces enough uncertainty into the observations for 1966 — 70 to make it unjustifiable to assert that a definite change has occurred in the period after the introduction of the scheme. That is all the more so because, in absolute terms, 1970 had more working days lost as a result of redundancy disputes than any previous year except 1962.

What has just been said is the best construction that can be put on the data to draw out conclusions that show the statutory scheme in the most favourable light. On the other hand a different picture emerges from the index of working days lost through redundancy disputes. For 1960 − 64 that index ranges from nearly 68, in 1963, to about 848 in the unusual year of 1962. After the Redundancy Payments Act got going, in the years between 1966 and 1970, the index of working days lost in redundancy disputes was as low as about 52 during 1967. That low was reached after an index reading of nearly 177 which was some 10 points higher than for the twelve months preceding the introduction of the Act. From 1968 the index started moving up again, and in 1970 it stood at nearly 419. In sum, the index moved about a lot before the scheme was brought in, and it continued to fluctuate throughout the period of operation. There is therefore no basis for saying that 1965 marked a turning point in the loss of days of work caused by redundancy disputes.

Number of stoppages

That is as far as it is possible to take the analysis of loss of working days, at least on a national and all-industry basis. But it is possible, and· illuminating, to consider the other two criteria that are available for assessing the gravity of stoppages. The available facts on the number of stoppages are contained in Table 24 (Appendix).

Taking 1965 as the base year once again, the index of the number of stoppages shows an over-all similarity to the pattern displayed by the index for loss of working days through disputes about redundancy.

The swings for the number of stoppages are much less extreme. Consequently the curve plotting that index in Figure 6 is much flatter than the one for 'days lost'. On this evidence the scheme's influence for good becomes still more questionable. For the five years before the Act the stoppages index was about 84 at its lowest (in 1960) and about 204 at the peak in 1962. If that year were to be left out of account, the variation is between 84 and 125. The Department of Employment's figures for stoppages directly attribut-able to redundancy disputes do not extend beyond 1969. But in that four-year span the extreme readings on the index were about 84 and 121. These are strikingly close to the range in the earlier period, if 1962 is left out of account.

The index based on changes in the share of total stoppages taken by redundancy disputes (see Figure 5) shows slightly more variation than its counterpart for the actual number of stoppages, but even so there is nothing in it to substantiate any kind of claim for the healing influence of the Act.

Workers involved

There remains one other criterion for the assessment of the importance of stoppages – the test of the number of workers involved. The basic figures for the total number of workers involved in all stoppages of work arising from industrial disputes are available as a published series. For 1960 – 69 only, there are statistics of workers involved in stoppages originating solely from disputes about redundancies.

In Table 25 (Appendix) both those series are set out and it also contains the number of workers affected by redundancy disputes alone put as a proportion of all workers involved in stoppages consequent upon industrial disputes arising from all the eight identified causes. Additionally the table (Appendix) shows the year-to-year variations of that proportion. Finally, with 1965 as the base year, variations in the actual number of individuals concerned in stoppages arising solely from disputes about the compulsory severance of employment are shown. Variations in those two indexes are plotted on Figures 5 and 6.

Starting again with the year-to-year variations in the shares of the redundancy-generated number in the total of all workers involved in stoppages, the most striking thing is the relative stability of the curve. The early peak on this index came in 1961, a year earlier than with the other two curves on Figure 5. Apart from that, the two parts of the curve on either side of 1965 are not dissimilar. Put another way, the number of employees who stopped work because of a dispute about redundancy did not represent a very different fraction of the total of all employees who, for one reason or another, were involved in stoppages before or after the scheme came into operation.

Moving on to variations in the index of the actual number of individuals who stopped work solely because of conflict about redundancy, the 'workers involved' curve in Figure 6 runs quite counter to the view that the Redundancy Payments Act was

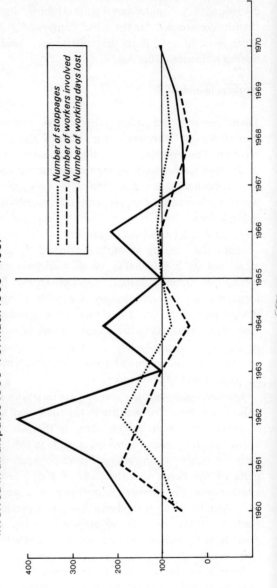

Figure 5
Variations in the indexes of number of working days lost,
number of stoppages and numbers of workers involved in
redundancy disputes expressed as a proportion of working
days lost, number of stoppages and numbers of workers
involved in all disputes 1960-70. Index 1965 = 100.

.... Number of stoppages
– – – – Number of workers involved
—————— Number of working days lost

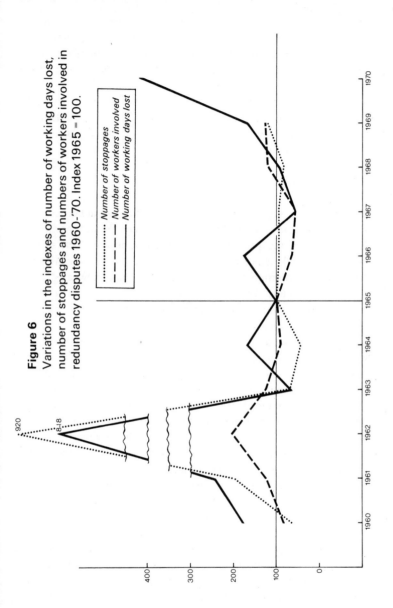

Figure 6
Variations in the indexes of number of working days lost, number of stoppages and numbers of workers involved in redundancy disputes 1960-'70. Index 1965 = 100.

.... *Number of stoppages*
‒ ‒ ‒ ‒ *Number of workers involved*
———— *Number of working days lost*

reducing the amount of tension about compulsory severance expressed through strike action. For (with the usual proviso about 1962), the years after the Act indicate no diminution of the involvement of individuals in work stoppages in protest against redundancy. While 1966 and 1967 both saw reduction on this standard, that is parallelled by 1963 and 1964 in the earlier period. And the two most recent years for which information exists show a growth in the number of workers implicated in stoppages caused by disputes about redundancy.

Variations by industry

Not much was known about the incidence of redundancies within different industries before the statutory scheme was brought in. Since the Act, the situation is not much improved. Yet, so far as policy making is concerned, a good deal hangs on the clarity with which the distribution of incidence of redundancy between different industries is understood and analysed.

How many redundancies were occurring in which industries? Has there been a sharper acceleration in some and not in others? To what extent have the differences resulted from reductions in product demand, with implications for future growth of the industry, and how much have they reflected technological change associated with higher total output, increased productivity per man, and a slimming down of the labour force? Without answers to these questions judgements cannot be made about things that need to be done about the allocation of manpower to different areas of activity. Nor can concepts be developed for assessing policy in the light of alterations in the main sources of demand for labour.

All of this goes beyond just manpower issues. So far as the differing rates of redundancy from one industry to another are a consequence of rising productivity, this raises a very complex cluster of questions, which has at one extreme the criteria for deciding the amount of capital which should go into particular types of industrial activity. At the other extreme of that cluster are a set of questions about the community's views regarding the ratio of work to leisure first, at places of work, and then, in the course of a person's working lifetime. These propositions outline the central nature of the need to know more about how redundancies are affecting different industries differently. For the present the focus is on trying to

Table 13 Working days lost through redundancy disputes in eight industry groups, 1960–1970 (total days, and index 1965=100).

Year	Mining & quarrying[1]		Metals & engineering		Shipbuilding & marine engineering		Vehicles		Textiles & clothing[2]		Construction		Transport & communication		All other industries & services	
	Index Number	Number	Index Number	Number	Index Number	Number	Index Number	Number	Index Number	Number	Index Number	Number	Index Number	Number	Index Number	Number
1960	3951	12,249	82	18,679	13	316	274	65,964	2	124	37	2,451	454	5,466	5	174
1961	2368	7,342	118	26,737	1048	24,637	302	72,768	3	140	108	7,167	287	3,459	162	5,563
1962	4282	13,273	476	107,753	2089	49,103	334	80,285	69	3,573	290	19,203	19519	235,202	176	6,056
1963	0	–	64	14,547	308	7,240	34	8,147	6	300	67	4,444	419	5,048	41	1,421
1964	41	126	94	21,246	52	1,229	270	64,870	1	25	139	9,196	265	3,194	34	1,173
1965	100	310	100	22,663	100	2,351	100	24,060	0	–	100	6,632	100	1,205	100	3,434
1966	936	2,901	125	28,244	3	64	105	25,359	100	5,215	67	4,426	2524	30,410	307	10,545
1967	0	–	82	18,464	72	1,680	14	3,429	0	–	85	5,658	31	374	62	2,124
1968	0	–	98	22,090	300	7,055	81	19,440	40	2,100	62	4,093	0	–	48	1,654
1969	0	–	113	25,622	303	7,126	159	38,190	20	1,065	167	11,060	291	3,511	466	15,993
1970	1778	5,513	522	118,384	270	6,352	297	71,548	19	809	256	16,949	78	934	983	33,743

Notes and sources

(1)   There were no redundancy disputes in mining and quarrying in 1963, and during 1967–69.
(2)   As there were no redundancy disputes in this industry group in 1965, the index is based on 1966=100.
        Data made available by the Department of Employment.

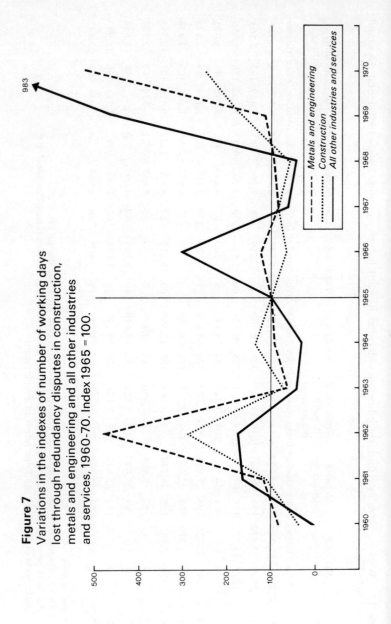

Figure 7
Variations in the indexes of number of working days
lost through redundancy disputes in construction,
metals and engineering and all other industries
and services, 1960-70. Index 1965 = 100.

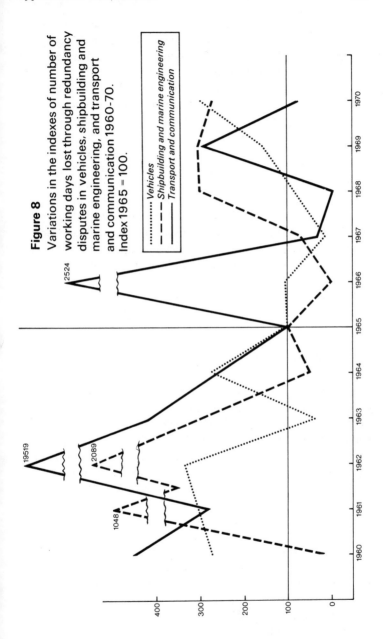

Figure 8
Variations in the indexes of number of working days lost through redundancy disputes in vehicles, shipbuilding and marine engineering, and transport and communication 1960-70. Index 1965 = 100.

.... Vehicles
– – – Shipbuilding and marine engineering
——— Transport and communication

establish whether an industry by industry examination of redundancy generated stoppages is possible, and the light such an analysis throws on whether or not the statutory scheme has led to a reduction of industrial conflict about redundancies.

Working days lost through stoppages caused by disputes about redundancy in eight broad industry groupings are tabulated in Table 13. Variations of the indexes for six of the broad industry groups are plotted on Figures 7 and 8.

The variations in the disputes index for mining and quarrying have not been graphed, as in four of the eleven years there were no stoppages in that industry caused by this type of dispute. The other industry group for which a curve has not been drawn in the figures is textiles and clothing. The difficulty there arises from the need to take 1966 as the base year for the index. That is necessary because in 1965 (the base year for all the other industries) there was no loss of working days in textiles and clothing through disputes about redundancy.

Year-to-year variations in the indexes are sharp, and quite random. This is true for all of the industry groups in Table 13.

Mining and quarrying

In mining and quarrying there is a particularly unusual pattern (see columns 1 and 2 of Table 13). Between 1960 and 1962 the loss of working days was high. In 1963 there were no disputes about redundancy leading to stoppages of work. Loss of working days in the year that followed was negligible. There was a ninefold rise in 1966, but that was a moderate level when contrasted with the first three years of the period. Between 1967 and 1969 there were no losses of working days through disputes about redundancy, but in the last year for which information is available the index rose twice as high as the highest previous level reached after 1965. A special redundancy scheme is operated by the Coal Board with government backing. These special arrangements swamp any effect that the 1965 statutory severance payments scheme might have had upon that industry. The interactions between the special provisions in mining and the general statutory scheme brought in during 1965 are too complex to be wholly disentangled.

Textiles and clothing

Textiles and clothing too are untypical. In part this is because of the nature of employment in the clothing component of that industry group, and it also stems partly from the large programme of reorganization launched with government support in 1959. Evaluation of the effects of the statutory severance scheme on redundancy disputes in particular industries has therefore to focus on the metals and engineering group; shipbuilding; vehicles; construction; and on the broad category covered by the heading of 'all other industries and services'. In transport and communication, there are again unusual circumstances. British Rail and the docks, both have specific redundancy schemes. Nevertheless the variations in the loss of working days in that industry are plotted in Figure 8.

Even the most cursory examination of Table 13, and the diagrammatic presentation of the information from it, is sufficient to establish the unwisdom of attempting to use that evidence to point to the statutory severance scheme's success in moderating disputes about redundancy.

In the metals and engineering group (Figure 7) the losses of working days were higher in 1970 than in any year before the introduction of severance payments legislation, even including 1962. In the fifth year after the statutory provisions had been brought in, days lost through redundancy disputes in the metals and engineering group were more than in three of the five years that preceded the legislation.

Shipbuilding and vehicles

For the shipbuilding and marine engineering group the record is rather better (Figure 8). But even there it would be stretching the evidence too far to suggest that the period after 1965 saw a consistent and continuing decline of conflict about redundancies. Of all the industry groups in Table 13, vehicles had the most consistently high level of days lost from redundancy stoppages before the 1965 Act. In the three years following things were a lot calmer than earlier. But events in 1969 and 1970 shattered the new-found peace.

There are absolute volumes and index changes for the textiles and clothing group in Table 13. There is a problem here of having to use a different base year for this industry. But here too the Act does not appear to have improved matters.

Transport and communication

Particularly because of the structure of employment in this industry group, loss of working days through stoppages has considerable volatility. The difference, for instance, between 5,000 days lost and 235,000 could be accounted for simply by a one-day national withdrawal of labour on British Rail. But national railway stoppages are rare events.

There is also the long drawn out grumbling about redundancies in the docks. But the days lost as a result of redundancy disputes in this industry group is quite small. And, interestingly enough, there is a marked and fairly consistent improvement in the loss of working time arising from disputes about redundancy. Ironically, the first year of the life of the statutory severance scheme brought, in 1966, a particularly high loss of working days from disputes about redundancy. All the same, the curve of the index for this industry group (see Figure 8) has tended to be lower than it was before 1965.

That solitary piece of evidence of more amicable dealings on redundancy since the inception of the scheme is some comfort in trying to establish the success of the Redundancy Payments Act by this standard of assessment of its achievements. That is just as well, because the final industry group covered by Table 13 points with a good deal of certainty to a worsening of industrial relationships about redundancies.

All other industries and services

This group takes in over half of the 27 Orders into which industrial activity is allocated under the UK Standard Industrial Classification and includes industries in manufacturing as well as services. In common with the groups already considered, this category had a flare up of loss of working days associated with redundancy disputes in 1962. In terms of the actual volume of days lost, however, the other industries category, even in that year, was a model of good behaviour.

This category also had, in common with the seven groups examined so far, sharp year-to-year fluctuations in the loss of working days from stoppages caused by disputes about redundancy. But unlike any of those seven it had a more moderate range of variation in the years preceding the Redundancy Payments Act than during 1966 − 70. Moreover during those later years the annual loss of working days was consistently higher than during 1960 − 64.

At no time after the introduction of the statutory severance payments scheme was the index (1965 = 100) of days lost in redundancy disputes as low as in any year in the period before the legislation.

As has been said, given the sharp year-to-year fluctuations there has to be a good deal of caution in interpreting the evidence. But developments in this category are firm enough to allow the conclusion that the scheme did not diminish the abrasion caused by redundancy to levels below those prevailing before the Act. In fact, during the life time of the scheme, there have been more redundancy-generated strikes. But such strikes might have been more serious still if there were no scheme.

Compensation for disruption

Cash payment, then, flowing from the statutory severance compensation scheme was designed to reduce general alarm and apprehension about disruption. That, in turn, was expected to work its way through to each particular situation where people's employment was to be terminated because of redundancy. With the shock of disruption moderated by the cushion of cash compensation, friction and strife on occasions of redundancy would tend to decline. That would show up in, among other things, disputes about redundancy. In the context of the time for which the 1965 legislation was dealing, the policy makers were content to leave it at that. For the job market was good, there were many vacancies, and it was thought that market forces would do the rest by way of ensuring desirable and beneficial redeployment of manpower. Indeed the word 'redeployment' was fresh minted at that time, and summed up the prevailing view that if only manpower resources could be made to flow in new directions, they would be wholly absorbed without a significant hiatus between the occurrence of particular redundancies, and the re-employment of those people in other jobs.

The outcome was not quite like that. From 1966 unemployment in Britain began to rise inexorably and year by year. The number of unfilled job vacancies declined sharply between 1966 and 1967, and then settled at levels well below that of the opening year of the decade. It is quite possible that if these big changes in the labour market had not happened, hopes about more peaceful handling of redundancies in industry might well have been fulfilled. For the cash compensation to have taken the edge off the general worry was only part of the set. For the thing to be won game, set and match, it was necessary to have continuing high levels of economic activity and tight labour markets. As it was, workpeople's apprehensions about being out on the cobbles were back in renewed strength within a year of the enactment of the statute. In those circumstances, the statutory severance payments scheme could do little to damp down industrial conflict about compulsory termination of employment. Consequently, it can be no real surprise that an examination of stoppages of work from disputes about redundancy fails to reveal any moderation that can be attributed to the beneficial influence of the statutory severance payments scheme.

10 Action on redundancy

In any situation where a firm considers it necessary to reduce its labour force, two principal issues arise. In the first place, there is the issue of the framework of judgement about the necessity for reduction of the labour force. Secondly, there is the task of easing the movement of the people concerned to new employment.

Who decides?

The first issue is one about policy, and it involves weighing up both economic and social considerations. The hiring and firing of men is in the firm's decision-making province, but that process is not wholly separable from the community's interests. The evaluation of the need for a particular redundancy, as much as the criteria applied in reaching that conclusion, can legitimately be held to be policy issues too important for the firm alone. Should individual enterprises be the sole judges of the necessity and desirability of redundancies? Recall that the 1965 Act is founded on the belief that redundancies are good. On top of that, the Act takes it as axiomatic that the sole judges of the necessity for some workpeople to be 'disemployed' are the firms employing that manpower.

On this major issue of principle the Redundancy Payments Act made no contribution at all. Where it does seek to inject the wider community interests into specific redundancy situations is at the stage when the firm's decision-making process is complete, and action is in sight to make employees redundant. Here, the approach incorporated into the statutory severance scheme is something that goes back into history. An item in the Ministry of Labour Gazette, for August 1948, stresses the importance 'to the country as a whole as well as to individual employers and workers that the time between a worker finishing in one job and starting in another should be reduced to the minimum'. In order to reduce that time lag 'provision has been made at Local Offices of the Ministry of Labour and National Service for assisting workers who are under notice to find other employment'. Then, the Gazette article, somewhat plaintively, continued 'but this help cannot be given unless the Offices know when workers are likely to become redundant'.

Commenting further on this service designed for the community's economic and social gain (17 years before the introduction of legislation on severance payments) the Ministry of Labour went on record with, 'many employers do in fact co-operate with Local Offices of the Ministry, by giving them advance notice of redundancies and by advising workers affected to register for alternative employment. Workers, too, are increasingly taking advantage of this arrangement. Some employers arrange with the Local Office for lists of vacancies suitable for the people about to be discharged to be available at the works. Others make provision for workers to be registered at their place of employment, and give them time off for interview by prospective employers'. But, not content with what had been achieved, the Ministry of Labour thought that there was 'scope for greater co-operation of employers and workers with Local Offices'. Well over a decade and a half after that was written, provision for advance notification of redundancy was incorporated in the 1965 Act.

Advance notice

Stripped of the Parliamentary draftsman's careful circumlocutions, the Act gave the Minister of Labour the power to obtain advance information from employers about their intention to discharge employees on ground of redundancy. The mechanism chosen to obtain employer compliance was roundabout and indirect. No attempt was made to impose a straight compulsory requirement that firms should notify the Department of Employment of forthcoming redundancies in good time, so that the public employment service could get on with the job of placing people in suitable new employment. Instead, the chosen approach was to tie this up with the payment of rebates to employers from the Fund established by the Act. The Department of Employment (strictly speaking, the

Secretary of State) has powers under the statute to make regulations about the basis on which employers are entitled to receive rebates from the Fund.

Rebates and notice

Although, under those powers, the Department of Employment has made regulations about the time limit within which employers must put in their claims for rebate (and for a variety of other conditions of entitlement), the point of interest here lies in the use made of those powers for getting information to the public employment exchanges in advance of actual redundancy. Here the Act enables the Department to ask an employer for a maximum of four weeks 'prior notice' of his intention of putting in a claim upon the Fund.

The Department of Employment is able, under powers given to it by the Act, to reduce an employers' rebates, up to a maximum of 10 per cent of their value, if the firms fail to give that advance notice. At first sight these arrangements appear shrewd in administrative terms, whatever limitations they might possess on a standard of judgement based on wider social and economic criteria. To get what the jargon describes as 'management control information' from 'financial control data' is an economical way of conducting an operation. Indeed the Department has taken a lot of trouble over the form employers have to fill. The form is designed in such a way that work done on setting out data for advance notification can be re-utilized in the putting in of the actual claim for rebate from the Fund. Thus two targets are hit at one throw: employers who unceasingly complain about the burden of form-filling put upon them by Whitehall are mollified, and the Department's local offices are able to have early detailed information regarding individuals who are about to be made redundant.

In principle, at least, that is how things stand. And so far as the financial control aspect of the procedures is concerned, the Comptroller and Auditor General is satisfied that the Department of Employment is conducting a satisfactory operation.[1] Quite evidently, the Department is painstaking in its investigations to check that employers do not put in fraudulent claims for rebates from the Fund. The reasons given by the employer for the redundancy about which he is giving prior notice of claim are examined at the Department's local office in the 'light of local knowledge' before decisions are made about the legitimacy of the claim.

If Departmental officials have doubts that the dismissals might not be due to redundancy as defined by the Act, a specialist officer from higher up the ladder pays the firm a visit. His object is to find out in detail the reasons for the dismissal, and to double check that workpeople who are being made redundant will not be replaced. Local offices also keep close watch over the employer to see that he is not replacing the dismissed worker 'in circumstances which cast doubt on whether he was ever really redundant'.

Fraud against the Fund

The Department of Employment has also made a check of a random sample (for 1965 – 66) of the information put in by employers in support of their claim to rebates. Evidently that check showed that 14 – 15 per cent of claims had had to be amended before payment, and something under 1 per cent had been rejected by the Department. All this adds up to pretty strenuous efforts against the Fund being exploited to provide rebates for compensation for false redundancy claims.

Quite genuine doubts can be held about the necessity of such rigorous financial control. In part the necessity for it arises from tales about individuals receiving large sums of redundancy compensation and being re-employed again by the same employer without even the decent cover of an intervening spell of unemployment. That sort of story, with just the right smack of scandal, provides fodder for Parliamentary Questions, and Whitehall must be seen to maintain its reputation for good housekeeping. But none of that rigorous and intensive effort is of much value in enabling the Department of Employment's public employment service to do a good placement and counselling job for the redundant employee.

It is here that the biggest shortcoming lies in combining management control information with verification of the legitimacy of the financial outflow from the Redundancy Fund. Nevertheless there can be no doubt about the Department of Employment's wish to develop a positive and major role for the public employment service in dissipating the effects of redundancy. A consistent theme, as we have seen, going back at least to 1948 in the Department's ideas about increasing the depth and value of its help to redundant employees, is the need to have as much time for preparation as possible. That objective, at least, the 1965 Act seemed all set to bring within reach.

Often, especially on occasions of large-scale redundancy, the public employment service has chalked up a considerable measure of success in helping workpeople to find new jobs.[2] Yet, there is apparently a curious diffidence about the Department's use of the powers available in the 1965 Act. Where that statute gave authority for the Department to ask for a maximum of four weeks' prior notice of forthcoming redundancies, in practice that length of notice has not been sought. If the redundancy is small, involving fewer than ten employees, all that the Department asks of the firm is 14 days' advance notice. When more than ten people are to have their employment terminated, the length of notice which the employer has to give to the local employment exchange goes up to 21 days.

It is odd that the Department of Employment has not used the full scope of the Act to gain time for its placement function. Another interesting, and again self-imposed, limitation is in the information that the Department asks the employer to furnish. The form on which the firm gives details about a forthcoming redundancy in its workforce asks for eight items of information. Of these, four are of some direct value to the employment exchange in its task of finding the person a new job. These are basic things – whether the individual is male or female, his date of birth, the length of his service with the firm, and the date when he is to be made redundant. The other half of the form is about items solely concerned with the financial aspect of the transaction between the employer and the Redundancy Fund.

Occupational information

Clearly, the demand for information from employers needs to be kept to the minimum, and confined to issues that are relevant and essential. Nevertheless a striking omission in this list is the absence of any occupational information. In order to form a view about what the individual's prospect will be like in the labour market, and for preparatory examination of the things that the employment exchange might be able to do for him, the occupational characteristics of the person being made redundant are of central importance. There are many difficulties about getting clear occupational definitions. Often different terms are put to the same jobs in different establishments. It is not always easy to set down a meaningful occupational description within the narrow confines of a form manageable in size.

These are good explanations for not asking employers to describe occupations. Nevertheless this is the key to an informed and selective process of counselling and placement. It is a measure of the bias of the statutory severance scheme that it does not generate an information flow on this central issue for effective manpower redeployment.

That the Redundancy Payments Act was not thought out as a part of general framework for manpower adaptation is clear from the minimal importance attached in it to developing information flows that could be put to use for making decisions on a coherent manpower policy. But even if that wider objective is left on one side, ·on more limited grounds there is a substantial case for a monitoring system in the mechanism of the scheme. That would have made a continuous assessment and evaluation of what was being achieved by that statutory measure possible. To launch a big scheme, uniquely different in its characteristics from the normal way of doing things in British industry, with purposes of great economic and social significance, and yet not associate with it systems for learning from experience through careful collection of data and the operation of feedback, is baffling.

A usual response to this kind of comment is that information systems and monitoring devices cost money. They also consume scarce research and administrative talent. When all that is said, however, the question still remains: how sensible is it to have spent £381 million over a six-year period with a particular purpose in view, and not had a system for establishing whether the community was getting value for money?

Not Whitehall's custom

Changes are coming slowly, but of course Whitehall does not usually function effectively in research and information matters. It is customary for the department concerned to make periodic reviews of events associated with a new piece of legislation. Yet it is strange that the idea has not been grasped that legislation like the statute establishing the Industrial Training Boards, or the statutory severance payments scheme, merits more than the traditional internal departmental mulling over. The contrast with the United States is extreme. Of course applied research in the social sciences is very much a part of the American way of life. Still that does not detract from the impressiveness of the decision of successive United States Administrations to incorporate a clause in all recent manpower and social affairs legislation requiring the commissioning of research about the operation of those statutes.

It seems self-evident that a Whitehall department with responsibility for something new like the statutory severance payments scheme would need, at the very minimum, well-established internal monitoring systems for observing and analysing what was going on. For one thing, if a professional job of observing, interpreting and reviewing the working of the scheme had been in hand, the undignified scramble to prevent the Fund from running out of money need not have arisen.

Limited though they were, the powers given by the Act to the Department of Employment are good enough to allow the development of a useful information system about redundancies. Something has been said already about the omission of occupational information from the details that the Department asks to be included in the advance notice of redundancies that the statute requires from employers. Division of view is possible about the merit of trying to do something to remedy this. But there can be no disagreement about processing the data that is already collected to form the basis for more informed managerial decisions by the Department's officials and as background for reviews of the working of the scheme.

During the main debate on the Bill that emerged as the 1965 Act, the Minister sponsoring the statute said that the provisions in Section 30 would mean that 'the employment exchanges will get advance notice of virtually all redundancies'.[3] Basic to the idea of getting advance notice to the employment exchanges is the intention that the Department's officials at local level should have a chance of assessing the labour market situation, and preparing themselves to offer help to the displaced employees in their search for new work.

Prior notice is necessary for the operational part of the public employment service's role to be discharged efficiently. It is, possibly, this operational orientation of the advance information about redundancies which explains the absence of aggregated data for determining whether the Department was getting 'advance notice of virtually all redundancies' as promised by the Minister. Otherwise it is difficult to explain why comprehensive statistics about all notifications of redundancies received by employment exchanges are not available right from the time that the scheme got going. Local offices of the Department of Employment have this in common with employers – they fret when Headquarters in St James's Square comes up with yet another demand for statistics.

Officials at employment exchanges think of figure grubbing as a waste of time that they could use much more fruitfully in doing real work. Added together, all of this goes some way towards explaining why the Department of Employment did not, evidently, begin to bring together any detailed information about advance notifications by employers of forthcoming redundancies. At any rate, that is what seems to have happened for the first three years of the lifetime of the statutory severance scheme.

Analysis of advance notice

Since 1969 something has been done. Figures of prior notifications received by employment exchanges have been collected month by month centrally at the Department. That information has been available to anyone who asked for it, though not officially published by the Department. For that there appears to be a sound explanation. In keeping with its usual cautious nature, the Department appears unwilling to take responsibility for information that might be questioned because the techniques used in its compilation might seem amateur. Such a view commands respect. But why were no attempts made to do a proper job?

Section 30 of the Redundancy Payments Act gave the Department authority to require, through regulations made by the Minister, advance notice from firms about redundancies which they were proposing to declare. When the regulation came to be made[4] under heading of 'Prior notice of expected redundancy', the proposition was plain: 'An employer shall give prior notice that a claim for a rebate may arise.'

A customary precaution taken by Whitehall departments against the incomprehensibility of the language of British statutes is the issuing of plain-words guides for use of people whose lives are affected by the decision of the legislature. In the Employment Department's Guide to the Redundancy Payments Act, the firm proposition of the Statutory Instrument appeared to undergo a sea change. 'An employer who is intending to dismiss employees because of redundancy', in the wording of that Guide, 'must, *wherever possible*, give advance notice to the nearest employment exchange'. That gloss did not, of course, modify the legal position. But clearly some soft pedalling was being done.

Wording and substance

Perhaps changes in nuances of wording do not in themselves constitute a difference of substance. Were that the only bit of evidence, there would not be much of a case. But add to that the fact that the Department of Employment denied itself the use of the maximum four weeks' prior notice it could have gone for under the Act. Then again, there is the tenor of the words in the Guide, which explain the reasons for asking employers for prior notice. The relevant paragraph runs:

> The purpose of advance notice is to enable the Department of Employment to clear up with the employer any queries about his claim for rebate as far as possible before the dismissals become effective and payments are made to the employees concerned.

That is the principal object. 'Advance notice will also help the employment services to take prompt action in finding fresh work for the employees made redundant.' It is not reading too much into this to think that the rigour of the book-keeping exercise is of paramount importance. And that would be all of a piece with the over-all high value attached to the financial control aspect of the Department's involvement in the running of the scheme.

About the interface between the public employment service and the scheme, there is a lot less rigour. In extolling the virtues of the proposed Act, the sponsoring Minister laid a great deal of emphasis on the benefits for the public employment service of the provision for 10 per cent reduction of rebate when employers are late in giving notice of an expected redundancy. Not only would that mean 'in effect, that the employment exchanges (would) get advance notice of virtually all redundancies', but the Minister had every intention 'to see that the utmost use is made of this to get ahead in good time with the placing of redundant workers in fresh employment, or with arrangements for retraining'. On the face of it that made eminent good sense. A good old-fashioned, no-nonsense money incentive was built in to encourage employers towards doing something that would be of value to the people who were losing their jobs, as well as to the community at large in its endeavours to help to reduce loss of productive manpower that could arise from avoidable extended job searches. It is illuminating to compare the design with the outcome.

Rebates withheld

In each of the financial years 1966/67 – 1970/71 rebates were withheld from employers because they had not complied with Section 30(6) of the Act requiring them to give prior notice of expected redundancies to the Department's local offices. The strength of this punitive measure can be gauged from the fact that the total sums of money denied to employers ranged from £7 in 1970 to £59 in 1969. In two of the remaining three years the cut back on employers' rebates amounted to £27, and in 1968 it was £22. For the whole quinquennium, the total sum of money of which employers were deprived came to £142. That was occurring over the same time span as a total rebate payment to employers of something over £217 million.

That amounts to as near perfection as seems possible in human affairs. Given that the arithmetical average of lump-sum payments to individuals for that period as a whole was £250, and assuming a 50 per cent rebate, there were evidently only about eleven of the employees who became redundant during 1967 – 71 whose impending termination of employment was not notified to the Department's local offices. This figuring is based on the annual accounts of the Redundancy Fund. For the first three years of the life of the scheme, none of this can be checked against actual figures of the advance notifications received by the public employment service. But from 1969 there are the statistics, about which the Department of Employment has reservations.

Though that information covers only 1969 – 71, and three years are rather a brief period of observation, it is possible to learn a fair amount from setting the advance-notification statistics against the total number of payments made each year. Those payments figures indicate the number of redundancies that did in fact take place, and they are more firmly based than the statistics of notifications about forthcoming redundancies.

Shortfall between notified and actual numbers

In all three years, the number of redundancies about which advance notice was given to the public employment service was smaller than the actual number of redundancies receiving severance compensation. In the course of the period, the difference narrowed year by year. For about 40 per cent of the payments made in 1969, employment exchanges appear not to have received early notification of impending redundancies. Things got better in 1970, when the corresponding figure was down to about 20 per cent. By 1971 the number of prior notifications was only 9 per cent below the actual redundancies eligible for statutory severance compensation (see Table 14).

Quite evidently the advance notification procedures became increasingly more effective during the three years about which information is available. True though that is, there is a big difference between the picture given by Table 14 and the conclusions drawn earlier by examination of the Redundancy Fund accounts.

Table 14   Prior notification of redundancies, and number of actual statutory severance payments, 1969−71.

	1969	1970	1971
Number notified in advance[1]	149,500	220,900	336,200
Number of payments[2]	250,800	275,600	370,300
Notified redundancies as per cent of number of payments	59.6	80.1	90.8

Notes and sources
(1)   Made available by the Department of Employment. Derived from returns limited to 20 or more workers, or closure, or more than five skilled workers, or at local discretion.
(2)   See Table 2. There is a small discrepancy between the figures in this row and corresponding figures in Table 2. This arises from (unexplained) differences in the quarterly data produced by the Department of Employment.

Yet, from Table 14, it appears that in 1971, the most recent and best year, alone, actual redundancy payment exceeded the number of prior notifications by over 34,000. Of course the extent of under-reporting at over 54,000 was higher still in 1970, with 1969 being worst of all when the number of payments was greater than prior notifications to the extent of 101,000.

A detailed explanation is possible, and is considered in full in what follows. Before that, it is as well to say why any of this matters. While it is wholly proper to have stringent accounting procedures for money collected from industry and channelled back to it through a scheme whose stewardship rests in the hands of a Whitehall department, and this requires expenditure of effort and ingenuity by civil servants, that cannot be the sole purpose of official involvement in a scheme of the kind established by the Redundancy Payments Act. More important is the use to which that early notice of an impending upheaval can be put in terms of achieving an efficient, quick redeployment of individuals to new productive employment.

Low level of notifications

For employers, there is clear gain in dealing with a redundancy with as little fuss and bother as possible. Except when the redundancy involves a lot of people, or is charged with difficulties for other reasons, the chore of giving detailed notice to the local employment exchange is additional bother which employers are naturally happy to do without. Building in the penalty of a withholding of a small part of the rebate was intended to help in overcoming that natural inertia.

From the low level of prior-notification figures for 1969, two inferences are possible. One is that quite a lot of employers implicated in redundancies were failing to do what was required of them right through into the fourth year of the life of the severance payments scheme. But from then on there was a change, and more firms chose to send in early notification. If that happened, then the explanation must lie in something other than the financial incentive to provide notice in good time, for the penalty was not, as we have seen, used in any substantial way at any time. The second possible explanation could lie wholly in the Department of Employment's record keeping. It could be that employer behaviour had been consistent, all the time, and had been at a high level of compliance with the statutory requirement. Information had come in at the same level all the time to the Local Offices, but the collation and assembly for Headquarters had initially been less good than it became during 1970 and 1971.

Before an opinion can be formed of the plausibility of either of those two explanations, it is necessary to delve into the basis of the figures on advance notification. In principle the law requires employers to tell the local offices of the Department of Employment what redundancies are in the offing. That obligation, of course, exists only with regard to employees who have the minimum two-years' length of service to qualify them for payment. And here is the first leakage from the system. Workpeople who do not have the necessary minimum of two-years' service, not only do not qualify for a statutory severance compensation, they are also not directly brought into the view of employment exchanges by the working of the mechanism established by the Redundancy Payments Act.

That is an issue with ramifications beyond this immediate context. For the present, it needs to be noted on two counts. Employment exchanges are denied an automatic interception of this stream of manpower flowing out of redundancy situations, and their steering and placement activities are in consequence more narrow in scope than is desirable.

A no less important consequence of there being no system for connecting up redundant workpeople ineligible for compensation under the statutory severance payments scheme with employment exchanges is the gap in everyone's knowledge about exactly how many people are losing their jobs through redundancy. Admittedly, that information gap is more important for over-all national policy about the prevailing rate of redundancy than for the operational needs of employment exchanges. In this field, however, the real loss almost certainly arises from the permissive nature of the Department of Employment's approach to firms which should be giving forewarning of impending redundancies but fail to do so.

But then, on that reasoning, how can the improvement for 1970 and 1971 shown in Table 14 in advance reporting be reconciled with the proposition that the Department of Employment has not become more punitive in its application of the penalty clause? It was suggested earlier that employers could have suddenly changed their ways and started, of their own volition, to inform employment exchanges more fully about impending redundancies from 1970 onwards. On the other hand, it could be that the Department of Employment was being more thorough, from 1970 onwards, in sweeping up from its local offices the information which they had been getting at a consistently high level even before that seminal year.

Possible explanations

To complicate the picture further, yet another factor needs to be taken into account. The statistics of redundancies notified in advance contained in Table 14 include an unknown number of individuals ineligible for severance compensation because they did not have the minimum length of service to qualify. Their impending redundancy was, nevertheless, notified voluntarily by employers to the Department's local offices. As a result, some part of the improvement from 1970 onwards in the statistics of redundancies notified in advance of the event to employment exchanges could be arising simply from the fact that, with the growth of the total volume of redundancies in the country, those employers who in any event would have told the Department's local offices early about their rebatable redundancies were at the same time voluntarily passing on information about workpeople who were going to lose their jobs without statutory compensation.

In other words, employer behaviour did not improve across the board in this respect. All that happened was that those who gave advance warning did so increasingly about everybody who was going to get the sack.

To this complexity, further complication has to be added. The closing of the gap between the number of advance notifications and of actual payments could have been arising from the nature of the method of compilation of the Department of Employment's statistics given at Table 14. Every month, Headquarters staff at the Department of Employment add up the figures of advance notices about impending redundancies received by employment exchanges in all parts of the country. That has been going on systematically since January 1969. Included in these figures are all workers, irrespective of their eligibility for statutory severance payment, whose impending redundancy is notified to employment exchanges.

That apparent comprehensiveness is, however, deceptive. Local offices are not, as we have already noted, particularly fond of being used as agents for the collection of statistics. One way of reducing the burden of this particular data-collection exercise has been the decision to confine record keeping (and passing on of information to Headquarters) to certain kinds of redundancies. Basically, there is a minimum size criterion. Employment exchanges are not required to go through this reporting procedure for occasions of redundancy where less than 20 people are affected. However this cut-off solely by reference to size is put in abeyance if the redundancies in a given situation are small but are a consequence of the total shut down of an enterprise. Additionally the size criterion for recording and passing on information to St James's Square is relaxed if at least five of the employees to be made redundant belong to skilled occupations.

Method of counting

With that basis for the passing on of advance notification data to the centre, the convergence of notified redundancies towards the number of actual payments in the course of 1969 – 71 could have been brought about by a changing pattern in the incidence of redundancies. Suppose that in 1971 employment exchanges received advance notices of redundancies which affected the same number of individuals as in the preceding year. Yet, if more of those individuals were affected by bigger redundancies, if, that is to say, there were more redundancies in 1971 which involved dismissal of 20 or more employees, that would increase the size of the final figure recorded by employment exchanges and reported to headquarters.

Likewise were there to have been an increase in redundancies among enterprises employing a greater proportion of skilled manpower, that too would be fed through by employment exchanges and, in turn, enlarge the size of the centrally collated total. Equally the total figure of advance notifications could be bumped up if the rate of closure among small establishments (with less than 20 employees) had risen from 1969 onwards.

All this is worth going into because these figures are the sole source of managerial information available within the governmental machine for assessment of current policy, and planning measures to take account of developing circumstances. All the indications are that the financial control data derived from applications for rebate from the Redundancy Fund are not of much use, and not much used, in making evaluations either of the success in attaining the wider objectives of the Act, or, more narrowly, in terms of the public employment service's ability to contribute to an effective redeployment of manpower.

As always an argument can be put forward on grounds of economy against gathering too much information which might or might not be useful for policy making. People whose job is to get on with the job are anyway understandably impatient about demands for information which, no matter how significant from a policy-making point of view, are remote from day-to-day activity and a distraction from the work in hand. While that, coupled with a worthy disposition towards thrift, can be an argument for lettings things run without too much probing and analysis, by the same token it can be the basis of a case for establishing a research and planning capability from the start of the operation of a scheme which has the degree of social and economic significance that attaches to the Redundancy Payments Act.

An established piece of conventional wisdom in Britain about redundancies is that training and retraining should be an intrinsic part of the programme of resettlement of individuals who have lost their jobs. Training in this context, at least for the overwhelming majority of redundant workpeople, is not a self-evident option. It is something that has to be brought within their frame of reference by deliberate action by someone. In a society whose *mores* are work-dominated, a redundant person is immediately at a loss. So far as manual workers are concerned, their training in Britain is directly related to their being in employment.

Trade unions in Britain have not had a tradition of involving themselves in training schemes for their members. There remains the government as the long stop. As neither employers nor trade unions have the inclination or the capability, retraining for redundant workers has to be supplied by the government acting as the custodian of the whole community's interests. But retraining cannot be given in the abstract. A lot of information is needed about the kinds of jobs which are being extinguished. A good deal of knowledge is required about the skills and occupations of those being made redundant.

Redundancy and retraining

In Britain the only access point to the system of retraining for manual workers is through employment exchanges. Consequently, personnel at those exchanges need time to analyse and prepare proposals for the clients who are going to be in need of their help in deciding whether or not they should involve themselves in the process of retraining. Back-up facilities, in terms of a big and flexible government retraining capability, have to be available for employment exchange personnel to treat this as a serious choice they can offer to redundant workpeople. And, most important of all, there has to be a reasonably clear view at policy-making level about the directions, by occupations and industry, towards which manpower flows should be encouraged. That policy, moreover, has to be under unceasing examination, continuously taking in new and more detailed information for updating the basis for judgement and action. A model of how this can be done is available in Sweden, and has been analysed in a previous PEP publication.[5]

All that is a far cry from the current reality in Britain. Far from there being a comprehensive infrastructure of manpower redeployment, there is not even a strong thrust to use fully the instruments of policy and mechanisms of administration that are available. All that has been said so far about advance notification of vacancies has to be seen in that context. It is not the technical inadequacies of the system of data collection that really count. What matters is the approach which that reflects, and the inadequacy of purpose revealed by it all. The Department of Employment has not used the penalty clause in the redundancy rebate scheme to get more employers to turn in advance notice of all redundancies, chiefly from fear of upsetting firms whose co-operation is needed by the public employment service on, for instance, notification of vacancies, which is wholly voluntary.

Yet the worst offenders in not giving forewarning of impending redundancy are very probably in the services sector, and employers generally in those industries are not singularly distinguished by their intensity of co-operation with the Department's local offices. There also seems to be every likelihood that many firms in the construction industry do not go out of their way to inform the employment exchanges, in advance of the event, of their intention to compulsorily terminate the jobs of some of their employees.

Given the tough tradition of that industry, many people would have no doubt at all that the worst way of getting co-operation from employers in construction is to take a soft approach.

Basis of policy making

What is being said here is conjectural. And yet, there is no option but to speculate, because neither the industry nor the occupational dimensions of the incidence of redundancy in Britain is known, much less understood. One possible rejoinder to this kind of criticism is to suggest that if all this is really important, no doubt someone somewhere would have done something about it. Even if British academics had a stronger tradition of applied research in the socio-economic field, the undertaking being discussed here would have been inappropriate to them. When it comes to informed policy making based on evaluations of the working of a measure like the Redundancy Payments Act, the most effective system is one containing information feedback to managers from the operational personnel out in the field. Quite evidently the body that should have done that job is the Department of Employment.

There is a tendency in Whitehall to adopt an air of weary scepticism whenever outsiders point to things that are not being done, or are being pushed forward without sufficient vigour. The weariness increases and the scepticism deepens, when such views are expressed about the basis of policy making, and both are most pronounced whenever there are suggestions that the making of decisions could be helped through systematic assembly of detailed information and continuing research into work done on a day-to-day basis in order to implement a piece of legislation.

What, it might be asked, would be the value for policy making of the exercise advocated here? It has to be said straight away that a question like that is very difficult to answer. Examples can be cited from other countries (see, for instance, an earlier PEP study, *Making Labour Markets Work*) where everyone involved is convinced of the value of good information systems. But a standard civil-service response to comparisons with other countries is a lofty superiority: it is all right for other chaps to go fact-grubbing; we, in Britain, know better.

Attempts to demonstrate the usefulness of collecting information and analysing it as a platform for policy, on the basis of British experience, are extraordinarily difficult. Chiefly the difficulty lies in trying to make out a convincing case for collecting information when there is very little existing information to go on. In fact, the best that can be done is to put the general principle that any sensible organization would want to keep track of the events it has set afoot, and to that end it makes sense to establish systems for feedback of information.

11 Britain's system for redeployment

A modest bit of analysis of the figures for prior notification of redundancies illustrates in a concrete way how useful interpretations can be squeezed out of existing information. An account has already been given of the limitations of the figures of redundancies for which advance notification was given to the Department of Employment for 1969 – 71. Nevertheless, as an experiment, those numbers have been plotted quarter by quarter for 1969 – 71.

On Figure 9 we have also charted the variations in the actual redundancy payments that were made. Information on this is, of course, available from an earlier date, and the curve showing actual payments, unlike the one about notifications, starts in 1966. From inspection of Figure 9 it is clear that the number of notified redundancies falls short of the number of actual payments in most of the twelve quarters. Nevertheless each quarter's advance notifications give a reasonably good guide to the number of payments made in the three months which followed.

Reflection confirms that such an outcome is not illogical. For the purpose of the advance notices is to foreshadow events. So a simple and straightforward thing to do is to plot the number of advance notifications which came in during one quarter against the number of actual payments from the Fund for the following quarter.

Figure 10 shows the number of redundancy payments lagged by one quarter, plotted against the number of redundancies which were notified in advance to employment exchanges. This gives a good linear relationship between the two. The two variables have a coefficient of correlation of 0.931 (the equation is $y = 0.72x + 34.1$; see Table 26, Appendix, for actual figures).

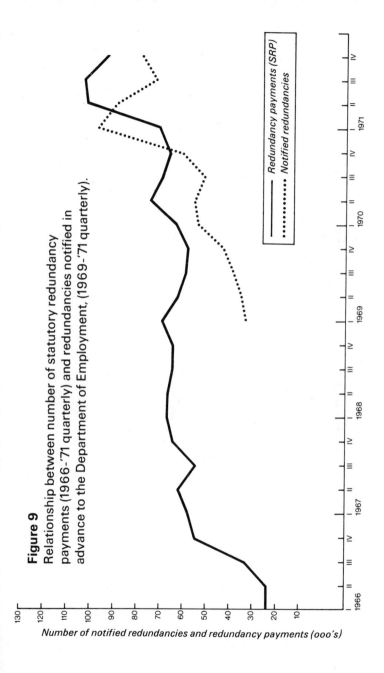

Figure 9

Relationship between number of statutory redundancy payments (1966-'71 quarterly) and redundancies notified in advance to the Department of Employment, (1969-'71 quarterly).

Number of notified redundancies and redundancy payments (ooo's)

Redundancy payments (SRP)
Notified redundancies

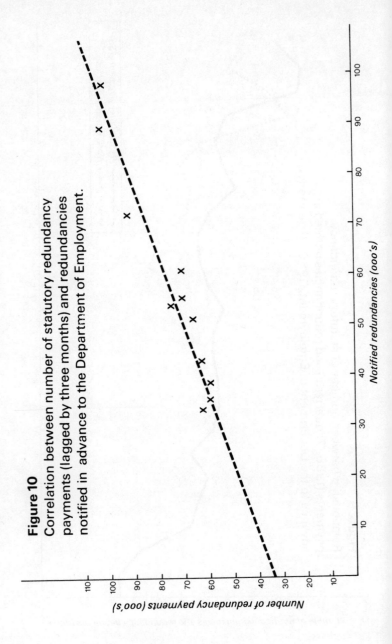

Figure 10
Correlation between number of statutory redundancy payments (lagged by three months) and redundancies notified in advance to the Department of Employment.

Notifications and payments

As was said earlier, this is not a profound piece of computation. Yet, assuming that the linear relationship continues to hold, it is possible to predict the actual number of claims likely to be made on the Redundancy Fund one quarter ahead of the advance notification data. Clearly that is quite a modest achievement. But, as we saw in Chapter 7, there has been a reasonably firm ratio of distribution of the incidence of redundancy by age category. By applying that to the forecast of redundancies likely to occur within a period of three months ahead of the time of forecast, it would have been possible to estimate a three-monthly cash outflow from the Fund.

That could have gone some way to prevent the apparently hand-to-mouth pattern of existence of the Redundancy Fund in the years preceding the 1965 restructuring of the rebate scheme. In one sense what is being said here is of no more than historical interest. But there is more to it than that. The significance of this example is in what it illustrates. If evaluation of progress towards reaching a goal is thought worthwhile, and given some information, quite elementary techniques can be applied to yield worthwhile assessments.

All kinds of scholarly technical objections can be raised about the illustrative and modest calculations presented here, and the use of them to point a wider moral. The argument of this chapter is based on the view that there was more in the legislation for a statutory severance scheme than paying compensation to people who got the sack because their employers' need for manpower had declined. That was part, but only a part, of what the sponsors of the Act had had in mind. Of course, it was the simplest aspect of the over-all design. Raising money by an impost on industry and paying it back again is a quite straightforward administrative job.

This aspect of the enterprise set out to associate redundancy, in the minds of workpeople, with the receipt of a lump sum, as well as the less disagreeable phenomenon of loss of employment. To say that this formed the passive part of the notion of a wider framework for redeployment is a fair representation of the view prevailing in Westminster when the statute was enacted. The word 'purposive' had a prominent place in the vocabulary of that Labour administration. And the purposive part of the approach to questions of redundancy was embedded in getting the public employment service, and systems of government training, much more thoroughly implicated with workpeople who lost jobs through no fault of their own. But while money was raised handsomely for the payment of compensation, there was no corresponding blossoming of resources for the Department of Employment's manpower service functions which were needed to complement the compensatory part of manpower redeployment. Consequently, whether by default or design, the whole thing became a market oriented exercise.

Market forces

Viewed in that light, the events associated with the life time of the statutory scheme become moderately comprehensible. The main object was to get a constraint relaxed and the money incentive was expected to take care of that. Afterwards, in a booming economy with lots of jobs, the authorities saw no pressing need for expensive and bothersome monitoring of what was happening in the labour market and how such events related to the statutory severance scheme.

Because the interconnections between the payment of cash to ease workpeople's opposition to redundancy and the purposive elements of redeployment were not spelt out except in barest outline, no deep engagement has developed between the public employment service and government retraining on the one hand, and the handling of redundancy on the other. Indeed, it was not until 1972, a full six years after the legislation on severance compensation, that a substantial restructuring of the public employment services was put in hand. Of course, in large-scale redundancies (or controversial smaller ones) the public employment service has put its best foot forward, and often emerged with great credit. Such occasional bursts of activity are easier to organize, and have far more immediate rewards, than systematic local office involvement in all the drab day-to-day occasions when employers decide that they no longer need some of the people who had been working for them.

Moreover, the oustanding, exceptional (whether in size or for other reasons) redundancies, where the public employment service has deployed its efforts with evidence of success, have tended to be occasions when it seemed pretty obvious that the labour market left to itself would be unable to reallocate the newly-freed manpower resources with reasonable efficiency. What seems to have happened is a failure to use the financial control information from the severance payment scheme to map out a clear outline of impending redundancies in the hinterland of each employment exchange. Instead, across the wide front of the public employment service as a whole, the Redundancy Payments Act has brought no real change. In the Department of Employment a good deal of discussion about improvements to the employment exchange service had been going on from time to time. But there is no evidence of urgency being imparted to those Departmental reviews in the context of legislation about severance payments.

Manning of employment services

For one thing, across-the-board activity by employment exchanges geared to provide a better service to redundant people has immediate repercussions for the manning of the Department of Employment's local offices. There was no significant change in the number of Department of Employment staff involved in the public employment and training services associated with the working of the statutory severance scheme.

This unbalance, between the effort and financial resources going into the cash compensation scheme, and the supportive measures for a better functioning of the labour market, was not particularly noticed nor generally regarded with concern at a time when the economy was fully stretched. From 1966 onwards conditions in the labour market changed enough and in a way which would have justified a big stepping up of the level and quality of the public employment and training services for channeling the flows of redundancy to get the maximum benefit for the community.

A sensitive and prompt response from the authorities to changing conditions in the labour market is not possible without a meticulous scanning of emerging events and analysis of what they foretell. This is why the weaknesses in the information system about redundancies matter. As the job market became tighter, the deteriorating placement prospects of people losing their jobs through redundancies should have been communicated by staff at employment exchanges to policy makers in St James's Square. But for that to happen, local offices would have needed to have had a lot of local labour market intelligence, and a disposition to interpret it and draw conclusions.

Such a continuous involvement of employment exchanges with both their local environment and the policy people at headquarters has obvious advantages. Exchange staff stand to gain a sense of involvement in a shared and worthwhile job. Senior officials at headquarters could be in touch with real outcome of policies that they had made. In an interactive context of that kind evaluation and assessment of the working of policy would become an automatic, inbuilt feature of the administrative process. For local office staff, getting statistics together would not be just another chore. The chief civil servants, in turn, would have no respite from the job of thinking up measures to keep the policy on course, or the pressure to re-examine original goals in the light of changing circumstances.

Development of the public employment service in that fashion would go part of the way to provide the active element in a manpower deployment strategy, the passive component of which is contained in the statutory severance compensation scheme. Given that sort of structure, the government retraining programme too can have more chance of relevance to the changing structure of the labour market. A framework would also exist for consideration of bigger manpower policy questions.

Within three years of the start of the statutory severance scheme demand and supply conditions in the labour market were sufficiently different to justify asking basic questions about the appropriateness of the view underlying the Redundancy Payments Act that redundancies were generally a good thing. By that time there were clear signs that shrinking job prospects were creating a new wave of disquiet among workpeople about the extinction of many enterprises, and established patterns of employment. Quite profound alterations in the pattern of employment as between different sectors of industrial activity were becoming evident. While the Redundancy Payments Act was the key for unlocking a rigid pattern of manpower use in the economy, the rapid change of the structure of manpower deployment, taken together with worsening over-all employment conditions, undoubtedly created a need, certainly by 1969, for a profound and fundamental review of that particular policy measure and the objects of manpower policy in general.

An active manpower policy?

Even if anyone in Whitehall had had it in mind to develop a strategy for an active manpower policy, the lack of information to which we have pointed would have been an impediment. The authorities have always intended that the publicly provided labour market services should facilitate a more effective deployment of manpower when workpeople are 'shaken out' from their jobs.

That there has been a shake-out is not open to question. Personnel and industrial relations policies from 1965 on, most notably illustrated in the technique of productivity bargaining, have led to a cut-back in the manpower input in substantial areas within manufacturing industries. There has been a thinning out of the labour force in the tertiary sector too. Employment in the distributive trades, for instance, having risen steadily during the first half of the decade, started to decline from 1966 quite rapidly. Experience, specifically in the United States, and more recently in Germany, indicates a big shift in the basic structure of employment in mature industrial economies. There is a reduction of demand for manpower in sectors of industry concerned with production of goods. On that basis, and taking account of developments in Britain's labour market since 1966, it is reasonable to argue that even rates of economic growth considerably higher than in recent years are unlikely to cause a rise in the demand for manpower in the goods-producing sector of the economy.

There is, then, the longer term trend in mature industrial economies for a contraction of employment in the secondary sector. In Britain the high level of unemployment since 1966 has arisen partly because total demand had to be kept under check in the early part of the period for balance-of-payments reasons. Another part of the explanation lies in the longer-term phenomenon of the goods-producing sector needing less labour. The shake-out of manpower, exemplified in the rising volume of redundancies, has superimposed a short-term contraction of demand for manpower upon the established underlying trend towards falling employment opportunities in the secondary sector. Added to this have been the employment effects of political judgements about desirable levels of employment in the services sector generally, and more particularly within the publicly provided services. The policies of successive administrations have worked to restrict the rate of growth of the tertiary or service sector. In introducing the Selective Employment Tax in 1966, the Labour Government erected a powerful disincentive to expansion of employment in all service industries. When the Conservatives returned to power, a central policy aim was to cut back public expenditure, and this too has had an adverse impact on growth of employment in the tertiary sector.

Different needs

All these developments have joined in making the labour market situation in Britain quite different in 1966 – 71 from what it was up to 1965. On that ground, and because of the failure of the more active strand of the initial strategy to emerge, the rationale for the Redundancy Payments Act which was valid in 1964 is now very much open to question. These questions are of two kinds. In the first place enough has happened since the enactment of the severance payments scheme to make it reasonable to ask whether the policy objectives, of which it was one instrument, are still as valid as they were in 1964. The second set of queries concern the machinery for the implementation of the Act, in terms of its appropriateness for the objectives of policy as they were initially visualized, and in terms of their relevance to altered circumstances since the legislation was brought in. In considering those questions much information and insight can be got by looking at other industrial countries'[1] experiences with redundancy policies.

Going back to the origins of the Redundancy Payments Act, it is not too much of an oversimplification to say that policy was based on the conviction that there was need for a lot of redundancies. Policy makers were clearly concerned to do what could be done to reduce the pain and discomfort imposed on individuals who would be caught up in this process. But there was no doubt that the process itself was necessary, and had to be encouraged because the economy would then grow faster.

Another component of that reasoning was the assumption that firms would not reduce their labour force unless they had determined by rigorous examination that substantial economic gains would result. That being the case, the accepted view was that public authorities would have no direct part to play in the determination of whether redundancies were in fact necessary in particular plants and establishments. Indeed there never was any question of involving the

public authorities in consideration of factors which lead managements to decide they need to contract their labour force.

At least, there was no such view about the generality of
redundancy situations. Occasionally governmental involvement was
an accepted custom when the scale of manpower outflow was going
to be big. Indeed, as in the case of the Cotton Industry Reorganization Act or with the Coal Board arrangements, the government frequently played a leading part in establishing the framework
within which the cut back took place. Such industry-wide programmes of reorganization for purposes of renewal of capital and
introduction of new technology were not, of course, everyday
occurrences.

Government involvement

Cotton textiles, the National Coal Board closure programmes, the
rationalization scheme for British Rail are outstanding industry-wide
exercises in cutting back manpower. In all these the government has
taken a hand, not only as the paymaster (though that has been its
principal role) but in the managerial analysis leading to the decision
to reduce the labour force. Besides those large-scale reorganization
schemes, government involvement of a rather different kind in baling
out firms in the private sector facing closure has often had, as its
mainspring, the wish to prevent the disappearance of jobs in
industries or regions which had already lost many jobs. Though the
main object of this kind of government involvement has been
facilitation of a smooth contraction of employment, the public
authorities have from time to time come in with financial and other
help to encourage private sector enterprises to look for ways of
dealing with their difficulties other than by reducing their payroll. A
characteristic of governmental involvement of that kind is that it has
been *ad hoc* rather than part of an over-all programme. Frequently
such operations have been carried out in parts of the country where
jobs are scarce, and unemployment is high.

More significant, when government help has come in order to
prevent or reduce job losses and redundancies, the official role has
extended to participation in managerial decision making within the
enterprises which were moving towards closures or large-scale
redundancies. The official attitute to these situations has differed
fundamentally from that displayed in the context of the Redun-

dancy Payments Act. There, the public authorities have merely had the mechanical and routine job of administering the Redundancy Fund and protecting it against abuses. The other role assigned to the public authorities was that of helping the redundant individual to resell his labour in the market. Whether or not that function has been well developed by the Department of Employment is another matter.[2] Of critical importance here, is that the public authorities have no part, or standing, in the enterprises' decision making which results in redundancies.

The central question about the British scheme and the structure of reasoning upon which it was founded is whether or not the good of the community, measured even by economic criteria alone, is best served by decisions about employment taken unilaterally by management. In France, and in a rather different form in Germany, the prospect of redundancies is an occasion for multilateral decision making. While firms have the right to decide the size and composition of their labour force, and when and how to expand or contract it, this right is formally, as well as in practice, circumscribed by rights vested in workpeople's organizations and public authorities.

While there was great buoyancy in the labour markets in all but the least prosperous parts of Britain, and there was believed to be the prospect of a great shortage of manpower which would hinder otherwise sustainable rates of economic growth, there might not have been grounds for questioning employers' decisions to cut back the labour input into their production processes. Nor, perhaps, against the background of a high demand for labour was there a particularly strong case for seeking a voice for workpeople and public authorities in prior consideration of the strength of the reasoning leading to loss of jobs in individual enterprises and particular places of work. Though the strength of the evidence pointing to fundamental shifts in the labour market in Britain can be argued about, it is impossible to deny that quite big changes in the total and sectoral demand for labour have appeared and are in prospect. Nor is there room for any real argument about the need for greater emphasis on keeping job opportunities available. In terms of action this implies deeper and fuller consideration in each and every situation where employers find themselves with what appears to be a stock of manpower surplus to their current and foreseeable requirements.

Alternatives to redundancy

In the exploration and planning of action other than redundancy, the Department of Employment's local offices should be entitled to participate in the employer's analysis which leads him to decide on redundancies. Early involvement of workpeople's representatives is essential.

Undoubtedly these propositions raise fundamental issues. Yet the idea that the community as a whole has a close interest in redundancy situations is already firmly established in British industrial relations and legislation. Does all this encroach on the principle enshrined in the phrase 'management must have the right to manage?'

Britain's long-standing, and expensive, programme of aid to the less prosperous regions of the country is firmly constructed on a close association between private sector firms and the public authorities. A central characteristic of this relationship is the active role of public authorities in the managerial decision-making process which leads to new activity or expansion. The trigger for the whole of this enormous programme is the wish to create new employment opportunities in the development areas and prevent, on a selective basis, the extinguishing of existing jobs. In this programme the right of management to manage is not, evidently, found to be under challenge. Equally there is no question of the public authorities being merely passive providers of fiscal and cash assistance. If close official participation in managerial decision-taking is well-established and acceptable for the purpose of growing new employment, can an equal involvement in situations where jobs are to be extinguished be regarded as reprehensible and revolutionary?

A role for public authorities

Then there is the established custom of sporadic governmental involvement to prevent closures or large-scale dismissals of employees. Official involvement in depth and details is not only accepted as a necessary evil because the government becomes the paymaster, but frequently welcomed as of positive benefit in sorting out long standing complications and establishing a new framework for the operation of the enterprise.

Governmental participation of this type is usually seen as a crisis

measure. There is often much drama about it. A good deal of
head-shaking and finger-wagging is done about the unwisdom, or,
contrastingly, the irresistible urgency of public involvement.
Opponents of baling-out, shoring-up and the supply of splints to
lame ducks warn about moral, social and economic dangers of
applying public resources. Yet, despite the best efforts of the
proponents of the virtues of a self-regulating market economy,
successive British governments have chosen, without serious dissent
from mainstream views in industry, to adopt the participative rather
than the spectator role.

But that kind and degree of involvement by public authorities in
redundancy situations has remained confined to the major threats.
As far as the more common occasions are concerned, public
authorities have played very much a residual role. Yet the principle
of governmental involvement in redeployment of manpower was
firmly grasped by the legislation for the statutory severance
payments scheme. What is being argued here is the need for the
community interest (represented through the governmental
machinery) to be brought to bear in all redundancy situations.

The disappearance of a job is something which concerns the
employer, workpeople and the community. Particularly against the
background of an unemployment level three times higher than
normal in Britain since the war, tripartite consideration of the need
for redundancies, and the possibility of alternative action, is evident
good sense. Is it, then, being argued here that the aim of manpower
policy should be an unchanging pattern of employment? If that were
the argument, would it not act as a brake on productivity, and the
sustainable rate of economic growth?

An end of over-manning

Available evidence is consistent with the view that the over-manning
which was characteristic of British industry until the mid-1960s is
now disappearing.[3] What the technique of productivity bargaining
did most spectacularly was to remove under-employment among
people at work. Productivity-based wage deals excised the leisure
that was built in within the working environment in British industry.
Where, until the mid-1960s, people who were employed had
quantities of leisure at work (the ratio of leisure to work clearly
varied from industry to industry), in more recent years employers

have slimmed payrolls and spread manpower more thinly over production processes.

It has not even always been necessary to have a much higher capital input. Reorganization of procedures and methods of work have contributed to reducing 'leisure at work', thus displacing manpower which was previously gainfully, if not fully, occupied. As labour forces in industry have become more thinly and productively spread, and in the absence of growth in the economy, unemployment has risen. Although it is doubtful whether the level of unemployment in Britain will ever return to what was normal for the years up to 1965, there is mounting evidence that higher total production can be achieved and maintained without a significant increase in the demand for labour.

Even on a solely economic evaluation there is little rationality in pushing forward a process where a diminishing proportion of the population is gainfully employed, and working at high levels of productivity, while ever-larger armies of unemployed people are sustained on welfare benefits financed by those in employment. Even if the time has not yet come to argue the case that the maintenance of employment is an objective rating higher priority than the achievement of greater labour productivity, the changing structure of the labour market in Britain during 1966 – 71 is sufficient foundation for the proposition that whenever jobs are at hazard, there should be thorough tripartite examinations to decide whether they should be extinguished.

Conclusions

Earlier discussion about the weaknesses in the information system associated with official policy about redundancies, as embodied in the Redundancy Payments Act, is significant most of all in pointing up the lag between existing measures and current needs. Had good information systems existed, emerging evidence for changes in policy would have been highlighted. Much the same result is likely to have come about if the Department of Employment's local offices had played a more consistent and effective part in the dispersion of the effects of redundancies whenever they occurred.

Indeed, a first and interim step to the creation of public-authority participation in the fashion that has just been outlined is an activation of the advance notification measure contained in the

Redundancy Payments Act. A wholesale, immediate and systematic engagement of employment exchanges in all redundancy situations can be made the principal objective of the new-look public employment service being groomed in the Department of Employment. A thrusting, self-confident role has to be played by employment exchange personnel. The tripartite evaluation of the case for redundancies, and the search for alternatives, cannot be set afoot without new statutory powers.

Statutory authority of that kind would almost certainly be best associated with the establishment of a National Manpower Board with responsibility for making policy and carrying out executive functions related to the more effective operation of labour markets. The case for such a body and an outline of its structure and functions have been considered in a previous PEP publication (*Making Labour Markets Work*, 1971). No matter how determined an Administration might be to establish an organization of this kind, the law making and administrative process is bound to take a minimum of two years. Though that is arguably the best context for public-authority involvement in the vetting of proposed redundancies, some progress is possible within the present legal and administrative structure.

Except in the rarer cases redundant workpeople, after compensation, are largely left to fend for themselves. As we have attempted to demonstrate, this is very much a truncated version of the scheme policy makers had had in mind. A good deal can be done to bring in the extra dimensions of the service for redundant workpeople which was originally envisaged.

The offer of services can be an automatic part of any redundancy situation. All that is involved is a willingness on the part of the public employment service to go out looking for business. But any widening or deepening of the activities of the employment exchanges creates demand for money and men. Our rough calculation in Chapter 2 showed that the annual rate of redundancies in Britain has been about 800,000 in recent years. In 1971 about 16,000 members of the Department of Employment's staff were occupied in the employment and training services. Of these some 7,000 people are engaged solely in placement activities. A substantial proportion are badly trained and poorly motivated. But leaving such qualitative judgements on one side, they have to put in most of their time on the administration of unemployment benefit and the problems of the long-term unemployed.

For the comprehensive and detailed servicing that is being proposed here to be practical in any sense, the public employment service would need a lot more, and better, people. This would cost more money. Ever since the establishment of the statutory severance payments scheme, massive expenditure has been associated with redundancies. The money has come, with very minor exceptions, entirely from industry. The Exchequer has not even borne the costs of administering the Redundancy Fund. Yet it was the government, as custodian of the national interest, which was most concerned about removing the stickiness in the labour market by eroding work-people's resistance to redundancy. Admittedly there are competing claims for public funds for a variety of worthwhile objects of policy. Nevertheless, in the company chairmen's favourite phrase, 'our manpower is our most precious asset'. In one sense it is not material where the money comes from. If serious difficulties are thought to arise in making, say, £30 million available to the Department of Employment to produce a spanking new public employment service, a small rise in the contributions employers now pay towards the redundancy scheme (together with an equally small piece of amending legislation) would rapidly bring in that much money.

12 An alternative strategy – France

No matter what part of the labour market or aspect of industrial relations is looked at, the sharpest contrast between Britain and other Western European countries lies in the part played by government. Although attention has usually focused on the contrast between voluntary collective bargaining on wages and conditions of employment in Britain, and the prominence of statutory provisions in the regulation of wage negotiation and conditions of work on the Continent, the sharpness of difference is quite as great on redundancy arrangements.

As a starting point for comparison it is useful to focus on the part which the Ministries of Labour play.

The French Ministry of Labour was given considerable statutory authority in 1945 to intervene in the working of the labour market. That year marked the abolition of private employment agencies, and the establishment of the Ministry of Labour's employment exchange system as the sole agency for the placement of job seekers. The part of the 1945 law which set out to achieve compulsory notification of all vacancies did not achieve any measure of success and was gradually quietly forgotten.

The Ministry's authorization was required for any job engagement to take place, or before any worker could be dismissed. In less than two years, a good part of this all-pervasive authority had disappeared. But the powers of intervention in redundancy situations, deriving from the 1945 statute, not only remained unmodified, but took on new importance. The all-embracing procedure for official authorization on recruitment and individual dismissal fell into disuse, partly because the whole thing was impractical, and in part because the courts decided that prior involvement of the public authorities is necessary only in dismissals which are based exclusively on the economic circumstances and performance of firms and enterprises.

Limited management prerogative

By British standards, the French employer is deprived of quite a slice of 'management's right to manage'. He is obliged to obtain Ministry of Labour approval before dismissing any of his workers on grounds of redundancy. Officials are thus automatically brought into the picture.

Once the Ministry of Labour is involved, it can say that officials in its Inspectorate of Labour need time to look into the employer's grounds for wanting to cause redundancy. The public authorities have this power not only to ask for postponement, but after their investigation they are entitled to discuss all sorts of alternative courses of action with the firm. Before considering the detail of what actually goes on, it is important to reflect again on the principle that is at stake.

In Britain an employer is asked to *notify* his local employment exchange of redundancies, in France the employer has to first *obtain approval*.

Powers available to the French authorities enable them to ask employers for detailed explanation of the reasons for the proposed redundancy. Officials are able to investigate whether workpeople's representatives have been consulted, and insist that the employer should do so to canvass their views about ways of resolving the firm's difficulties without having to resort to dismissal.

A prime consideration in the minds of the Ministry of Labour officials is the effect that the proposed redundancy would have on the local labour market. Where job opportunities are plentiful, the Labour Inspectorate gives its consent to proposed dismissals on economic grounds more readily than in regions where jobs are in limited supply. When, as in times of a dip in national economic activity, or because particular local labour markets are slack, Ministry officials take a more stringent view of proposed redundancies, they can propose a wide variety of measures which the employer is obliged to consider, and put into operation as alternatives.

Ministry's rights

In 1962 when labour supply rose sharply, and there was concurrent rapid employment growth, the Ministry told its officials that they should go about the vetting of proposed dismissals bearing in mind the need to use the 1945 statute in such a way as to avoid consequences 'often unhappy for wage earners'.[1] Thus, when an employer sets out a case for running down his labour force, officials of the Ministry of Labour do not automatically accept these as sufficient reason to justify redundancies.

In principle, the Labour Inspectorate is entitled, in all redundancies involving more than 20 employees, to examine the firm's evidence about the need to cut back.[2] It is then, for instance, open to the official from the Ministry of Labour to revoke the Departmental authorization for overtime working in the enterprise, bringing down the permissible working week to 40 hours. This enables the spreading of work amongst a bigger work force as an alternative to making some employees redundant. Banning overtime is a traditional response among workpeople in Britain to a threat of dismissals when there is not enough work to go round. Traditionally this reaction has come in Britain specifically from the place of work, rather than in the form of a national set of rules established by workpeople's organizations.

With the deterioration of employment prospects, and the growing slack in the demand for manpower, characteristic of Britain since 1966, workpeople's organizations at the national level, including the TUC, have recommended work-sharing as an alternative to the reduction of manpower in firms faced with the economic necessity for a cut back of their payrolls. Yet, trade unions have both philosophical and practical difficulties in going for an across the board policy of work-sharing as an alternative to redundancies.

British trade unions are particularly sensitive to charges that they are responsible for holding back new technology, and in a more concrete way, union members at individual places of work are not always in favour of solutions that are alternatives to dismissal of some of their mates, but which lead to a reduction of the earnings levels for everyone that remains in employment. Many of these difficulties just do not arise in the French situation. There, it is not the workpeople's representatives who have to obtain employer consent to a proposal for work sharing. It is the outsider, the official of the Ministry of Labour, acting as a representative of the community as a whole, who takes responsibility for suggesting this as an alternative to the sacking of people proposed by the employer.

Shorter working week

Banning overtime working, or more general work sharing, is the least positive of the measures available to the French public authorities in situations of impending redundancy. Another course the Ministry can urge on an employer is the reduction of the working week, even when no overtime is being worked. Beyond these constraining measures the Ministry of Labour can actively sell employers a retraining scheme for workpeople who are facing the prospect of redundancy.

Retraining schemes come in a wide variety. That variety is more than a matter of the content or range of courses. In terms of finance of retraining, provision of money for income maintenance while individuals are undergoing retraining and places where training is given, a considerable range of choice is available and used with great flexibility. Quite unlike Britain's programme, where financial compensation is the principal, and arguably the only, buffer between a man and his redundancy trauma, training and retraining is central to French redundancy policies.

Retraining programmes can be associated with the employers' keeping on workpeople whom he was previously intending to make redundant. If, after consultation between the public authorities and the employer, such a scheme is not sufficient to eliminate the need for some redundancy measures, officials still have a considerable say in how they are to take place and who is to be affected.

When the Ministry considers the local employment situation to be particularly difficult, it has powers to restrain and stagger the rate of lay-offs. There is evidence to suggest that the Ministry's officials quite frequently withhold their consent for dismissal until the workers have been placed either in training or in other work. This staggering of the impact of a redundancy connects up with the statutory provision, made originally in 1958, for notice to be given to employees whose jobs are to be terminated. Under that initial statute workpeople who had a minimum of six-months' continuous service became entitled to one months' notice. In 1967 a new statute raised the length of notice to two months for anyone who had put in two-years' continuous service with his employer.

Period of notice

At first sight, this is not spectacularly different from the legal requirements in Britain about notice of dismissal. Indeed the requirements of the Contracts of Employment Act 1963 have been substantially widened, in this respect, by the Industrial Relations Act which went on the statute book in 1971. Workpeople in Britain now are entitled to seven days notice of dismissal once they have had 13 weeks of continuous service. This rises to two weeks after two years' service; four weeks for anyone with 5 – 9 years' service; and six weeks for 10 – 14 years. The top limit is eight weeks after 15 years or more with the same employer.

In France cash severance compensation is not as universal as in Britain, and the sums of money involved are quite small. Yet the provisions in Britain with regard to both notice of dismissal to the individual and the cash payment, are apparently ends in themselves, and this is where the contrast with the French approach is most clearly marked.

With notice of dismissal the principal aim is to smooth the path of redeployment of the individual worker to a new job. From the very outset, in their 1967 statute, the French were attempting to establish not merely a period of passive notice to employees of impending dismissal.

Embedded in the legal requirement for either a month or two months' notice (depending on length of service) was the intention to organize things in a way to make the notice period productive. Additional point was given to this intention of putting the emphasis on jobs by the wide-scale and virulent industrial upheavals of May 1968. A measure indicative of the major difference of tone and intent between the French and British measures is the right given by law to employees under notice of dismissal to have at least two hours off work each day to look for new employment.

Transition from old to new job

In fact, to talk about the period of notice of dismissal, as though it is synonymouus with the meaning of the term in Britain, is misleading. In the terminology of the French statute it is 'le délai-congé', or a period of 'suspended leave'. Employees who have between six months' and two years' service are entitled to one month suspended leave. Those with more than two years' service have one of two alternatives open to them. They may receive two months' leave or a different package, where one month of the leave is replaced by a special cash indemnity. Precisely which package is offered is determined in the light of specific circumstances, and this is one situation where the employer has the final word. Although all this is impressive enough in itself, perhaps an equally striking part of the over-all approach is the encouragement provided through the statute, and by the public authorities' behaviour, to the voluntary negotiation between employers and trade unions of collective agreements which improve on this basis established by statute.

Since 1967 the notice of dismissal has had a direct connection with the objective of deliberate redeployment of manpower. Though the public authorities' wider powers of intervention in redundancy situations originate from 1945, these too have taken on a sharper focus since 1967.

The check on the employer has been twofold. In the first instance, the statutory obligation requires each employer to have established internal procedures and general rules governing the order of dismissal. By these rules account has to be taken of the family responsibilities of those likely to be affected by a redundancy, their length of service in the establishment, and their qualifications. Here what the statute set out to do was to require each employer to have a set of criteria by reference to which he is able to draw up the list of people to be made redundant when such action becomes necessary. The second check upon the employer arises from the powers available to the Ministry of Labour. So far as the establishment of an internal predetermined procedure within firms is concerned, case law built up over the years has removed the stringency of this constraint upon the employer's freedom of action at times of redundancy.[3]

Internal procedures

As things stand, management can incorporate criteria of its own choosing in the dismissals procedure. Although these procedures are required, by law, to be submitted to the firm's works' council, that body is entitled to an opinion only, and has no statutory right to negotiate on the content. There are known to be some collective agreements, whose number is increasing, which now build on the foundation provided by the law. But, though rapid developments are taking place, the number of workpeople covered by such negotiated procedures is still small.

The real check – and the one of greatest interest – on the French employers' rights to dismiss workers on grounds of redundancy is the public authorities' participation in the firms' run up to the decision about redundancy. Before we look at what the public authorities are able to do about the content of the outflow of manpower associated with a redundancy accepted as necessary, it is useful to compare the internal dismissal procedures within French and British enterprises.

In France the establishment of procedures within enterprises for dealing with redundancy situations has its origin in a statute. Such efforts as have been made in this direction in Britain are based on exhortation. In *Security and Change*, produced in 1961, and indeed in earlier documents, the Ministry of Labour in Britain set out to encourage employers to establish predetermined procedures for dealing with situations when redundancy is unavoidable. More recently the Department of Employment and Productivity has put forward a set of guidelines for the establishment of redundancy procedures by employers.[4]

Those guidelines are derived from the practice of firms who have thought it worthwhile to prepare themselves for the contingency of redundancy. Additionally they embody the collective wisdom of the representatives of the Confederation of British Industry and the Trades Union Congress. Like all pieces of exhortation, the ideas set out in *Dealing with Redundancies* have nothing more than moral authority, and managers of enterprises are at liberty to ignore any, or all of them. Employers are offered no rewards or punishments if they fail to introduce domestic procedures for handling redundancies. In view of the need to establish a consensus among the co-sponsors of the recommendations in *Dealing with Redundancies* it comes as no surprise that the set of measures proposed does not include the settlement of the terms for dealing with any redundancy which might arise by *negotiation* between workpeople and management. The most that the Department of Employment and Productivity document could do about this was to point to 'advantages for managements and unions in including provision for meeting redundancies in their joint long-term planning'.

Formal coverage

So far as the form is concerned, the Department of Employment and Productivity guidelines cover all the points that are likely to crop up when employers judge that redundancy is necessary and un-avoidable. But it is all pretty passive. And curiously (for a document produced under the auspices of a Labour Administration) emphatic about the prerogatives of employers. 'In all arrangements for discharges, managements will want to show themselves conscious of the need for careful and sympathetic handling of individual cases'. That proposition, in both its sentiment and wording, is poles apart from the intention of the French statute which sets out to establish rights for workpeople, rather than leave them to the conscience of the employer.

All that can be said for the efforts made by government and the national organizations of employers and workpeople in Britain to encourage the development of plant-level procedures for handling redundancy is that, by going through the motions, they have taken pre-emptive action against accusations of utter inactivity. That the steps taken in Britain are small and, in practice, ineffectual, is not seriously open to question. Having produced what was, for a government publication, a surprisingly attractive-looking document, no further provision was evidently thought necessary to establish how employers were in fact responding to the advice embodied in *Dealing with Redundancies*.

This is where the French provisions are most significantly different. Being based on a piece of law, they contained automatic follow-through. Although decisions of the French tribunals have been such as to modify the constraint upon employers to work within a set of predetermined criteria in deciding who among their workforce should bear the brunt of redundancy, nevertheless the fact of the existence of the legal provisions kept the issues open. Moreover as the stringency of the legal provision has been eroded, and left a gap, that in itself has given an impetus to the incorporation of procedural arrangements regarding dismissals into collective agreements between employers and unions.

Again, by contrast with the British approach of *Dealing with Redundancies*, employers in France are obliged to inform workpeople's representatives in advance of any proposed dismissals on grounds of redundancy. This requirement was introduced by statute in 1966, and it enables workpeople's representatives (through the works' council) to say what they think about the employer's proposals, and the procedure envisaged for their implementation. Workpeople's representatives are entitled to little information however. For instance the firm does not have to give them a list of all the people to be dismissed. But management does have to say what it has in mind by way of a timetable for dismissals, and the attempts it has made to diffuse the need for redundancy by means of internal transfers.

Employee representatives are also given the legal right to receive a report from management about steps that it has taken, or proposes to take, for helping those to be made redundant. In providing that information, management has to explain why staggering of dismissals is, or is not, possible; it has to report on its attempts to investigate available vacancies in the local labour market, and on the discussions between the firm and public agencies about the placement of redundant employees in training courses. Apart from these measures the employer has specific obligation to give an account of the particular ways in which he has sought to give aid to the older (over-60) workers affected.

Workpeople's reactions

After this parade of differences between provisions in France and arrangements in Britain, there is one thing both countries have in common. Employee representatives in France, though they get notice and considerable detailed information about an impending redundancy, and are better off in this respect than their counterparts in Britain, tend to react to the news in very much the same way as workpeople in Britain. Most of the time, French employee representatives in the works' councils simply raise a shout of protest against the proposed redundancies, and set out to gain support from public opinion for their opposition.

One explanation for the apparently negative behaviour on the part of organized workpeople in France lies in the unions' unwillingness to become implicated in the administration of a redundancy. The possibility of mitigating the effects of the proposed dismissals by detailed discussion and negotiation with the employer is rejected by the unions for fear that they would share guilt by association with him. As in Britain trade unions have consistently turned their faces against the idea of negotiating redundancy procedures with employers.

Though the approach of organized workpeople's representatives in both countries has been similar, the consequences of that have had different implications. Failure by representatives of the workpeople to grasp the rights given them by the statute of 1966 does not enable the French employer to decide unilaterally the extent and manner of the cutback. In Britain the Department of Employment remains, for the most part, a spectator and ultimately sweeps up the pieces. Not so, however, in France. There, irrespective of the posture adopted by the representatives of the workpeople threatened with redundancy, the public authorities remain very much at the centre of the stage. This has implications at two levels. Both parties to the redundancy can be regarded as appealing to an outside administrative authority.[5] The presence of the public authorities in the run up to the redundancy as well as in the handling of it, brings in advantages for both employers and workpeople.

Public authorities' contribution

From the employers' viewpoint, the public authorities are bound to be more receptive than the unions to arguments justifying the redundancy. To the workpeople, the public authorities are not only more accessible (for the law requires them to be on the spot) but also much more impartial. Additionally, as representative of the community, the Ministry of Labour and its officials are a lot more likely than the employer to pay attention to the social costs and disharmony which are inherent to redundancies.

One level, then, on which the presence and detailed involvement of public authorities has a profound effect has to do with the over-all industrial and social climate within which enterprises have to go on operating. How much sense of security this brings to workpeople generally is anyone's guess, but the French have opted for winning security through a referee.

That general principle highlights one of the differences between the alternative ways of dealing with redundancies in Britain and France. It is arguable that the detailed involvement of the public authorities as soon as the decision in principle about the necessity of

the particular redundancy has been taken helps to dispel some part
of the insecurity of the threat of the sack. There is no counterpart to
this in the British system.

The manpower services in France can enter into the mechanics of
the actual redundancy in considerable detail. Once the main issue
has been settled, the firm gives the Ministry of Labour officials a list
of the people it proposes to make redundant. Information is made
available about their age, length of service and their occupations,
providing opportunities to the French manpower services for an
operational role in the dismissals that are to take place.

Protecting the more vulnerable

Officials of the French Ministry of Labour have the right and the
obligation to propose alterations in the employer's list. Such changes
could be made on the ground that the employees concerned might
have more than normal disadvantages in looking for new jobs. In
principle Ministry of Labour officials can refuse permission for
workers over the age of 60 to be made redundant unless specific
provision is to be made for them, either by way of placement in
another job, or for income maintenance through funds made
available by agreement by the Ministry itself.

Hard evidence of the number of occasions when the public
authorities use their right to withhold permission is not available. It
is, however, a generally held view that such steps are by no means
uncommon. But statistical information about redundancies is even
more difficult to come by in France than in Britain. It is odd that
the large-scale operational involvement of the French manpower
services in the handling of redundancies produces so few statistics.
Of course this means that there is not even as much scope as in
Britain for assessing the closeness of fit between what *should* be
happening and what *is*.

In terms of statutory requirement, the French manpower services
have a good deal on their plate. Over and beyond the
traditional placement activities common to the manpower services of
all Western industrial countries, the Ministry of Labour in France is
involved in detail not only in the handling of redundancy processes,
but also in a multiplicity of training and retraining enterprises, as
well as in the establishment and operation of special income-
maintenance schemes. The Ministry also has the traditional task of

running an inspectorate to look into the safety and health conditions at places of work. On top of all this, there is the monitoring and enforcement of statutory requirements concerning the representation of workpeople in factory committees and through trade unions, as well as watching over collective agreements and seeing that they are in line with legally defined social and labour relations objectives. In parallel with this, the Ministry carries the responsibility for the administration of the national minimum wages legislation, and is the custodian of the legal provisions governing the hours of work in industry.

Work load on French manpower services

Although the French Ministry of Labour is less burdened than its counterpart in Britain by the systems for paying out unemployment benefit, official involvement in the labour market and the jobs to be done by officials in France are wider in range, and more demanding of detailed participation than is the case in Britain. Yet there are only 250 – 300 officials in the French Ministry of Labour and they have administrative charge of the execution of the whole variety of statutes affecting the labour market. Consequently, despite their wide scope for intervention, the public authorities' real capability for influencing the actual circumstances relating to particular redundancies cannot be very large. Indeed it is a widely held view within the French trade unions that much of the Administration's statutory authority is merely a matter of form, with little practical effect.

Then, again, there is the issue of enforcement. Although, by law French employers are required to do a great variety of things in the preparatory stages of a redundancy, and in order to diffuse its repercussions, there is no clear evidence about the consequences to firms of being in breach of their obligations. In principle, penal sanctions can be invoked against employers who have failed to take account of official views about methods of dealing with a redundancy situation. In practical terms, what the French structure of rules appears to have done is to enable the public authorities to claim a right of presence in all redundancy situations.

Beyond that, statutory powers provide only a foundation for the public authorities to try their powers of persuasion on both parties involved in a collective termination of employment. The law, in

other words, is not so much a bludgeon to be used against
recalcitrant employers, as a means for the public authorities to open
up a discussion with employers in order to ensure that before,
during, and after the taking of a decision to 'disemploy' people, full
consideration is given to their interests and the implications of the
redundancy for the community.

An important element in the public authorities' presence on
occasions of redundancy is their ability to offer direct help, either to
enable the employer to avoid the need for a redundancy, or to
reduce its scale. Because the Ministry of Labour has tangible things
to offer, there is less need for it to wave penal sanctions round
employers' heads. Firms are, generally speaking, not at all hostile to
having representatives of the public authorities implicated in the
planning and execution of a redundancy. For their presence has
psychological value in lowering the tension of confrontation
between workpeople and employer, and officials from the manpower services can tap government resources to aid the process of
redeploying the individuals facing dismissal.

Institutional peculiarities

Administratively, and in institutional terms, the French structure for
aiding and abetting redeployment is complex and, to outside
observers, fairly confusing. Some things are done by the state
working on its own. In those activities the finance and back-up
personnel are provided by the government and controlled by the
Ministry of Labour. At the same time there are a host of joint
enterprises with a variety of institutional structures, and a wide
range of functions. The whole set up is further complicated by the
difference in scope of coverage of the many joint organizations.
Some are at a national level with the whole of the country and all
industries and services as their catchment area. Others, though
operated on a national plane, focus on individual industries, both for
purposes of securing money and a management structure and for
recruitment of their clientele.

All this can be baffling to the outsider. But the multiplicity
appears to provide a rich source of alternative courses of action and,
rather surprisingly, a scope for speed and flexibility. Disentangling
all the interlocking pieces of machinery that function in the labour
market in France is a formidable task. A hurdle to ready

comprehension is the French tendency to give independent-sounding names to different bits of the Labour Ministry's budget: a particular head of expenditure, which in the United Kingdom has significance only in Parliamentary and Whitehall accounting terms, emerges in France with the resounding title of the National Employment Fund. That particular Fund, set up in 1963, nicely illustrates how the public authorities concerned with the labour market in France set about allocating resources and administering an active policy of manpower redeployment.

In 1963 powers were taken by the government and entrusted to the Ministry of Labour to enable official involvement over a wider range of labour market issues. The money allocated to the Ministry of Labour for this purpose is described as the National Employment Fund (*le Fonds nationale de l'emploi*). These powers were an enlargement of activities initiated in 1955, when the government made provision in the budget for money to be available for a threefold purpose. In the first place, funds were to be provided to encourage modernization of plant and equipment in industry. Secondly, money was to be paid out in pushing forward a programme of regional development and the decentralization of industry from Paris. The final strand of that design was the provision of government money for retraining and resettlement of manpower. That last element within that over-all set of measures for government assistance to industry was a part of the Ministry of Labour's budget. But though the other two aspects of that package of activity were the responsibility of other ministries, the whole thing was wrapped together as the Economic and Social Development Fund (FDES).

When the Ministry of Labour was given much wider powers in 1963, and money to put them into operation (through the National Employment Fund), its operations originating from the 1955 scheme, financed through the Economic and Social Development Fund, did not immediately come to an end. For more than five years, the French Ministry of Labour was running training and resettlement programmes for workpeople financed from two separate bits of its budget – and this was more than a simple matter of keeping the books straight.

Between 1967 and 1969 allocations under the two financial headings were in fact used for running different kinds of retraining schemes. Though all this gave scope for flexibility of operation, the advantage was probably outweighed by the scope for confusion, and

in 1969 the Ministry of Labour unified the financial basis for
retraining activities directed specifically towards redeployment. One
purpose of setting all this out here is to give something of the flavour
of the French machinery for intervention by public authorities in
the labour market.

Of key importance in assessing what the authorities set out to do
in redundancy situations is the role of the French Ministry of
Labour in establishing training programmes as a response to
redundancies.

Adult vocational training

A big programme of adult vocational training has been a basic
ingredient in French labour market activity for more than two-and-
a-half decades. It all began in 1946. At the time the the entire drive
was directed to the reconstruction of an economy severely damaged
by war. The principal need for skilled manpower was in construction
and engineering.

Instruction centres were set up by the Ministry of Labour to give
accelerated training. Courses were intensive, generally of six months'
duration, and specifically adapted to the needs of industry. Where
initially the purpose of training was to build up a big supply of
skilled manpower for the rebuilding of the economy, with changing
times the object of the French governmental adult vocational-
training schemes has altered. In part, of course, the purpose is still to
increase the supply of skilled manpower. But quite as important is
the object of giving individuals opportunities for upgrading or
refresher training. Additionally, and of increasing significance, is the
role of adult vocational training to adapt workpeople to changes in
technology and the shifting pattern of skill demand in a dynamic
economy. How the French training centres are organized, the skills
which they teach and the methods by which they and their clients
are financed, all these have evolved in the light of experience and
through a déliberate process of experimentation.

Adult vocational training, in centres run directly by the French
Ministry of Labour, is strictly comparable with what is attempted in
the Government Training Centres in Britain. In the government run
adult training centres alone some 42,000 people were trained during
1969. Over and beyond that, the French Ministry of Labour has
consistently gone in for the joint financing and administration of

another set of centres. Most of these joint centres are run by a tripartite body containing Ministry of Labour nominees, representatives from employers' organizations and trade unions.

In the language of the political vocabulary brought in by the Conservative administration in Britain since 1972, that French institution would qualify as a 'hived-off' agency. ANIFRMO, the National Industrial Association for the Rational Training of Labour, operates well over 100 of these jointly controlled centres for adult vocational training. Adding the ANIFRMO adult vocational training capability to that of the centres wholly controlled by the Ministry of Labour, France had a normal adult training capability which gave courses of between six months and one year to something over 82,000 people in 1970. In that year, government training centres in Britain provided courses for almost 17,000 trainees.

Training centres in Britain and France

In Britain, unlike France, the only vocational training centres available for adults are those run direct by the government. Though the Department of Employment is now embarked on diversification and expansion of the adult vocational training programme, on present plans total government sponsored adult training will rise to 60,000, and possibly as much as 70,000, by 1975. In that year, given the best possible outcome, the United Kingdom's adult training capacity will still be some 15 per cent lower than the actual accomplishment of the French programme in 1970.

There is much that is interesting in the organization of adult vocational training in France. The way that a lot of the centres are governed by public authorities working in close association with workpeople's representatives and employers is especially striking in the context of France's not particularly harmonious set of relationships between organized workers and management. Of particular present interest is the part of adult vocational training in the dissipation of the less desirable consequences of redundancy. Availability of a fairly large adult retraining capability helps from an organizational viewpoint, and in more direct ways, when the time comes to deal with redundancy.

The fact that there is an ongoing pattern of negotiation between the Ministry of Labour and individual firms for government subsidization of adult training activity enables the same techniques to be employed without too much difficulty in emergency situations. Building on the existing normal adult training provision, the special powers available to the Ministry of Labour in the context of the National Employment Fund, can be deployed to give greater flexibility and speed to providing training for redundant workpeople. The Ministry of Labour builds a second intensified block of training provisions on top of the normal facilities available. What tends to happen is that the Ministry negotiates either with the firm that is about to make people redundant, or with any other enterprise that is ready to take on the redundant employees specifically for the purpose of giving them retraining.

Big training programmes

In terms of the contrast between British and French arrangements, more striking than the difference in the size of the available capacity, is the gulf between the techniques employed by the two public authorities to enfold the displaced employees in a training programme. British adult training is, with minor exceptions, all at centres run by the Department of Employment. The French also have additional capability in the authorities' framework of training for redeployment of manpower. One of these is the jointly run training centre (ANIFRMO-administered) which is without parallel in the British system.

Having two separate but interconnected streams of provision for normal adult vocational training gives the French more flexibility in the kinds of things that people can be taught at the centres. Moreover that flexibility allows scope for centres to take in workpeople who have appeared on the scene unexpectedly.

On top of this, there is retraining by employers under contract to the Ministry of Labour. This particular enterprise started in principle, and on a small scale, as far back as 1954. When the Ministry got its new powers packaged under the heading of the National Employment Fund, it started to give a lot more attention to developing the use of training on employer premises as yet another device for coping with the disappearance of jobs.

Training contracts with employers

In 1963, when the contracting out of retraining was first started by the French authorities systematically, the programme was quite modest. But the basis of its administration, the objects to be sought, and the intention to develop the system further were already quite clear. The Ministry of Labour can back its suggestions to enterprises with money.

Officials have finance on tap, and statutory authority, to go out to firms that are in good shape and induce them to take on workpeople made redundant by other enterprises, solely with the object of giving them retraining. The way in which this scheme has evolved since 1963 is illuminating. After a fairly slow start the programme was beginning to build up into something sizable by 1968. In that year, the French Ministry of Labour negotiated 40 agreements for training on employers' premises for redundant workers. Britain, too, has now made a start on this type of programme.

In making this kind of arrangement with firms, the French Ministry of Labour is usually responding to the employment situation in a given area. A common reason for setting up temporary training facilities on employers' premises is that demand for manpower in the local labour market is low and declining. In that kind of situation the permanent government, or government sponsored, vocational training centres in the immediate neighbourhood are often unable to cope with the increasing numbers of displaced employees who could be placed on retraining courses.

Sometimes the public authorities take the view that more is to be gained by the workpeople, and the donor employer, from training given on a firm's premises than by sending the redundant workpeople to the permanent centres within the normal adult vocational-training system. This kind of assessment is made possible by the public authorities' detailed knowledge of the local labour market, and their feel about the likelihood of growth of new jobs in firms that start off with just the special training programme.

Training schemes contracted out to employers involve the Ministry of Labour, the people running the permanent vocational-training capacity and, through that – as well as in more direct ways – representatives of workpeople. In deciding the content of the training, the public authorities use the knowledge, experience and personnel from their normal vocational training centres. Officials of the Ministry of Labour, together with personnel from the permanent adult training scheme, agree jointly with the contracting

employer the basis on which individuals are to be selected for the
in-plant training course. A collective decision, among the same
people, is taken about the pay that the trainees are to receive, and
the division of the cost of that, as well as of the training programme
as a whole, among various sponsors.

Diversity of means

There are so many different measures available to the public
authorities in France, and which they apply to retraining geared to
redundancy, that a summary account is bound to differ from what
actually happens. The alternative is to plunge into a tangle of
statutory and administrative procedures all of which bear on the
action taken by the public authorities in these situations. At least,
since the packaging together of the powers associated with the
National Employment Fund, there has been a reasonably clear basis,
from 1963, for identification of the over-all objects of the public
authorities' purposes in intervening in the operation of national and
local labour markets.

The contribution of training programmes towards resolving the
disruption of redundancy can be considered in broad terms. The
detail continues to vary from situation to situation. That variation is,
as we have noted, an in-built part of the strategy for dealing with the
complexity of real-life situations. An agreement between the public
authorities and an employer for a training programme on his
premises might, for instance, have its origin in the notification to the
Ministry of Labour by an entirely different firm of its intention to
make some part of its labour force redundant. That triggers off a
whole chain of public authority involvement, some of which has
already been considered. On the specific training front, the initiative
comes from the Ministry of Labour which approaches a likely-
looking firm in the area where the redundancies are about to
happen. Everybody makes a big attempt to see that arrangements are
made in good time so as to enable workpeople to go on to the
training programme straight from their previous jobs.

To get employers to engage in adaptation training of this kind,
the French Ministry of Labour offers cash. Basically, the public
authorities' object is to make the operation costless to the employer
who agrees to set up a training programme on his premises. A quite
thorough costing exercise is done, and the firm and the public

authorities make out an agreement detailing the basis of calculation of the amount of money that is to change hands. Once the thing gets going, the public authorities keep periodic check on the programme, usually as a preliminary to making payments to the employer.

In principle, the Ministry of Labour can pay the wages of everyone involved in the training enterprise. The tendency is to avoid getting involved in anything that is to run for less than three weeks and keep to a maximum of five months. While the Ministry agrees to finance all or part of the direct wage bill of those being trained as well as their instructors, it also pays the other elements of labour costs. All expenditure on machinery and equipment as well as material to be worked on is covered by the Ministry. When there is need, the Ministry pays the costs of training instructors, usually drawn from the firm's own employees. Alternatively the employer who is contracting to provide the training course can send some of his employees for brief instructor-training courses at the Institute for Adult Vocational Training (which is run by the Ministry of Labour).

Another thing for which the public authorities are prepared to pay is a psychological aptitude test for workers to find out the kind of training that will suit them. Provision is also made for money to be available for unforeseen contingencies.

Some idea of cost

A detailed analysis of costs of this scheme is not possible as there are no published statistics. However in the first year of the Ministry of Labour's exercise of its new powers its budgetary allocation under the heading of National Employment Fund was about £2 million. And that money had to cover not just the topping-up training for emergencies arising from redundancies, but was also intended to finance other contingencies and measures associated with the adaptation of manpower to economic and technological change. Part of this money was to be used for the payment of some kind of cash compensation, but quite what that was to be, was left unclear except for the specified older-worker category of employees. By 1970, not only had the resources available to the Ministry for these purposes risen threefold to nearly £6 million, but other arrangements had been made for the finance of a system of severance compensation brought into operation from 1968.

Obviously the financial resources available are quite modest. In considering the weight of this programme, it is necessary to take account of two points other than the availability of funds. One thing to be noticed is that these resources are intended to provide a top layer above the basic (nearly £24 million in 1970) provision for training and retraining in the permanent centres. The second point of importance is that this head of expenditure allowed the Ministry of Labour to do a lot of pump priming. In a way, this has been uncommitted money, not attached to specific projects planned in advance: on the contrary, it has been available to the Ministry of Labour to inject into situations where the authorities have judged quick action to be necessary.

Such evidence as is available appears to suggest that training places for between 18,000 and 19,000 people were provided in 1969 and 1970 as a direct result of the existence of this flexibly deployed but relatively small sum of money. It is these elements of speed and flexibility which have brought the Ministry of Labour's National Employment Fund to the forefront of the newest phase of the French attempts to develop systems for dealing with redundancies. These attempts have their origin in the major industrial conflicts during 1968. In order to comprehend the latest phase of French policy, a fair amount of detail has to be looked at.

Collectively bargained arrangements

Superimposed on the provisions for training and redeployment established by legislation since 1945 is a new and growing layer that is being added to through continuing collective bargaining at national and industry level between employers and trade union representatives. The French government watches the process. And it takes steps to modify or elaborate existing legislation to take account of progress made in collectively negotiated arrangements between employers and trade unions. This interaction and dynamic was precipitated by the industrial disputes which swept across France in the spring of 1968.

One aspect of the underlying causes of that confrontation was a demand by workpeople for more comprehensive unemployment compensation. The focus of the unrest among workpeople lay in a disquiet about security of employment, and the extent to which that appeared to be under threat from changes in the structures and management of enterprises, in alterations in technology, and from

changes in product demand. Although employers and their organizations were unwilling to respond to employee demands for new and
more effective procedures for dealing with security in employment,
they gave in under pressure from the government and joined in
serious negotiation with trade unions.

Much of what has happened since 1969 in France for handling
redundancies stems from a joint agreement made that year between
the Government, France's central employers' federation and all the
national trade union federations. That document[6] itemized all the
issues that employer and union representatives would discuss, and
set out a timetable for the completion of discussions. The item with
the most direct bearing on the treatment of redundancies was
headed 'Employment and training'. On that the central employers'
federation and the trade union confederations bound themselves to
start talks before the autumn of 1968, with the intention of
finishing up with an agreement on security of employment.

It was understood by both parties (and the Government) that the
proposed agreement would set out the things to be done by
employers, the workpeople's representatives and by the State to
assist redeployment of manpower whenever that becomes necessary,
particularly as a result of mergers and takeovers. On the same theme,
but with a wider scope, employer — trade union discussions were to
arrive at proposals for the establishment of Joint Employment
Committees. The terms of reference of those committees at both
regional and national levels, and their constituents in terms of
industries and branches of economic activity was to be decided
through negotiation beginning in the winter of 1968.

The French line

Events since then have been complex and manifold and much
remains unclear about the detail of what is happening. But events in
France have clarified the depth of contrast between that country's
way of looking at redundancies, and the approach to this issue in
Britain.

A big change of direction in French policy since 1968 is a new
emphasis on collectively negotiated agreements between employers
and trade unions about the manner of handling redundances. None
of this has, however, meant an opting out by government from this
sphere of activity. True the main agent of change in policy and for

the things actually to be done for people who lose their jobs is not a new set of statutes. Yet the force that has propelled central organizations of employers and workpeople towards negotiated solutions has come very largely from the Government. Moreover the Government is steadfastly maintaining its attitude that public authorities must remain deeply involved in partnership with employers and trade unions for the purpose of managing the national labour market and, more importantly, in assisting sub-markets for labour, whether regional or occupational, to work more effectively. Since 1969, developments have taken place on three aspects of the handling of collective dismissals on economic grounds. In the first place, the role of workpeople's representatives when redundancy is in sight has now become clearer and more substantial. And all the indications are that workpeople's representatives at enterprise and plant level will have scope to increase their authority, as agreements at those levels flesh out the framework established by the national accord between the central employers' and trade union organizations.

That is one new dynamic element in the French industrial-relations system for dealing with redundancies. A second big change is clarification of the steps to be taken by everyone in preparation for, or at times of, redundancy. The third change in this field, precipitated by the industrial unrest in 1968, was the start of a process of collective bargaining at national, enterprise and plant level, for improvements in the terms of the package available to workpeople whose jobs had come to an end despite attempts to find alternative courses of action. An account has been given in this chapter of the statutory powers available to the French Ministry of Labour in relation to the collective dismissal of workpeople on economic grounds. The role and powers of workpeople's representatives at plant level in such situations has also been considered. Since 1969 the emphasis has shifted away from the public authorities' regulatory rights and there has been a move towards extending the authority of workpeople's representatives at national and workplace level.

Joint Employment Committees

On the national plane, all this underlay the setting up of Joint Employment Committees, industry by industry, or for a group of industries. Arrangements also exist for these committees to develop regionally. Nationally and regionally they are to 'assist in the redeployment of workers whose dismissal cannot be avoided'. Additionally, they have the responsibility for ensuring that all existing facilities are mobilized and put to use in finding new employment for dismissed workpeople.

The paramount importance of co-operation in redeployment is re-emphasized by the composition of the committees. They are made up of equal numbers of workers' and employers' representatives. As the programme gets under way inter-industry committees are to be set up at regional level. Through these bodies programmes are to be developed for inter-industry redeployment of manpower.

Joint Employment Committees are developing close contacts with the public authorities' permanent training facilities, the government sponsored but privately operated training capability, as well as ANIFRMO vocational training centres. Particularly strong connections are expected to develop with the Ministry of Labour's manpower and placement services. Those aspects of the Ministry's activities have since 1967 been brought together in the National Employment Agency, and there is a strong likelihood that employee representatives will be asked to join it.

It is evident that a structure of considerable complexity has been created for monitoring developments in the country's labour market. How much these bodies will be able to do beyond providing trade union representatives with a platform for expressing disquiet about the pattern of events in the labour market is a matter of conjecture. But it is beyond question that scope has been provided, for a continuing conversation between employers and trade unions at national level about the changing employment prospects.

Scope for developing good practice

There is no certainty that the trade unions will be able to make use of these opportunities to develop rational and humane practices for the handling of redundancies. Though the French have a long tradition of complicated committee structures associated with the National Plans, a proper scepticism about the practical outcome of the new Joint Employment Committees is not out of place. Specifically, all they have to do is meet at least twice a year, and prepare an annual report on the employment situation and likely developments for the industry falling within each committee's scope. In order to do this, and for other activities that they might wish to undertake, they each have available the services of a secretariat provided by the employers' organizations.

None of this has been going for very long, certainly not long enough for any well-founded assessment to be made of possible achievements, or their ability to influence broad lines of policy. Any outside observer is bound to be struck by the complexity of the whole exercise. In part that is a reflection of the French style of public administration and system of relationships in industry between employers and workpeople. But the key purpose of the intricate intermeshing of a large structure of committees is decision taking through participation. That again is entirely in keeping with methods used by the economic planning machinery which France has so successfully operated since the war. What stands out is that developments since 1969 have created a set of consultative bodies which have as their purpose the review and analysis of employment issues. There is, of course, nothing in Britain which corresponds to this. The nearest analogy is with the Industrial Training Boards, but their scope and purposes are much more circumscribed.

That panoply of committees for dealing with redundancies and other causes of change in the structure of employment is only one tier of the structure of consultation and decision making which the French have been developing. The national agreement on Joint Employment Committees did not give them a role in activities in the place of work. Here, at the sharp end of collective dismissals, the new arrangements amplified the rights of workpeople's representatives.

Trade unions who were parties to the national discussions for the new manpower institutions did not like the idea that the Joint Employment Committees should have no say in the decision taking at the workplace on occasions when redundancies were being considered. Employers, however, wanted it that way, and their views prevailed. What they did concede was a much clearer statement of management obligation to consult employees through works' councils. Though the rights and role of works' councils remain much as they were before 1969, it is likely that, as the new ideas work their way through into practical situations, workpeople's representatives will be able to have more say in the plans and programmes of individual managements.

Employee participation at workplace

Most of the changes made are to do with procedures. Managements
still do not have an obligation to negotiate with their works' councils
about a redundancy. It still remains a matter of providing information about what is proposed and allowing opportunity for
consultation. The new agreement does not oblige employers to tell
the works' council which employees are going to be made
redundant. Works' councils are now (as previously) entitled to have
information about the number of dismissals. Beyond this the
employer has to say what occupational categories are involved, state
reasons both for the number being what it is and the basis for
selection of the categories of workers to be affected.

   None of this is new, but there is a new distinction between the
provision of information associated with redundancies arising from
different causes. Two categories of circumstances are identified.
Redundancies which arise from 'economic circumstances' form one
category. The second type is associated with mergers between firms,
or concentrations of activity in particular places within a given
enterprise, or the need for a cut-back in the labour force in
connection with a substantial modernization of the techniques and
machinery of production. These two causes of redundancies have to
be treated in different ways, because dismissals associated with
mergers or internal reorganization are subject to the direct control of
management, but a falling away of product demand is much less so.

Mergers and modernization

Employers have to give workpeople's representatives different
periods of time for deliberation on the plans proposed by management. Irrespective of the cause of the impending redundancy, the
purpose of the consultation remains the same. One object is for
management and workpeople's representatives to examine together
the extent to which there is a genuine case for a reduction in the
workforce. The second object of the consultative process is to
establish the best means of assisting dismissed workers. Here there is
a specific requirement upon the employer to embody in his
proposals to the works' council ideas about making use of the

Ministry of Labour's resources through the National Employment Fund. For a variety of reasons this is an important and remarkable requirement. In the first place it establishes an obligation on the employer to consult the public authorities before he puts redundancy proposals to the works' council. As was pointed out earlier in this study, this is in striking contrast to the practice in Britain.

There is an in-built element within the French system which propels the parties confronted by a redundancy to turn to the public authorities. This propulsion is not achieved solely by legal means. The French Ministry of Labour has resources which it is worthwhile for employers and workpeople alike to tap. For the employer, prior discussion with the Ministry of Labour has the clear advantage that he could, having gained access to subsidies from the National Employment Fund, come to his employees with proposals that blunt the edge of his intentions. Moreover an employer offering proposals based on his discussion with public authorities would have gone through a prior vetting of the reasonableness of his intentions and the validity of the reasons for the course of action on which he was proposing to embark.

The obligation on the redundant worker's representatives to enquire into the employers' plans to use facilities provided by the public authorities begins a process of involvement of a kind seldom achieved in Britain.

Better terms at plant level

What is being outlined here is not by any means the fullest range of possibilities within the French system. When the central employers' organization and trade union confederations made their agreement in 1969, it was clearly understood that only the minima were being established. From that point on it was open to employers and trade unions to negotiate improvements through agreements made not only industry by industry but also in individual plants.

Talks of that kind have been going on since 1970, and the rate of progress as well as the outcome of the discussions vary from industry to industry and from one plant to another. There is not yet enough information for a systematic assessment to be made. Consequently an analysis of the arrangements at plant level for dealing with redundancies in France has to confine itself in the main to a consideration of the basic arrangements set out by the 1969 agreement.

This cautionary digression has relevance to what happens when an employer gives formal notice to his works' council about an impending redundancy. The time for deliberation by workpeople's representatives before management can go ahead is determined by whether the proposed redundancy is caused by economic circumstances beyond the control of the firm, or is the result of a deliberate policy of structural change. But the length of this deliberative period is also one of the matters on which plant-level agreements can build above the floor laid down by the 1969 national settlement between the central organizations of employers and workpeople. Staying with the minima set out in the national framework agreement, the chief point of interest is the difference in the treatment of the two types of redundancy. For redundancies from both causes, a further variable affecting the length of the period of reflection is the number of workpeople to be dismissed.

In principle, the greater the number of dismissals, the longer the length of notice to which works' councils become entitled. In the kind of redundancy that the employer attributes to a decline in the market demand for his product, the consultative period for a dismissal affecting 10 – 49 people is eight days. When the number of people affected is greater than 50 but under 100, the consultative period rises to 15 days and to one month when 100 or more people are involved.

Collective notice and individual notice

It is important to be clear that these periods of time available to workpeople's representatives are a prior step to the issue of notice to individuals whose jobs are going to disappear. In other words, when an employer is proposing to make a hundred or more of his employees redundant, not only will the firm have, in due time, to give each of them individually anything up to two months' notice, but before that stage is reached employee representatives will have had another full month's notice about the impending redundancy.

This pre-redundancy deliberative period is substantially increased when the proposed dismissals are a consequence of mergers between firms, or of concentration of production in selected organizations within the same firm. Structural or technological reorganization leading to a cutback in the labour force, entitles workpeople's representatives to as much as one month's notice when the dismissals are likely to affect as few as 10 people. The length of the consultative period doubles when the proposed redundancy covers 200 – 299, and rises to three months for numbers over 300. On top of this there is scope for extension of consultative periods by plant-level agreements.

Clearly an established right to have early warning of management redundancy plans is quite a gain, especially as all employers are now pledged to this procedure. Here too the situation is better from the employee's viewpoint in France than under either the statutory redundancy provisions or such rudimentary collectively bargained agreements as exist in Britain. The essential point is not that there are no arrangements in Britain between employers and employees about consultations preparatory to the implementation of a redundancy. The difference lies in the scale and range of the operation in the two countries.

Across-the-board, comprehensive provision in Britain exists only with regard to the payment of cash compensation as established by the 1965 Act. Even that, as we have seen, is not wholly comprehensive for there are people with short periods of service who are not eligible for cash compensation. But when all is said and done, the British scheme for giving cash compensation is the most substantial severance payments arrangement anywhere in Western Europe. It does not detract from this merit to point to the barrenness of the British scene for other methods of assisting the redeployment of displaced employees.

French statutory provisions for the involvement of public agencies in helping to steer redundant workpeople to new employment are without parallel in Britain. And developments since 1969 have focused on building in new sets of participative processes which implicate employers, trade unions (at national level) as well as workpeople at the plant and, as the third equal partner, the public authorities. This participative structure is at all levels. There is engagement of all three parties at the industry level for consideration of an over-all policy of manpower deployment. The Joint Employment Committees have that job. Then there is consultation in which workpeople directly concerned at factory or plant level are given clear and specific rights in the procedure for arriving at a programme for handling a particular redundancy.

Objects of the French system

On substantive issues, too, the French system provides a range of guarantees for workpeople faced with the prospect of loss of employment. Here it is not a damaging over-simplification to say that the concept and detail of the French approach is to regard redundancy as redeployment of the last resort. There is no suggestion that redundancies are to be rejected or opposed. The emphasis is on orderly and controlled systems that allow changes in the structure of employment, by industry, occupation and, indeed, by geographical region. The purpose is to achieve flexibility in the use of manpower, to be accomplished through a secure framework within which workpeople can change jobs without falling out of the stream of employment. In essence, the object is not to restrict the pace of change, but to modify its impact on people whose jobs and ways of life are at hazard. In this, the purposes motivating the people responsible for the French system are no different from those of policy makers who drew up the Redundancy Payments Act in Britain.

In Britain the main hope of bringing about security was pinned on money compensation at times of redundancy. The French have opted for a package over and above the statutory protection against collective dismissal which they have had since 1945. Individual establishments have undertaken, by agreement with trade union federations and the public authorities, to do all that they can to avoid redundancy. When collective dismissals are unavoidable, firms are pledged to find ways to keep the redundancies as low as possible.

One way in which firms should implement this objective is spelt out in the 1969 agreement – employers must fully explore the scope for internal transfers of individuals from one job to another, either within the establishment, or to other establishments under the same ownership. A key feature of the French national framework agreement on security of employment is the formal undertaking given by employers that when a cutback in manpower is made necessary, because of a merger or other structural reorganization, employers will work to get the reduction through natural wastage or voluntary redundancies. One part of this idea enables the older members of a firm's workforce to leave with favourable arrangements for social benefits. When job changes within an establishment (or between establishments of the same firm) are used as a device for minimizing a possible redundancy, and the whole situation has arisen because of a merger, the national agreement binds employers to avoid downgrading the individuals affected.

Transfers and downgrading

Despite the best will in the world, firms might not be able, in the context of a new organizational or production structure, to transfer employees to other jobs, while at the same time maintaining their pay grades. The people responsible for the 1969 agreement were wise in the ways of industry, and knew that this kind of situation could give rise to interminable bickering, and erode goodwill. That appreciation of the realities, coupled with their predilection for intricate solutions, led them to work out surprisingly detailed provisions about this contingency. They also seized the opportunity to draw the public authorities into the resolution of this tricky situation.

If the loss of earning is less than 10 per cent of the previous wage, the signatories of the agreement expect the worker to simply grin and bear it. But if the man stands to lose more than that, two possible courses are open to him and to the employer. For a maximum period of six months in the job to which he has been transferred, the individual has an entitlement to an allowance. How much cash he gets depends on whether the employer himself chooses to pay it, or if the Ministry of Labour comes into the picture.

Essentially, the cash allowance is intended to bridge the gap between the individual's earnings in his new job and his wages in the job from which he has been displaced. The principle is borrowed from a system pioneered by the European Coal and Steel Community, which applied the system to good effect in the process of the restructuring of those industries in the member countries.

When the allowance becomes payable, the cash amount is bigger than in subsequent months. But right from the outset the amount of money paid is less than the actual shortfall between his new and previous earnings. As each month passes, the gap becomes wider. Now, quite how much of a gap there is depends on the arrangement that has been chosen by the parties. Either the employer can pay the whole sum of money or he can make an agreement with the Ministry of Labour whereby a subsidy from the Ministry's National Employment Fund can be made available.

If such an agreement is made, two things follow. The cost to the employer is reduced and there is a gain for the employee because the allowance, jointly financed by the Ministry and the firm, brings his new wages nearer to his former earnings. The whole thing is quite complex, but it should be evident from what has been said so far that there are built-in incentives to the employer and to workpeople to opt for the involvement of public authorities in the financing of the wage maintenance.

Temporary income maintenance

Once again, through the interlocking procedures, the public authorities are brought directly into the handling of redundancy, or near-redundancy, situations. Furthermore, this illustrates the kind of practical issue to which works councils can apply themselves. Although there are examples in Britain of analogous income-maintenance arrangements for particular groups of displaced employees, they are specific to particular industries and of small impact in terms of number of workers covered.

So far as cash payments are associated with redundancy, or near-redundancy situations in France, this temporary income maintenance of workers whose jobs have had to be changed in order to prevent their dismissal can be regarded as a sort of severance compensation.

Mention has already been made of the small amount of provision which exists in France for a direct cash indemnity when people are dismissed on grounds of redundancy. And there is a little more to be said about it. What is of interest at this point, however, is the difference between the French and the British strategies for achieving the same goals. While the purpose of policies in both countries is to get the conditions right for a more flexible deployment of manpower, the key element in the French programmes is a deliberate application of measures to bring this about without turning to redundancy except as a last resort. Hence the complex deliberative processes. Equally the emphasis is on building up not a cash compensation for loss of employment, but access to systems whose purpose is to re-engage the individual in the labour market as quickly and effectively as possible. While the approach in the United Kingdom seems mainly to compensate a man for loss of his employment by providing a lump-sum severance payment, on the other side of the Channel the prevailing view appears to be that the best compensation for the loss of a job is another job.

Given that context, much of what has already been said about the earlier statute-based provisions governing redundancy, and the new developments taking shape since 1969, appears logical and sensible. Though there can be doubts about the practical effectiveness of a system as complex as the one which the French have constructed, the validity of their reasoning is not easily questioned. It is that same set of reasons which accounts for the relatively slight emphasis on cash compensation. The pattern of compensation has woven into it concern for rapid progress towards re-employment. This is true more of the statute-based universally applicable provisions about redundancy than in industry and plant-level agreements.

In the statute-based scheme, the amount of redundancy pay is calculated solely on the basis of length of service. Or at least that is the case for employees up to 60 years of age. For manual workers up to the age of 60 the basic legal indemnity for dismissal is 10 hours' pay for each year of service. The French worker is then entitled to one week's severance pay for every four years of service. As cash compensation for redundancy, this is much less favourable than the basic week per year in Britain. Moreover the British scheme associates a higher level of entitlement to compensation for years of service put in after the age of 41.

Collectively bargained compensation

Although the statute-based French scheme made somewhat more generous provision for non-manual workers, even that does not compare with the British scheme. But from about 1970, industry and plant-level collective agreements in France have been attempting to increase the amount of severance compensation over and beyond the legally established minimum. One effect which this has had is to reduce the (small) disparity of treatment between the hourly paid and the non-manual monthly paid employee. Although more collective agreements are being made in France with improved cash compensation for redundancy, their coverage is still fairly restricted, and there are considerable differences between one industry and another. Systematic and detailed information does not exist about the cash compensation collectively negotiated across French industry. But the general impression is that wherever these agreements are being made, some improvement above the statutory minima is being achieved.

In what is perhaps the most favourable arrangement from the workpeople's viewpoint, the chemical industry agreement has introduced severance compensation which at the top end of the range yields higher compensation than under Britain's statutory scheme. While the agreement in the chemical industry covering some two-and-a-half million French workers has succeeded in bumping up the cash compensation for redundancy, the greater emphasis has gone on devising methods for avoidance of redundancy. One of the chief objectives is extension of the principle that individuals should be found jobs within the new structure of the enterprise; this holds particularly if the threatened job loss is a result of a merger or concentration of production facilities.

Trade unions have used scope allowed by the 1969 national agreement to build in an improved variant of the income-maintenance scheme into the chemical industry provisions for the handling of manpower displacement. For as long as eight months, under the industry agreement, a man transferred to a new job can go on getting an income-maintenance allowance designed to bridge some part of the shortfall between his new and previous pay. Effectively, in this respect, the industry agreement has doubled workpeople's entitlements. On the issue of provisions for retraining the chemical industry agreement does not break new ground. But at about the time when it was being negotiated, talks were proceeding between the central organizations of employers and workpeople on this issue, and resulted in a national agreement in mid-1970.

Older people

Quite clearly embedded in the over-all national strategy for manpower redeployment in France is the object of enabling employees over the age of 60 to opt for redundancy. What is striking about this is the further reinforcement it provides to the concept of a purposive redeployment of manpower which appears to underpin all the bits and pieces of policy and administrative activity under-taken in the manpower field in France. Moreover the principle of employer, government and workpeople's participation in resolving issues of manpower employment or 'disemployment' is epitomized in the arrangements for special provisions for older workers.

For a start, the Ministry of Labour (using National Employment Fund resources) is in a position to propose a cost-sharing agreement with the employer when the idea of special treatment for people over 60 is mooted. The initiative might come from the Ministry of Labour, or the employer may propose the idea; yet another possible source is the works council of the plant. The basic criteria for making the special income-maintenance arrangement for older workers are to do with the state of demand for manpower in the local labour market, or more widely in an occupational labour market. There is ample scope for the exercise of judgement by the public authorities, for if they think that a spate of redundancies is likely to jeopardize the employment situation in a particular place, they can use the special provisions.

In effect a bridging operation is put in hand. This enables individuals (and the emphasis is always on specific consideration of individual circumstances) over age 60 to retire on a 'pre-pension'. Retirement pensions in France, as in Britain, become payable at 65. In Britain the man who becomes redundant at age 60, or any time between then and retirement age, could have a lump-sum severance compensation equivalent to 30 weeks' pay and then, if he fails to get a job, unemployment benefit, replaced after 312 days by a supplementary benefit. His counterpart in France can be provided with a package of financial assistance which recognizes he is no longer effectively in the labour market. French 'pre-pension' arrangements are financed by the bringing together of the Ministry of Labour's resources from the National Employment Fund, a contribution from the employer and funds from the general unemployment benefit scheme.

Before this package becomes available an agreement has to be reached between the public authorities and the employer. In other words, there is no across-the-board application of this scheme, and until early 1972 the central organization of medium and small firms had not agreed to join in the programme. Partly because of this, the number benefiting from these arrangements was quite small, between 4,000 and 7,000 during 1968 — 70. But here, as much as in the other complex of provisions in France for handling redun-dancies, progress is being made in industry and enterprise agree-ments, and the number is beginning to build up.

For the present, the real significance of this scheme lies in its clarity of purpose. Re-employment of older workers affected by redundancies presents problems everywhere. In Britain the social security arrangements do provide income maintenance for older people awaiting their retirement pension. But the contrast between that and the 'pre-pension' scheme in France is one of passivity as distinct from a deliberate grappling with a clearly identified difficulty.

Latest training measures

As from the end of 1970, French workpeople whose jobs disappear as a result of redundancy are guaranteed their previous wages for anything up to one full year, if they spend that time undertaking retraining. Though that sounds simple enough, and is a logical extension of what the French had already been doing for redeployment-oriented retraining, it is a bold step in implementing more fully the ideology of redeployment.

With present techniques and the current state of technology in industry, there are few jobs for manual workers which require more than one year's training. Consequently, the newest phase of retraining in France is offering displaced workers an unfettered choice to adapt to the requirements of any new occupation which they find attractive. The only constraint is the individual's own ability to incorporate new knowledge and skills.

Incentive to train

More remarkable even than the guarantee of income during training identical to the individual's previous earnings level is a built-in provision to attract people in their middle years. Even the Swedes, with their enormous programme of retraining have had difficulties in inducing workers past their early middle age to take courses to acquire new skills and proficiencies.

While the French may not be among the most prone to acknowledge the existence of any worthwhile idea that they have not themselves thought of, it is quite likely that, having looked at countries with big retraining programmes, they decided to do something about this difficult problem. Also in keeping with the French propensity for never going for a simple solution when a more complex one can be found, the idea of providing a special inducement to redundant workers in their middle years to take up retraining was spliced together with the other long-standing objectives of the manpower programme.

What is done is immensely logical but quite astounding. If certain conditions are fulfilled an individual over the age of 30 in a retraining course can receive an allowance that is 10 per cent higher than his earnings in his previous job.

The French effort is highlighted by contrasting it with the sense of pride and achievement of the British public authorities when (in 1971) trainees at Government Training Centres began to get training allowances marginally better than their entitlement under the unemployment benefit scheme. Another striking aspect of the boldness of the French public authorities is their decision to bring in the added incentive at 30 rather than 41 – the starting point for special treatment in the cash compensation scheme in Britain.

To check through the conditions in which a French worker can get retraining yoked to a training allowance of 10 per cent more than the wage he was earning provides a résumé of the aims and methods of manpower redeployment in France. There are a lot of characters on the stage. Each has a part, and unless they all join in, the show fails to get on the road. Before a person can get the 110 per cent of previous earning level of training allowance, a set of conditions has to be met. One method by which this can be achieved is by agreement between the employer and the Ministry of Labour before the firm embarks on a redundancy.

Now, if the workpeople in a plant know that this possibility is open, they are very likely to be motivated to ask, through their works' councils, that their employer should get on with making an agreement with the Ministry of Labour as soon as he has formed the view that redundancies are necessary. There is, thus, an interlocking set of pressures. Moreover once the public authorities are brought on the scene, they can induce the employer to range over all possible courses of action. Pressures operate on the employer in another way. Having examined all options, if no choice remains other than to terminate the jobs of some of his employees, there are obvious industrial relations advantages in demonstrating that he is going all out to safeguard their interests. And short of finding another equally good job immediately, what could be better than getting some of his erstwhile employees 10 per cent more pay than previously while they go on a training course?

Public authorities long stop

Just in case none of this works, there is a built-in fail-safe device. If the participative roles assigned to all who are involved in the planning and administration of a redundancy are not played, or poorly done, the worker whose job has disappeared can get himself the favourable rate of training allowance — provided he asks the Ministry of Labour for retraining within six months of his redundancy. In sum, the French provisions for dealing with redundancy are complex. There is an in-built dynamic in them. The scope for growth and development of policy and administration can be exploited by interaction between public authorities, employers and workpeople's representatives; and it is open to any of the three parties to initiate that process. Assessment and evaluation of the actual outcome of the French strategy cannot be attempted until the schemes have had time to mature and it would be helpful if the French public authorities were as inclined to collect information in this field as they are on other economic and social issues.

13 Experiments in Germany

Interestingly, the basic statute (*Kundigungsschutzgesetz*) governing dismissals of employees in Germany, enacted as far back as 1951, contains the concept of 'socially unjustified' terminations of employment. A mass of case law has accumulated around the 1951 Act, and all of it is exceedingly complex. That is to be expected, for the German Labour Courts have had the job of spelling out the circumstances in which an employer's decision to dismiss an employee is socially unjustified.

One thing has been established: the concept comes into play only when a worker loses his job through no fault of his own. That begins to make it sound much like the situations which in Britain are labelled 'redundancy'. But what the law gives with one hand it takes away with the other. For when the dismissals are caused by 'necessary operational changes' in the establishment, the Courts have refused to rule them to be socially unjustified. When new technology extinguishes jobs in which men were previously employed, firms maintain that such a change is an 'operational necessity' and the Courts have not ruled against that view. Not just technological change, but structural reorganization of firms, modification of production techniques and even a decline in product demand have all been found acceptable grounds for the sacking of workers, and not contrary to the concept of prevention of 'socially unjustified' dismissals.

Why, it is tempting to ask, go to the bother of having a law like that? And why, when on the Metal Workers Union's reckoning some million-and-a-half individuals were being displaced annually from their jobs, did no one think fit to do anything about the situation?[1] One, and the biggest, part of the explanation for the apparent unconcern about implementing a law which brought in a striking and unique concept lies in the fact that in all except two years of the decade from 1960, unemployment in Germany was between 0.7 and 1.0 per cent of the employed labour force. And the rise in the level of unemployment to the, by German standards, dizzy heights of 2.1 per cent in 1967 led, as we shall see, to startling changes in manpower policy. But leaving that fairly effective cause for the absence of disquiet on one side, the *Kundigungsschutzgesetz* had two items of merit. That statute put some check on employers, and no matter how gentle that constraint, workpeople were given rather more security against arbitrary dismissal in Germany than was extended to their counterparts in Britain, some twelve years after the enactment of the German statute. The second achievement of the *Kundigungsschutzgesetz* was in what it did to involve the Public Employment Service in all significant redundancies.

A role for the public employment service

Despite the pervasive feeling in Germany that the government should keep out of the running of industry, the 1951 statute gave the public authorities a good deal of say in situations when firms proposed to make a cutback in their labour force. What is even more striking is that these constraints on the German employer were being imposed at a time when the Ministry of Labour in the United Kingdom was trying to persuade employers, rather plaintively, of the virtues of co-operation with the public employment service when workpeople were going to be made redundant.

In identical circumstances, the German employer is obliged by law to tell the public employment service that he is proposing to make some of his employees redundant. Not all proposed redundancies have to be notified by employers in this way. Unlike the French rules, the German statute lays down conditions for exemption. One feature of interest in this procedure is that it is worked out with reference to the size of the impending redundancy, and the total labour force employed by the firm. A small enterprise which employs more than 20 but less than 50 people has to give information to the public employment service if more than five are to be made redundant. The middle-size firm with 50 – 499 employees has to send in advance notice of redundancies if 10 per cent of its payroll, or more than 25 people are going to be made redundant. All large establishments (with a payroll of more than 500) are required to tell the public authorities of their intention to declare redundancies if a minimum of 50 of their employees are to be involved.

The public authorities' rights in relation to the redundancy, once it is above the exemption limit, are the same irrespective of the size of the enterprise. When the public employment service is informed about an impending redundancy it puts this before a standing committee made up of representatives of employers, trade unions and the state (*Land*) government. Neither this committee nor the employment service as such can prevent or prohibit the redundancy from taking place. Nor, unlike the conditions in France, does the German employer need the specific consent of the public authorities in order to proceed with the dismissal.

Delaying redundancies

The public authorities can, however, postpone the proposed redundancy for another month. Effectively the employer retains the right to sack his workpeople because of changes in his level of demand for manpower, but the public authorities are by law brought into the picture. They are able to examine what the employer is proposing to do in a tripartite committee constituted so as to enable it to take a view about the repercussions of the redundancy beyond the firm in which it is about to occur. Moreover the public employment service has an opportunity, but not the legal right, to examine what alternatives to the redundancy might be open with the employer. Officials of the public employment service have an opportunity to suggest the kind of measures, such as early retirement, a halt to recruitment, a reduction of the working week, which in France can be imposed on the employer by the public authorities under their statutory powers.

Good grounds exist for saying that the public authorities concerned with the labour market in Germany have more rights than their counterparts in Britain – but less than those of the French authorities – to bring the community's interests to bear. The involvement of the German public authorities has continuously been directed to the primary purpose of allowing the lapse of sufficient time between the employer's decision to cut back on his labour force, and the actual event of the redundancy. This has made sense because of the conditions in the German labour market. Unemployment, as we have seen, has been strikingly low. Throughout the 1960s, with two exceptions (1967 and 1968), there have been at least two vacancies for every unemployed person, and in most years the ratio of unemployed people to job vacancies was more like 1:4. Added to this is the quite exceptional record of achievement of the German public employment services in placing people in jobs.

These two phenomena, the tightness of the labour market and the effectiveness of the German public employment services in their placement activities, go a long way to account for the absence of any widespread alarm in Germany about redundancies. Yet another factor damping down disquiet about redundancies is the job security enjoyed by something approaching two-and-a-half million people employed in the public services. About half of these are what the United Kingdom terminology calls 'non-industrial' civil servants. They, as is the case with their opposite numbers in Britain, have their jobs for life.

But the other half, both non-manual and manual, of German public servants, whether employed in the railways or the post office or any other part of the industrial civil service, are also (unlike Britain) covered by collective agreements which give them protection against involuntary redundancy. Big technological changes and schemes for modernization of the state-owned railways in Germany have been carried out since the late 1950s, with the active co-operation of the Railway Workers Union. The lower manpower demand in the industry has been met only to a minor extent through redundancies, whose impact was directed almost without exception to the younger, shorter-service men. For the longer-service employees, there was retraining and internal redeployment without any downgrading and loss of wages. All of that was expensive and the costs were borne by government.

Collective agreements

Three aspects of the protection available to employees in Germany against redundancy have so far been mentioned. On each of these aspects of protection against redundancy, changes of varying extent have come in since about the mid-1960s. But before turning to those, two other things stemming from the early 1950s need to be cleared up. Quite separate from the procedure for giving advance notification to the public service, the employer is required to give notice of dismissal to people to be made redundant. Between 1951 and the enactment of a series of statutes in 1969 on labour market policy, the period of notice for all manual workers was a minimum of two weeks. Salaried, non-manual employees had to be given at least one month's notice, and in their case the length of warning of dismissal rose on the basis of seniority. Entitlement to notice could be as much as six months for white collar workers who had put in a dozen years of service. For manual and non-manual alike, the law ignored years of service put in before a certain minimum age.

Legislation in 1969 maintained the difference in treatment between hourly paid and salaried workers, but the gap is now less wide. Much more important, there is a built-in discrimination in favour of older employees in both occupational categories. Up to 35 years of age the German manual worker earns nothing by way of extra rights in the matter of notice of dismissal. British legislation does not, on the other hand, explicitly feed in this.

Special rights for older workers

A manual employee in Germany with ten years' service, all of which have been put in after the age of 35, is entitled by law to be given two months of notice. Anyone in Britain, on the other hand, who has 15 years' service, irrespective of age, is entitled to eight weeks' notice of dismissal.[2] While that is the maximum statutory entitlement to notice available to anyone in Britain, the Germans have built in a higher rate of protection still for employees whose job prospects decline with increasing years. Thus someone with 20 years' service (at a minimum age, that is to say, of 55) becomes eligible for no less than three months' notice. All this legislation, in common with analogous statutory provisions in Britain and France, applies to individual as much as to collective dismissals.

British observers, especially if they are trade unionists, look at the German works councils with suspicion, bewilderment and a tinge of awe. In their modern form, these bodies were established by the *Betriebsverfassungsgesetz* (Works Constitution Act) of 1952. Nineteen years later, the German Federal Parliament brought in a new Works Constitution Act. Though the central trade union organization (DGB) is persuaded that the 1971 version of the Act requires the employer to be more responsive to the interests of workers, so little time has passed since the enactment of this legislation that nothing very sensible can yet be said about its practical outcome. The law requires that all establishments employing more than 20 workers must have a works council. A wide range of management decision taking is formally open to consideration by these bodies. The weight of influence that they are able to exercise varies in practice from enterprise to enterprise, and there is division of view about the extent to which works councils are in any real position to induce managements to modify courses of action they have in mind.

On things like starting and finishing times, breaks for meals and workpeople's relationships with supervision, the works councils have the legal right to joint decision making with managements. They have similar rights on matters of pay in so far as these concern plant agreements on piecework rates and premium payments. There are areas of management decision taking involving the regrading or redeployment of individuals on which those bodies are entitled to express views and, most important for our present purpose, the employer must obtain the council's consent if he proposes redundancies.[3]

Quite how much legal authority is available to works councils on occasions of impending redundancy is not wholly clear. In time, the 1971 statute will probably dispel some of this obscurity. Works councils do not have co-determination rights (with management) on issues of technological and organizational change affecting the place of work and the personnel employed. These, and changes in product demand, are of course triggers for redundancy. Consequently, such influence as the German works councils can exercise is something that comes into play after management has unilaterally taken its decision.

Works councils' powers

Even so, workpeople's representatives in Germany have had much more of a right to consultation on redundancy than in Britain. And, as the works councils exist in all establishments of any size in Germany, there is a far wider range of employment over which employee representatives are able to conduct discussions as of right when redundancy is foreshadowed. This process is much helped by the statutory requirement that the employer's advance notification to the public employment service of an intended redundancy must be accompanied by the works council's opinion on the proposed dismissals.

Concretely, this ensures that in any establishment in Germany, workpeople's representatives will rarely have less than six weeks' notice of redundancies. As far as individuals are concerned, some of them, particularly those whose prospects in the labour market are likely to be difficult, have a much longer period of notice. In fact, it is quite possible to take the view that the provisions of the *Arbeitsförderungsgesetz* (Employment Promotion Act) of 1969, taken together with the conditions laid down by the 1951 statute, mean in effect that the involuntary inclusion of older employees in a redundancy is ruled out for all practical purposes. With that background, it might have been thought that there was no further need to increase the influence which works councils have on employers planning collective dismissals. Nevertheless the 1971 Works Constitution Act has considerably strengthened these bodies' scope for action at times of redundancy. Examination of the changes brought in during 1971, and of the deeper and more wide-ranging implications of the Employment Promotion Act 1969, involves the core of the experiments in manpower policy now going on in Germany.

In principle, the 1971 Act has cleared up some of the uncertainty about the kind and the limits of authority available to works councils when the employer comes forward with a redundancy proposal. Under the 1952 Act, works councils have had the right to state their views whenever the employer has proposed changes in the running or organization of an enterprise involving disadvantages for the whole of the workforce or for a substantial part of it. Strictly speaking, the law has given works councils scope to tell the employer that he must take account of their views whenever a process of rationalization of ownership or activity is envisaged. If a firm, for instance, wants to reduce its capacity by closing down sections of the enterprise, the works council has had the right to discuss this and make proposals of its own.

Similar rights have been available when the issue has been one of a merger between enterprises. Moreover works councils have had the right to be associated in discussions preceding the introduction of new methods of work. But in all of these apparently substantial provisions for workpeople's representatives to influence management, there have been loopholes. These have either arisen from the law itself, or from case law handed down by the Labour Court. In addition, works councils were precluded from joint consideration in advance of the introduction of new technology, even when it could be clearly foreseen that such changes would lead to a decline in the demand for manpower within the enterprise.

Changes since mid-1960s

A variety of events from the mid-1960s have combined to produce big changes in the scope available to works councils to participate in policy connected with redundancies. These developments stem, in part, from the growth of collective agreements at industry level between unions and employers, designed specifically to take account of the accelerating pace of technological change, and to establish procedures for minimizing the adverse consequences of that upon workpeople. Modernization arrangements introduced in the state-owned railways from 1959 provide the earliest example of collectively bargained special provisions for the introduction of new technology. Right from the outset everyone concerned accepted that productivity-raising and labour-saving innovations should be brought in, while ensuring that the consequential decline in the demand for manpower did not impinge adversely on railway employees. In a sense, that was a special case. It was, after all, the public sector: the government was the paymaster. The railways were making a loss, and something had to be done about their long-term future. On all these grounds generous guarantees of maintenance of previous levels of earning were given, together with substantial severance payments for those who chose to leave the industry.

Arrangements in textiles

In the private sector, moves in the same direction were first made in 1965, on a small scale. There, as in the large number of collective agreements negotiated throughout German industry since then, the central aim is to focus on means for resolving the problems of resettlement likely to be encountered by anyone more than 35 – 40 years of age.

Industry-level agreements between unions and employers on rationalization and technological change include substantive and procedural provisions for handling any displacement of manpower likely to result from those causes. An integral part of the procedure laid down in these agreements is that in the process of handling the repercussions of technological change or other rationalization, management must take joint decisions with works councils in their establishments. On substantive matters too works councils are given scope to improve, if they can, on the provisions incorporated in the industry-wide agreements. All this appears to have been consolidated by the 1971 Works Constitution Act.

Within the terms of the new statute, it is now possible for these plant-level bodies to demand an agreed programme of redundancy when changes in the establishment make it necessary to reduce its labour force. If management and the council cannot reach agreement they are able to resort to the services of an *ad hoc* conciliation board to which they each nominate a representative under a jointly agreed independent chairman. Findings are not binding on the parties, but even when they are not wholly acceptable to either management or employees, a new foundation is provided for further negotiation.

What with the accomplishments in the industry-based collective agreements for the protection of employees' interests against rationalization measures, and the 1971 statute, the German unions have now established, both in substance and procedure, the joint management with employers of redundancy situations. Unlike the French structure for dealing with these things, the public authorities in Germany remain outside the operational framework for redundancies at the point at which they occur. But the public authorities, too, have been busily engaged since 1969 in setting up placement and training arrangements to complement industry's agreements for the orderly redeployment of manpower.

Coverage of agreements

Collective agreements between German trade unions and employers for the protection of workers from the adverse consequences of rationalization began, as we saw, in 1965. By 1971 agreements were in existence covering about 7 million (of the nearly 9 million) workers in industry, 1.6 million government employees (some of whom are properly classifiable with the workers in industry), and a fairly small proportion of the 4.7 million people working in the service occupations.

These agreements are now an accepted feature of the collective bargaining scene in Germany. They are being refurbished periodically, extending coverage in terms of numbers of workers and deepening the qualitative and quantitative protection available to individuals. They are fixed-term, like the basic agreements on wages and, as they fall due for renegotiation, new and better provisions are incorporated. By the standard of number of individuals embraced within the agreement, and the terms of 'protection' available to them, the most outstanding is the agreement between the Metal Workers Union and the employers' organization in that industry. This 1968 agreement covers all 4.5 million manual and non-manual workers in that industry.

Quite a clear idea of the purposes of agreements for employee protection against the harmful effects of rationalization, and of the methods for accomplishing those purposes, can be got from a close look at the product of negotiations between the Employers' Association for the Metallurgical Industry and the Metal Workers Federation IG-Metall. In the first place, there is procedure. As soon as it becomes clear to the employer that the changes he has in mind will have consequences for his workforce, he is under obligation to inform the works council and engage in joint studies.

From then on, all issues relating to the manpower effects of the employer's planned programme of changes become a matter for implementation by joint agreement. In substance, the agreement sets out not to oppose but to contain and modify the adverse effects. Changes are defined under three headings: introduction of equipment and machinery with higher levels of technical performance; new methods of work related to new kinds of machinery and equipment; major alterations in the organization of the firm on economic grounds. Included under this last category are mergers and the concentration of production.

Redeployment before redundancy

In the Metal Workers Federation agreement, as with analogous settlements in other industries, the principal object is the retention and redeployment of manpower, taking in spells of retraining, as and when necessary, for this process. Dismissals are regarded very much as a last option when all other solutions have been explored and exhausted. So the first thing that the IG-Metall agreement does is establish that the main endeavour in the personnel field, associated with the introduction of new technology or other changes affecting work, will be to offer the individuals other, nearly equivalent, jobs within the establishment. If that option is not immediately available, then the people affected can be put on other work with a guarantee that they would be re-employed in jobs comparable to their old ones as soon as vacancies appear.

Meanwhile, the older worker who, having put in at least 10 years of service, has had to accept a transfer to a lower status and less well-paid job, is guaranteed his previous wage for a minimum of at least three months. If, after that period, the individual is not re-established in a job comparable with his previous one, the gap between his current and original pay continues to be bridged to a declining extent for a maximum of another six months. This arrangement, except for the age qualification, is comparable with the 'degressive' income-maintenance arrangements in France.

As the basic principle of the metal workers', and other similar agreements is the retention and redeployment of workers, there is a premise that retraining could be a necessary condition for adapting workpeople's skills to new requirements. When this retraining is a prelude to the placement of the individual in a job where his pay will be similar to before, his income is maintained at its original level throughout the period of training. That training-related income guarantee operates for up to six months. All other training costs are borne by the employer.

All this applies even if the training is obtained outside the employer's premises, and in that case the arrangement for finding a training place elsewhere is an employer responsibility. To give the employer some protection against loss of investment, reciprocal obligations are accepted, by the agreement, for the worker. If the individual decides to abandon his training, the employer has a right to recover part of the wage paid in the course of the training period that has lapsed. A similar right of recovery exists if the employee who has been trained leaves the firm without having put in service of a duration equal to the time he had spent on his training programme.

Metal workers' agreement

If all else fails, dismissals are accepted under strictly defined terms. Where the IG-Metall agreement stands uniquely on its own is in the prohibition of compulsory redundancy for individuals between 55 and 59 years of age with at least 10 years service with the enterprise.

Employees in the age bracket 59 – 64 can be made redundant with a specific link up with the national retirement pension scheme's provisions for early retirement. The viewpoint underlying this provision is of considerable significance, and requires amplification. What the metal workers' agreement has done is to establish the principle that a worker who is 55 years of age should not be made unemployed through the need to modernize and rationalize industry. It is a different matter if he has reached an age when he can obtain an early retirement pension. But until he has reached the qualifying age (60) he should not be deprived of employment.

For the alternative to loss of employment at 55 years of age is almost certain to be not another job but unemployment. The issue here is of enormous policy significance. Even in Germany, where all collective agreements about the effects of rationalization are emphatic on giving special protection to older employees, the metal workers' settlement is unique. Additionally, its importance lies in the fact that it covers 4.5 million workers, so is a significant marker to the direction of policy. Though other, later, agreements have not incorporated this provision, the fact of its existence focuses attention on the issue.

In France, as we have seen, the awareness of the poor prospects in the labour market of older workers is embodied in provisions for early retirement. But withdrawal from the labour market into the state of being a 'pre-pensioner' is not possible until he has reached 60. A like provision exists in Germany. Where the arrangements negotiated by IG-Metall have gone further is in making explicit acknowledgement of the fact that someone in his mid-50s is also in need of protection against almost certain unemployment.

Looking across the board at collective agreements made in Germany, this principle of giving protection to older workers is most clearly brought out in their negotiated schedules of severance compensation. With exceptions so minor as not to matter, these agreements all stipulate a minimum period of service and a basic qualifying age. With some exceptions, mainly for white collar workers, the minimum qualifying age tends to be 30. Add to that the almost universal criterion of a minimum of 10 years' service before entitlement to severance compensation begins, and the age of 40 marks the threshold to cash compensation for dismissal on grounds of rationalization.

Cash compensation

In common with France, but unlike Britain, Germany has no statutory provision for cash compensation for redundancy. The system which the Germans have devised, falls somewhere between the methods employed for dealing with redundancies in Britain and France. Of interest is the arrangement in Germany for cash compensation payable to a redundant worker. Apart from the textile-industry agreement affecting 480,000 workers, collectively bargained provisions for redundancy stipulate a rising scale of payments determined by age and length of service. As is to be expected, there is variation from industry to industry in the extent of compensation to which people become entitled. This arises partly from the fact that as unions have negotiated agreements in industries which did not previously have them, they have set out to get better terms than negotiators in other industries had already achieved.

Table 15 shows the matrix of compensation established in the IG-Metall agreement.

Table 15   Lump-sum severance compensation under German Metal-workers Federation Agreement (1968).

Age at time of redundancy	Years of uninterrupted service				
	10–13	14–17	18–21	22–24	25
	Number of months' wages paid				
40–46	2	3	4	5	6
47–52	3	4	5	6	7
53–58	4	5	6	7	8
59–64	5	6	7	8	9

Source

Metal Workers Federation of the Federal Republic of Germany; agreement on protection against rationalization.

A comparison with Britain

A straight comparison between workpeople's entitlement to cash severance compensation in Germany and Britain is difficult. Britain's arrangements are statute-based, and they enable all employees with more than two years of service to qualify for cash compensation. Trade unions in Britain are also beginning to negotiate compensation terms which improve on the statutory provision. Not much is known about such collective agreements, but available evidence suggests that they are not very widespread, and where they exist their general effect is not so great as to bring about significant improvements over and beyond the terms of compensation established by law. In Germany, by contrast, all severance compensation agreements are established by collective bargaining between unions and employers.

Though the spread of these agreements is now very wide, they still do not cover all employees. The circumstances in which compensation becomes payable are narrower in Germany than in Britain. That narrower scope for entitlement is, in the first place, a consequence of the exclusion of workers under 35 − 40 from having rights to cash compensation, irrespective of the number of years of service they have put in before they are made redundant. The second limitation in the German agreements comes about because they are specifically concerned to provide protection only against the adverse effects of technological and structural changes affecting workpeople and do not if redundancy is caused by changes in the demand for products.

A fuller analysis of these points of difference is made elsewhere in this chapter. What needs to be looked at now is the single issue of how workpeople fare in the two countries on the specific matter of cash compensation. In Britain, the most that anyone can get under the statutory scheme is 30 weeks' pay. A workers' years of service entitling him to benefit are taken into account only for a maximum of 20 years. With the IG-Metall arrangement, as with other collectively negotiated agreements in Germany, the maximum reckonable service is as much as 25 years.

This loads the balance further in favour of the older redundant employee. Consequently, a worker made redundant at age 60 could, under the metal workers' agreement, get 39 weeks' pay as against the 29.5 weeks' compensation to which his counterpart is entitled through the British statutory severance payments scheme. Moving down to the lowest age point in the older worker range, the German metal worker in the 40 − 46 bracket can get as much as 26 weeks' pay in compénsation for redundancy by contrast with the 19 − 23 weeks' wages top compensation available to anyone in that age category in the British scheme.

Newer agreements in Germany

Though the IG-Metall agreement marks a breakthrough in getting collectively bargained arrangements for reducing the harmful effects on workers of technological change and rationalization in industry, since 1968 when that was negotiated, unions in other industries have been working at getting an even better deal for their members. From what has been said so far, it is quite evident that the scheme set a pretty high standard of compensation for redundancy, when dismissals had to be made failing all attempts at internal redeployment of surplus manpower within an establishment. It has not been easy for German unions to improve on the terms of the metal industry agreement. Indeed, the agreement covering something over half-a-million workers in chemicals and ceramics, made within months of the Metalworkers' scheme, did considerably less well in establishing a scale of severance payments.

A worker made redundant at age 60 in the chemical industry has a maximum entitlement to 26 weeks' pay in severance compensation, which is 13 weeks less than his more fortunate colleague is able to get in the metal industry. By contrast, there are three agreements, negotiated in 1969, which have succeeded in pushing up the ceiling of compensation quite substantially.

Workers with 25 years of service, at age 60, employed in the production of margarine, are eligible for redundancy compensation equivalent to 56 weeks' pay. Employees with the same age and service qualifications in the manufacture of sugar also have a severance compensation right equalling that in margarine making. The sugar agreement has five age steps for the calculation of separate levels of compensation, and employees in the 40 − 55 bracket do rather less well out of it than their counterparts engaged in the production of margarine. Compensation levels are highest, and most generous in terms of age limitations, in the agreement covering workers employed in the manufacture of cigarettes. Under its terms, a worker aged 40, who has fifteen years of service, is entitled to a full year's wages on dismissal on grounds of redundancy. This rises steeply to 20 months' pay for anyone with 25 years of service who is 50 or more years of age.

Limitations of German schemes

Enough has been said to establish that the collectively bargained arrangements for redundancy compensation in Germany are substantial for the older worker. The focusing of benefits on the older employee is sharper in Germany than in Britain; and the sums of money received are bigger, sometimes considerably so.

Another difference between the two countries is the exclusion of younger people from entitlement to compensation for redundancy in Germany. Before returning to the issues of retraining and the over-all involvement of public authorities in the dispersal of redundancies, it is necessary to consider the limitations of the collectively bargained measures in Germany industry. To begin with there is a problem of definition. In the British scheme the dismissal of the employee becomes a redundancy if it is caused by:

'1. the fact that his employer has ceased, or intends to cease, to carry on the business for the purposes for which the employee was employed by him, or has ceased, or intends to cease, to carry on that business in the place where the employee was employed, or

'2. the fact that the requirements of that business for employees to carry out work of a particular kind, or for employees to carry out work of a particular kind in the place where they were so employed, have ceased or diminished or are expected to cease or diminish.'[4]

In common parlance, this has been put as an entitlement to severance compensation whenever an individual loses his job through no fault of his own.

Entitlement to cash compensation for redundancy under the German agreements is far less widely founded. Though this is not often spelt out in so many words, the unions, employers and public authorities in Germany are at one in the view that ups and downs in the level of economic activity and contractions in the demand for particular products do not justify severance compensation being paid for redundancy.

This view is fundamentally different from the basis on which the statutory scheme was established in Britain. There are also problems in Germany about the interpretation of the terms of the agreements for severance payments when workpeople are being displaced by changes that are within the control of the employer. In each of the German agreements a basic condition of binding the employer to help his employees to adapt to rationalization, or to receive compensation, is the necessity of making a change in the methods of production.

There is scope for debate about what precisely does constitute such a change. Moreover there is room for dispute about circumstances in which changes in the organization of either the enterprise as a whole, or in a particular production process, can be classified as rationalization giving rise to the benefits laid down in the collective agreements. In practice, the implementation of the metal workers' agreement has proceeded on the basis that structural or organizational changes must be such as to reduce the firm's costs per unit of output. Only then do the protective measures contained in the agreement come into play. It is important to bear in mind that though these detailed difficulties about definition arise from time to time, they are not very big or particularly difficult to resolve. Specific solutions for particular situations are worked out through the comprehensive negotiating procedure available to the works councils.

Action by public authorities

So long as unemployment remained at a fraction of 1 per cent, no one was excessively bothered in Germany about redundancies. But from the mid-1960s concern began to build up about the speed with which technological change was affecting employment within firms and industries, even where it was not feeding through into redundancies and higher unemployment. The collectively bargained agreements set out to soften the impact of redundancy and allow time and opportunity, which would be costless so far as the employee is concerned, and enable him to do all within his power to adapt to new requirements.

The employer undertook to make the process as productive as possible by agreeing to provide retraining, and training-based transfers to other jobs within the enterprise. Neither unions nor employers were particularly keen to involve the public authorities too closely. So far as a role was assigned to the public employment service, this was to act as a long stop when all else failed, and reasonable arrangements could not be made within the enterprise by agreement between workpeople's representatives and the firm, and the involvement of a third party was judged likely to be helpful.

Despite the substantial powers available to the public authorities, they too were ready to acquiesce in this arrangement from a conviction that that was the best way of running things. Moreover the public employment service was well placed to find jobs for anyone who came to it, for, after all, there were jobs in plenty.

Events in 1967 substantially altered the public authorities' approach to labour market questions. While this did not involve their seeking a direct role in the matters which unions and employers were tackling through collective agreements on the effects of rationalization in industry, the public agencies embarked on a big programme to facilitate job changes within the economy as a whole. These programmes have as their chief object the creation of avenues for workpeople to acquire new skills to meet alterations in the pattern of demand for manpower initiated either by technological change, or the shifts required in the labour force. Though the public authorities were prompted to introduce a new framework of manpower policy, partly by the relatively high level of unemployment in 1967, their main concern was not to respond to that transitional phenomenon, but to go over to a policy of active support to enable a smoother process of redeployment of manpower. The authorities embodied this new objective quite explicitly in the Employment Promotion Act of 1969.

In essence, the switchround of policy was away from a residual supportive role for the public authorities to a posture where it has become an active provider of opportunities and initiator of action. It is now the authorities' intention to create conditions so that emergencies do not confront the individual who has to cope with the flux of labour market conditions. In all of this the Germans are advantageously placed in having ready to hand a central agency for making and administering manpower policies.

The Federal Institute of Labour

The Federal Institute of Labour is a self-governing body run jointly by employer, worker and public-authority nominees. It is an essential part of the principles determining the activities of the Federal Institute that ministries cannot issue directives or instructions which are binding upon it. But in all situations where questions of power relationships between government departments and independent agencies are concerned the degree of detachment from political control is difficult to define, and varies from time to time. Nevertheless the Federal Institute enjoys great powers of initiative and, perhaps more important, has an independent budget of its own. Until 1969, by statute and in its own attitudes, the Federal Institute of Labour was principally oriented to administering the system of unemployment insurance, and the placement of job seekers. Its revenue for these purposes is raised through a levy on all employers' wages bills. In 1969 that levy brought in something over £384 million. For 1970 the rate of levy was raised to 1.7 per cent of the wage bill (from 1.3 per cent) and the receipts of the Institute increased to about £458 million.

Before the Federal Institute launched its new programme under the impetus of the 1969 Employment Promotion Act, it had in its accumulated reserves some £770 million, half of which was put aside in long-term investment. One measure of the distance between the German and British economies, as well as the conditions in their individual labour markets, is that the Federal Institute spent £90 million in 1970 on paying benefits to 149,000 people who were without jobs. In Britain during the same year there were rather more than 600,000 people unemployed, in receipt of benefits totalling £143 million. The fact that unemployment was so much lower in Germany is of some significance. Perhaps there is as much in the much higher level of unemployment benefit that was available in that country to people without jobs. But what is of paramount significance is that the Federal Institute of Labour spent rather more than £500 million, or well over five-and-a-half times its expenditure on unemployment benefit, on other labour market activities – well over double the cash flows, taking together public, quasi-public and private expenditure on all labour market supportive expenditure in Britain.

Personal incentives to retrain

With the German public authorities' clear aim of providing the maximum possible inducement to individuals to adapt to alterations in patterns of manpower demand, it is not surprising, but still remarkable, that the Employment Promotion Act has, since 1969, given people a legal right to financial assistance from the funds of the Federal Institute of Labour for retraining. While the actual level of income to which individuals are entitled during retraining courses is not as high as it can be in France, the German provisions for income maintenance through training allowances are considerably more generous than is the case in Britain. How much an individual gets in maintenance allowance during his training period depends partly on his earnings level in the job which he has left or lost and on his family circumstances.

Moreover the maintenance allowance is increased if the training period extends beyond a year, and raised further at the end of two subsequent periods of six months each, thus making it possible for individuals to take long training courses without a significant loss of income. In the first six months of the training period the basic allowance (to which family supplements are added) is something over one-third higher than the income-related unemployment benefit to which the individual would have been entitled. For a subsequent six months' period the basic allowance is 140 per cent of the workers' unemployment benefit entitlement. It has been calculated[5] that a married man with two children could get a maximum of 95 per cent of his previous net income for a programme of training extending to a twelve-month period. And of course, because of the provision for rises in allowances for training lasting longer than a year, it is quite possible that the maintenance allowance paid by the Federal Institute of Labour might give the individual, in the final stages of training, an income which is higher than his net earnings in his last job.

All this helps explain why the Federal Institute of Labour was spending nearly £47 million solely on the maintenance allowances paid to people who were undergoing retraining and further training in 1970. This might reasonably be contrasted with the total expenditure of £25 – 40 million envisaged in the British proposals for the finance of a refurbished national training structure proposed for 1972–75. That planned expenditure in Britain is intended to cover all costs of a national training strategy. In other words, the full total of resources to be devoted to the promotion of adult vocational retraining, and the maintenance of an incentive scheme to employers for their normal training activities, would amount to some £7 million less than was spent by the German labour market authorities in income maintenance alone for participants in their adult retraining schemes during 1970.

Before 1969, the number of workers getting training under the auspices of the Federal Institute of Labour was not much more than 50,000 in each year. With the change of emphasis marked by the Employment Promotion Act, the number of trainees financed by the Federal Institute was 50 per cent up in 1970 and was over 200,000 by 1972.

Over-all strategy

Looking at the over-all strategy for dealing with redundancies in Germany, it is possible to identify three clear aspects. Employer responsibility for doing something about displaced workers arises from two sets of circumstances. Though the legal obligation upon employers to refrain from 'socially unjustified' dismissals is not much used as a piece of law, it has served the purpose of making explicit the community's expectations. Much more concretely, collective agreements between employers and unions have enumerated managerial responsibility at times of redundancy directly attributable to decision taking by the enterprise on matters which are within its own control.

Those agreements establish procedure, and lay down substantive provisions regarding the steps to be taken by the employer to achieve redeployment of affected manpower, or to pay cash compensation if jobs cannot be found within the enterprise and the individual has the stipulated length of service above the minimum qualifying age.

Workpeople's representatives play a part in the arrangements for redundancy at two levels. In the first place, trade unions are the initiators of the protective agreements against the harmful effects of rationalization, and it is their pressure on employers which has enabled the widespread development in Germany of these collectively bargained provisions. Workers' representatives are more directly and intimately associated with the treatment of redundancy at places of work through works councils. At that level, they have established rights of joint decision taking with the employer on questions of training, transfer or dismissal.

Works councils are not wholly constrained by industry-level agreements as to the limits of what they can do when facing the implications of a programme of rationalization. They can bargain about the specific proposals made by the firm, and demand the use of a conciliation process involving an independent outsider.

Support and initiative from Federal Institute

While they have a good deal to contribute, the public authorities do this as a back-up facility. Though they have, by British standards, significant coercive powers which can be deployed against an employer, these are less strong and more sparingly used than in France. It would be untrue to think that the Federal Institute of Labour is a passive body performing residual functions, with all important decisions being taken and arrangements made about labour market activity through collective bargaining between employers and unions. Probably the best way of grasping what is involved is to regard the Federal Institute as being concerned with over-all labour market environment, coming into the picture at enterprise level only to the extent that such involvement is necessary for the fulfilment of its wider objectives. It is on that reasoning that the Federal Institute has bumped up its training programme. It is too soon to say that the separate pieces for producing efficient adjustments in the labour market are fully geared in with each other. But there is increasing clarity in the objectives being sought by the public authorities nationally, and employers and unions at the enterprise level, and an interlinking of the two.

While employers and unions have since 1965 worked through collective agreements to devise methods for redeployment within the individual enterprise, and have worked out methods of compensating individuals who lose their jobs, the public authorities have set out, since 1969, to organize the framework within which inter-firm, inter-industry and inter-sectoral transfer of manpower can be accommodated with the minimum adverse effect on workers faced with the need to change jobs. Manpower transfers frequently require occupational changes, and for that purpose, as well as with more general objectives of skill replenishment, the public authorities have launched their large-scale reorganization of adult vocational training.

In order to do this, the Federal Institute of Labour had to make arrangements to take account of the demands for retraining which are likely to arise from changes within enterprises leading to redundancies. Anywhere, other than in Germany, that would be described as 'manpower planning'. Yet, despite the deep-rooted view in Germany that the public authorities should remain at a decent distance from the concerns of the individual enterprise, the Employment Promotion Act has given the Federal Institute of Labour a unique and substantial instrument for influencing manpower flows within the whole economy. That, of course, is not inconsistent with steering clear of what is done by individual firms. But the startling thing is that while the purpose of the public authorities' new power is to enable the over-all labour market to work more effectively, the means for doing this imposes a quite important constraint on employers.

Earlier we saw that the public employment service operated by the Federal Institute in Germany is statutorily entitled to advance notice from employers of their intention to dismiss members of their labour force. Those notification requirements are stringent. More constricting still to the freedom of the employer is the amendment to the *Kundigungsschutzgesetz* (General Protection Law) in 1969, requiring that once the public employment services have agreed to the cutback, the firm must get on with it and complete its discharge of manpower within four weeks. Failing that, the firm must renotify the public employment service and the whole procedure begins all over again. Though this is striking enough, especially when contrasted with the total absence of any say on the part of the public employment service in Britain in analogous situations, it is the lesser of the powers conferred on the Federal Institute of Labour in this respect.

Planning redeployment

Under the *Arbeitsförderungsgesetz* (Employment Promotion Act) employers are placed under an obligation to tell the Federal Institute's public employment service a full year in advance if they can foresee changes within the enterprise that are likely to cause alterations in their pattern of demand and deployment of man-power. The Act does not require this to be done when the employer envisages an increase in his labour force. It is only when the firm's plans and programmes are likely to lead to an addition to the labour supply in the local labour market that the obligation of long-term notification comes into play. A statutory requirement compelling employers to tell the public authorities twelve months in advance about a likely discharge of manpower would be noteworthy in any set of circumstances. That this happens in Germany makes it doubly so.

To compound the confusion among adherents of the 'letting market forces rip' school, the anti-planning German authorities do not stop simply at that. An individual employer is required, by statute, not only to give long-term advance notice when he can anticipate the need to sack some of the people on his payroll; he has the further obligation to inform the public employment services of plans likely to cause the internal transfers to jobs with lower earnings.

From the viewpoint that people have the right to maintenance of what they have achieved by their efforts, this makes evident good sense. And the public authorities' concern is to allow such an individual the scope to find employment or retraining at the same wage level. In considering the wider implications of this approach it is necessary to bear in mind the matching of obligations between employer and the public authorities. To adopt such a programme requires confidence about the ability of the whole economy to go on producing enough jobs for full employment. Equally it implies the willingness and ability of the public authorities to retrain a worker suitably to handle new work where the financial reward is close to the pay level of the job which has disappeared.

These two aspects of the labour market external to the enterprise are clearly, in the German authorities' views, closely interlinked. Having a high level of demand for manpower is not by itself enough to mop up the increased labour supply caused by rationalization and structural change. What is more, even if that mopping up were to be possible entirely as a consequence of market forces, the resulting deployment of manpower would not be as effective as when there has been fresh training during the transition from the extinct job. It is to make sure that the skill-raising process does go on, that the Federal Institute of Labour has gone out to do a selling job, and handed out big sums of money to give a powerful incentive for entering retraining schemes.

Programmes and outcome

That, the sceptic might say, is all very well in theory, but what is there to prevent employers from simply ignoring all these things expected of them? Part of the answer lies in the established tradition of the conduct of industrial relations in Germany within a legally expressed set of the community's expectations. Specifically, the *Arbeitsförderungsgesetz* ties in this employer obligation with the authority available to the public employment services to delay the approval of dismissals. Beyond that, and possibly more importantly, that statute also enables the public authorities to recover from the non-compliant employer the full cost of retraining the dismissed worker for a maximum of six months. In that embodiment of a free-enterprise, free-market economy, the public authorities have since 1969 had the right to compel an employer to finance retraining of employees whom he has discharged, if that dismissal has been the result of an evident lack of planning.

Even yet, the picture is not complete. Workpeople's representatives at enterprise level are also assigned a role in the twelve-month forward plan about manpower which the Employment Promotion Act effectively demands from all managements in Germany. For the year's advance notice of an impending shake-out of manpower obligatory upon the employer must be accompanied by views from the enterprise's works council. Not all the ramifications of this have yet become evident. That it provides great potential scope for long domestic negotiations between employer and the representatives of his workforce about the best way of dealing with the need for a reduction of the labour force is beyond doubt. How effectively workers' representatives will be able to use this room for manoeuvre remains to be seen. What is already established is a clear right of those whose jobs are going to be at stake to join in consideration of ways and means of averting or reducing the upheaval of redundancy. Quite possibly the biggest advance of all is that the workpeople are not at the receiving end of cut-and-dried managerial decisions on matters affecting their livelihood. The statutory requirement imposed on employers to look well ahead at their manpower needs, taken together with the collectively bargained protective measures against the adverse effects of rationalization, appear to give the German worker a basis of security that can provide economically desirable labour mobility without the associated horror of being on the scrap heap.

A concept of redeployment

To suggest that, even with the major reforms brought in since 1969, the Germans have a manpower policy which goes like clockwork would be entirely misleading. Some, for instance, of the large-scale, generously funded training programme is, it is sometimes suggested, simply a centrally financed replacement for training that was already going on. Again, in the retraining context, there is the problem that it is mostly younger people who take up the opportunities, though everyone is agreed that the greatest need is among those over 40.

In the collectively bargained arrangements for cash compensation for those who lose their jobs because of technological change there is clear discrimination in favour of the older worker. On one set of criteria that is logical and sound. Yet questions of inequity between one worker and another are raised by this approach. In the role of the public authorities, especially in relation to their monitoring of the long-term changes of employers' manpower requirements, there are uncertainties about the effectiveness with which their available powers are exercised. There are also a whole range of minor shortcomings at which criticism can be aimed.

Yet, when all that is said, the fact remains that there is a national commitment to a programme of making labour markets work. Institutions have been devised with this end in view, and financial resources on a large and growing scale allocated. A framework exists for redeployment of manpower at a macro, national, level, as well as on a micro, intra-enterprise, basis. At both levels the aims are the same. In the telling phrase which formed the title of a Ministry of Labour publication in Britain, the entire endeavour is about security and change. Adult vocational retraining, together with financial compensation and income maintenance, are the prime instruments for making manpower flow towards new occupational and sectoral directions throughout the economy. As important, and being developed with as much care, is the effort to make these transfers across a bridge of occupational retraining and income guarantees within enterprises, so as to minimize the need for displacement through redundancy. What is being made secure is not one particular job, for the lifetime of an individual, but security of employment and of income through a succession of jobs without cold intervening spells of unemployment.

References

Chapter 2

1. *Effects of the Redundancy Payments Act,* OPCS, HMSO, 1971.

Chapter 3

1. *Adjusting to Change*, National Commission on Technology, Automation and Economic Progress, US Government Printing Office, Washington, DC, 1966.

2. William Allen, *'Part Time Britain?'*, Sunday Times, 1 March, 1964.

3. Security of Employment (Service Contracts) Bill 30, 17 November 1950. Looking back on this, in 1972, perhaps the most striking feature is the collection of people who supported Mr J. Rodgers in the presentation of his Bill – Mr R. Carr, Mr R. Maudling and Mr E. Heath.

4. *Security and Change*, Ministry of Labour, HMSO, 1961.

5. *'Redundancy in Great Britain'*, Ministry of Labour Gazette, February 1963.

6. *Growth of the United Kingdom Economy to 1966*, National Economic Development Council, HMSO, 1963.

Chapter 4

1. House of Commons, Hansard Vol. 711, April 26—May 7 1965.

2. See, for instance, Ray Gunter, Hansard, Vol. 711, Col 33, 26 April 1965.

3. A.D. Smith, *Redundancy Practices in Four Industries*, OECD, 1966.

Chapter 5

1. *Positive Employment Policies*, Ministry of Labour and National Service, January 1958.

2. *Security and Change*, Ministry of Labour 1961.

3. *'Redundancy in Great Britain'*, Ministry of Labour Gazette, February 1963.

Chapter 6

1. Santosh Mukherjee, *Making Labour Markets Work*, PEP broadsheet 532, January 1972.

2. Santosh Mukherjee, *Changing Manpower Needs – A Study of Industrial Training Boards*, PEP broadsheet 523, November 1970.

3. *Redundancy Rebates Act, 1969*, HMSO.

4. House of Commons, *Hansard*, Vol 776, 20 January 1969.

5. See 2.

Chapter 7

1. W.W. Daniel, *Whatever happened to the workers in Woolwich?*, PEP broadsheet 537, July 1972.

Chapter 8

1. Mr Robert Carr, Hansard, 30 January 1969.

2. Mr Roy Hattersley, Hansard, 30 January 1969.

3. W.W. Daniel, *Whatever happened to the workers in Woolwich?*, PEP, 1972.

4. *Ryhope: A Pit Closes*, HMSO, 1970.

5. J.B. Wood, *How Much Unemployment?*, IEA, 1972.

Chapter 9

1. See Part One, 'Introduction and Interpretation', in *The Effects of the Redundancy Payments Act*, OPCS, HMSO, 1971.

Chapter 10

1. *Redundancy Fund Account, 1965–66*, HMSO, 1967.

2. This is shown particularly in W.W. Daniel, *Whatever Happened to the Workers in Woolwich?*, PEP, 1972.

3. Mr Ray Gunter, Hansard, Vol. 711, April 26–May 7, 1965, HMSO.

4. SI 1965, No. 1893.

5. Santosh Mukherjee, *Making Labour Markets Work*, PEP 1971.

Chapter 11

1. A fuller study is under way at PEP covering France, Germany, Italy, Netherlands, Sweden and the USA, which examines severance payments systems as well as other instruments of manpower policy such as the public employment services, systems for training and retraining and regional policies.

2. Santosh Mukherjee, *Making Labour Markets Work*, PEP, 1971.

3. Information on this point is massive and a detailed examination is not possible here. As an example compare the rate of decline in employment in Britain to that in the USA during recessions from 1951 to 1971 (Table 27, Appendix). The striking acceleration, in the percentage decline in employment for each percentage decline in output in Britain since 1966 illustrates the extent of the shake-out since the Redundancy Payments Act. By contrast, the figures for the USA, though initially higher than for Britain, have remained relatively stable over the period.

Chapter 12

1. F.M. Meyers, *Ownership of Jobs: A Comparative Study*, Institute of Industrial Relations, University of California.

2. L. Lucas, *International Trade Union Seminar on Active Manpower Policy*, Supplement to the Final Report, OECD, 1964.

3. Y. Delamotte, *The Social Partners Face the Problems of Productivity and Employment*, OECD, 1971

4. *Dealing with Redundancies*, DEP, 1968.

5. This argument is developed by J. D. Reyneaud, and is cited, amongst other places, in Y. Delamotte (see 3 above).

6. Y. Delamotte, *The Social Partners Face the Problems of Productivity and Employment* (see 3 above), is a useful source about the events set afoot by the discussions in May 1968.

Chapter 13

1. J. Stiebel 'Manpower Adjustments to Automation and Technological Change in Western Europe', incorporated in Appendix Vol. III of the National Commission of Technology, Automation and Economic Progress, US Government Printing Office, Washington, DC, 1966. The metal workers' estimate of job displacements is strenuously contested by the public authorities in Germany, who

claim that the number is much smaller, but do not state alternative figures.

2. Industrial Relations Act, 1971, HMSO Section 19(2).

3. R. Vollmer, *Industrial Relations in Germany*, (Mimeo) 1971.

4. Section 1(2) Redundancy Payments Act, 1971, HMSO

5. R. Vollmer, *Social Security in Germany*. (Mimeo) 1971.

Appendix

Table 16 Cash payments and number of payments made under the 1965 statutory redundancy scheme, 1966—71.

		Number of payments	*Total amount paid (£000s)*	*Of which[3] paid from Fund (£000s)*	*paid by employers (£000s)*	*Annual[4] average payment per head*
1966[1]	I	24,130	4,904			
	II	24,130	4,904			
	III	33,792	7,522			
	IV	55,157	9,458			
Total[2]		137,208	26,488	19,876	6,612	£193
1967	I	58,713	11,720	8,832	2,888	
	II	62,218	13,242	9,955	3,287	
	III	55,669	12,078	9,107	2,971	
	IV	64,981	13,173	9,827	3,346	
Total		241,581	50,213	37,721	12,492	£208
1968	I	67,500	14,578	11,030	3,549	
	II	66,500	15,334	11,449	3,885	
	III	65,292	16,441	12,210	4,231	
	IV	65,208	15,483	11,688	3,795	
Total		264,500	61,837	46,377	15,460	£234
1969	I	69,925	16,751	12,656	4,095	
	II	62,447	15,632	9,815	5,817[5]	
	III	59,698	14,990	8,223	6,767	
	IV	58,694	14,513	7,885	6,628	
Total		250,764	61,886	38,579	23,307	£247

1970	I	63,954	15,654	8,446	7,208	
	II	75,415	19,792	10,897	8,875	
	III	69,907	19,353	10,253	9,100	
	IV	66,287	17,742	9,360	8,382	
Total		275,563	72,541	38,956	33,565	£263
1971	I	70,642	20,388	10,691	9,697	
	II	102,057	27,943	15,124	12,820	
	III	103,601	30,909	16,037	14,872	
	IV	93,921	29,009	15,243	13,766	
Total		370,221	108,249	57,095	51,155	£294

Notes and sources

(1) For 1966 the complete quarterly figures are not published. Information is given for the period 6.12.1965 to 30.6.1966. This had been averaged to estimate figures for the first two quarters of 1966. Data covering the nine months from 6.12.1965 to 30.9.1966 were published so that figures for the third quarter can be calculated by subtraction.

Information for the last quarter was obtained by subtraction from the total for the year which was published in the Gazette.

Thus:-

Published data for number and amount of payments

6.12.65 − 30.6.66   (1)
6.12.65 − 30.9.66   (2)
1.1. 66 − 31.12.66   (3)

The quarterly estimates were obtained as follows:

quarter   I   and quarter   II   =   (1) ÷ 2
quarter   III   = (2) − (1)
quarter   IV   = (3) − (2)

(2) The annual total for 1966 covers the period 1.1.1966 − 31.12.1966

(3) Information for breakdown of amount paid available only for the year 1966, not for the quarters

(4) To nearest £1.00

(5) After the first quarter of 1969 the employers' contribution was increased.

Department of Employment Gazette; quarterly breakdown taken from February, May, August and November issues.

Table 17 Extra costs to individual employers of payments to redundant workers in different age groups due to 1969 Redundancy Rebates Act.

			40 and Under	41–50	51–60	61–64
(a)	(1)	Estimated redundancy payments at 1968 wage levels				
		Males	£113.40	£249.60	£387.20	£429.30
		Females	£ 46.50	£ 93.00	£148.50	
(b)	(2)	Amount borne by employer prior to 1969				
		Males	£ 37.80	£ 55.50	£ 86.00	£ 95.40
		Females	£ 15.50	£ 20.70	£ 33.00	
(a)	(3)	Estimated redundancy payment at 1970 wage levels				
		Males	£129.00	£284.70	£444.40	£496.80
		Females	£ 55.50	£107.00	£173.30	
(b)	(4)	Amount borne by employer assuming pre-1969 level of rebates at 1970 redundancy payments				
		Males	£ 43.00	£ 63.30	£ 98.80	£110.40
		Females	£ 18.50	£ 23.80	£ 38.50	
(c)	(5)	Amount borne by employer after 1969 Act at 1970 level of redundancy payments				
		Males	£ 64.50	£142.40	£222.20	£248.40
		Females	£ 27.80	£ 53.50	£ 86.70	
(d)	(6)	Extra costs to employers after 1969 Act assuming 1970 level of redundancy payments				
		Males	£ 21.50	£ 79.10	£123.40	£138.00
		Females	£ 9.30	£ 29.70	£ 48.20	

		40 and Under	41–50	51–60	61–64
(e) *Per cent increase in employer's contribution after 1969 Act assuming 1970 level of redundancy payments* (7)	Males	50%	125%	125%	125%
	Females	50%	125%	125%	
(f) *Per cent increase in employers' costs of redundancy payments since 1968* (8)	Males	72%	157%	158%	160%
	Females	77%	158%	163%	

Notes and sources

(a) See Table 18.

(b) Prior to 1969 employers could claim rebates of $\frac{2}{3}$ the cost of redundancy payments for employees aged 40 and under, and $\frac{2}{3}$ of one basic week's pay per year and the whole of the additional half a week's pay per year for employees aged over 41. This is an approximate $\frac{7}{9}$ rebate for workers over 41.

(c) In 1969 the Redundancy Rebate Amendment Act imposed a uniform 50 per cent rebate for all age groups.

(d) (5) − (4)

(e) (6) − (4) × 100%

(f) [(5) − (2)] ÷ (2) × 100%

Of this overall increase in employers' costs since 1968, a proportion is accounted for by increases in weekly pay.

Table 18 Estimated redundancy payments by age group in 1968 and 1970.

	Males				Females		
	40 and Under	41–50	51–60	61–64	40 and Under	41–50	51–60
Length of service[1]	6 years	11 years	15 years	18 years	5 years	8 years	11 years
Weekly pay in 1968[2]	£ 18.90	£ 19.20	£ 17.60	£ 15.90	£ 9.30	£ 9.30	£ 9.00
Estimated redundancy payment in 1968[3]	£113.40	£249.60	£387.20	£429.30	£46.50	£ 93.00	£148.50
Number of payments in 1968[4]	67,024	48,110	53,434	41,657	16,523	14,830	15,797
Cost of redundancy payments in 1968 (£000s)[5]	7,601	12,008	20,690	17,883	768	1,379	2,346
Weekly pay in 1970[6]	£ 21.50	£ 21.90	£ 20.20	£ 18.40	£11.10	£ 10.70	£ 10.50
Estimated redundancy payment in 1970[7]	£129.00	£284.70	£444.40	£496.80	£55.50	£107.00	£173.30

	Males				Females		
	40 and Under	41–50	51–60	61–64	40 and Under	41–50	51–60
Number of payments in 1970 [4]	70,595	48,538	54,550	40,489	19,102	18,023	19,684
Cost of payments in 1970 (£000s) [8]	9,107	13,819	24,242	20,115	1,060	1,928	3,411

Notes and soures

(1) Calculated from information provided by the Department of Employment.

(2) *New Earnings Survey 1968.* Table 9 (lower quartile, gross weekly earnings by age, full-time manual men and women). A weighted average was calculated for the 21 – 39 age group.

(3) Calculated from *Redundancy Payments Scheme*, Appendix B.

(4) Department of Employment.

(5) 3 × 4. Total calculated is £62,675,137. The Department of Employment's total for 1968 is £61,837,000.

(6) *New Earnings Survey 1970*, Table 77. Weighted average calculated for 21 – 39 age group.

(7) Calculated as in (3), assuming constant average length of service since 1968.

(8) The total calculated is £73,682,338. The Department of Employment's total for 1970 is £72,541,000.

Table 19 Additional costs to employers of 1969 Redundancy Rebates Amendment Act.

Financial Year	Rebate from Redundancy Fund to employers [1] (£s)	Total paid out by employers [2] (£s)	Amount payable by employers assuming no change in rebates [3] (£s)	Extra costs to employers due to alteration of rebates [4] (£s)
1966–67	24,127,523	32,604,761	—	—
1967–68	37,336,849	50,455,201	—	—
1968–69	45,796,737	61,887,482	—	—
1960–70 [5]	30,292,702	60,585,404	44,833,199	14,540,497
1970–71	35,945,652	71,891,304	53,199,565	17,253,913

Notes and sources

(1) Redundancy Fund Annual Accounts
(2) Calculated; up to March 1969 employers received rebates to the value of approximately 74% of their payments; after March 1969 the rebates fell to 50% of their payments.
(3) Calculated by estimating 74% of total paid.
(4) (3) – (1).
(5) Redundancy Rebates Amendment Act operative from 1 April 1969.

Table 20   Number of redundancy payments by age group (quarterly, men and women) 1966–71.

Men

		Under 40 yrs	40–49 years	50–59 years	60–64 years	Total
1966	I	5,395	3,892	4,483	2,787	16,557
	II	7,410	5,405	6,704	4,947	24,466
	III	8,342	5,820	7,046	5,194	26,402
	IV	15,143	9,290	10,242	6,889	41,564
Annual total		36,290	24,407	28,475	19,817	108,989
1967	I	16,684	11,166	12,580	8,689	49,119
	II	15,619	10,459	11,483	8,105	45,666
	III	14,945	10,423	11,611	8,473	45,452
	IV	16,465	11,798	12,884	10,777	51,924
Annual total		63,713	43,846	48,558	36,044	192,161
1968	I	17,500	11,981	13,169	9,765	52,415
	II	16,450	11,804	12,928	9,545	50,727
	III	16,357	12,211	13,865	12,283	54,716
	IV	16,717	12,114	13,472	10,064	52,367
Annual total		67,024	48,110	53,434	41,657	210,225
1969	I	17,446	12,111	13,755	11,523	54,835
	II	15,317	10,838	12,065	9,603	47,823
	III	13,873	10,204	11,464	9,150	44,691
	IV	15,499	10,897	12,090	8,874	47,360
Annual total		62,135	44,050	49,374	39,150	194,709
1970	I	17,863	12,157	13,833	10,075	53,928
	II	19,284	13,443	14,755	10,628	58,110
	III	15,889	11,040	12,688	9,863	49,480
	IV	17,559	11,898	13,274	9,923	52,654
Annual total		70,595	48,538	54,550	40,489	214,172
1971	I	20,497	12,956	15,031	11,316	59,800
	II	29,932	18,056	20,058	14,614	82,660
	III	24,550	15,882	17,817	14,362	72,611
	IV	28,731	17,732	19,985	16,257	82,705
Annual total		103,710	64,626	72,891	56,549	297,776

Women

		Under 40 yrs	40–49 years	50–59 years	Total	Total men & women
1966	I	1,748	1,475	1,756	4,979	21,536
	II	2,556	2,177	2,542	7,275	31,741
	III	2,579	2,433	2,723	7,735	34,137
	IV	3,943	3,461	4,086	11,490	53,054
Annual total		10,826	9,546	11,107	31,479	140,468
1967	I	4,383	3,812	4,328	12,523	61,642
	II	4,346	3,988	4,272	12,606	58,272
	III	4,161	3,777	4,137	12,075	57,527
	IV	4,071	3,898	4,354	12,323	64,247
Annual total		16,961	15,475	17,091	49,527	241,688
1968	I	4,258	3,947	4,374	12,579	64,994
	II	4,085	3,700	4,017	11,802	62,529
	III	4,059	4,001	4,061	12,121	66,837
	IV	3,221	3,182	3,345	9,748	62,115
Annual total		15,623	14,830	15,797	46,250	256,475
1969	I	4,263	4,039	4,209	12,511	67,346
	II	3,869	3,477	3,679	11,025	58,848
	III	3,670	3,592	3,960	11,222	55,913
	IV	3,831	3,782	3,968	11,581	58,941
Annual total		15,633	14,890	15,816	46,339	241,048
1970	I	4,315	4,341	4,494	13,150	67,078
	II	5,121	4,918	5,434	15,473	73,583
	III	4,573	4,306	4,788	13,667	63,147
	IV	5,093	4,458	4,968	14,519	67,173
Annual total		19,102	18,023	19,684	56,809	270,981
1971	I	5,647	4,672	5,503	15,822	75,622
	II	7,892	6,212	7,060	21,164	103,824
	III	6,619	5,478	6,471	18,568	91,179
	IV	6,969	5,644	6,692	19,305	102,010
Annual total		27,127	22,006	25,726	74,859	372,635

Source
Calculated from information made available by the Department of Employment.

Table 21 Distribution of employees according to length of service in all industries and services 1968 (full-time manual and non-manual men and women).

		Completed 1 year or less	Completed 2–5 years	Completed 6–9 years	Completed 10–14 years	Completed 15–19 years	Completed 20 +
Men	*Manual*	25.3	24.0	13.5	11.6	8.6	15.8
	Non-manual	19.0	24.0	13.8	11.4	9.1	21.5
Women	*Manual*	36.5	31.6	13.0	7.9	4.1	5.2
	Non-manual	34.4	33.4	11.8	7.3	4.4	7.5

Source

Calculated from *New Earnings Survey 1968*, Department of Employment, HMSO, 1970.

Table 22   Proportion of employees not qualifying for redundancy payments (i.e. with less than 2 years service) in 1968.

	Manual Men	Non-Manual Men	Manual Women	Non-Manual Women
All industries and services	25.3	19.0	36.5	34.4
Agriculture, forestry and fishing	19.7	–	–	–
Mining and quarrying	9.8	5.8	–	–
Food, drink and tobacco	27.2	17.8	39.7	33.9
Chemicals and allied industries	20.3	17.5	38.0	32.8
Metal manufacture	19.8	16.6	–	32.2
Engineering and electrical	25.9	20.4	35.6	37.3
Shipbuilding	22.1	–	–	–
Vehicles	16.3	16.4	34.0	32.4
Metal goods	25.1	21.6	32.6	34.2
Textiles	27.5	11.4	30.7	39.2
Clothing and footwear	24.7	19.8	30.0	34.0
Bricks, pottery etc.	26.5	18.8	36.8	–
Timber, furniture etc.	33.3	19.4	–	–
Paper, printing and publishing	20.1	21.3	31.0	37.7
Other manufacturing	27.9	21.9	36.9	–
Construction	43.1	28.2	–	43.2
Gas, electricity and water	11.9	9.4	–	27.8
Transport and communication	21.1	11.3	28.0	26.4
Road haulage contracting	37.8			
Sea, air transport	36.0			
Distributive trades	31.4	18.9	41.6	32.4
Insurance, banking etc.	25.6	18.6	–	32.1
Professional and scientific	23.2	23.9	34.9	35.4
Miscellaneous services	37.5	26.6	47.2	48.9
Public administration and defence	20.5	15.6	33.3	28.0

Source

Calculated from *New Earnings Survey 1968*, Department of Employment, HMSO, 1970.

Table 23 Estimates of numbers of redundancies by age group with proportions kept constant[1] at the average level for 1966 (men).

Years and Quarters	Under 40			40-49			50-59			60-64		
	Actual numbers	Calculated volume at 1966 proportions	Error 2	Actual numbers	Calculated volume at 1966 proportions	Error 2	Actual numbers	Calculated volume at 1966 proportions	Error 2	Actual numbers	Calculated volume at 1966 proportions	Error 2
1966												
I	5,395	5,514	−119	3,892	3,709	+183	4,483	4,321	+162	2,787	3,017	−230
II	7,410	8,147	−737	5,405	5,480	−75	6,704	6,386	+318	4,947	4,453	+494
III	8,342	8,792	−450	5,820	5,914	−94	7,046	6,891	+155	5,194	4,805	+389
IV	15,143	13,840	+1,303	9,290	9,310	−20	10,242	10,848	−606	6,889	7,565	−676
Annual total	36,290	—	—	24,407	—	—	28,475	—	—	19,817	—	—
Quarterly average	9,073	—	—	6,102	—	—	7,119	—	—	4,729	—	—
1967												
I	16,684	16,357	+327	11,166	11,003	+163	12,580	12,820	−240	8,689	8,940	−251
II	15,619	15,207	+412	10,459	10,229	+230	11,483	11,919	−436	8,105	8,311	−206
III	14,945	15,136	−191	10,423	10,181	+242	11,611	11,863	−252	8,473	8,272	+201
IV	16,465	17,291	−826	11,798	11,631	+167	12,884	13,550	−666	10,777	9,450	+1,327
Annual total	63,713	63,990	−277	43,846	43,044	+802	48,558	50,154	−1,596	36,044	34,973	+1,071
Quarterly average	15,928	15,997	−69	10,962	10,761	+201	12,140	12,538	−398	9,011	8,743	+268
1968												
I	17,500	17,454	+46	11,981	11,741	+240	13,169	13,680	−511	9,765	9,540	+225
II	16,450	16,892	−442	11,804	11,363	+441	12,928	13,240	−312	9,545	9,232	+313
III	16,357	18,220	−1,863	12,211	12,256	−45	13,865	14,281	−416	12,283	9,958	+2,325
IV	16,717	17,438	−721	12,114	11,730	+384	13,472	13,668	−196	10,064	9,531	+533
Annual total	67,024	70,005	−2,981	48,110	47,090	+1,020	53,434	54,869	−1,435	41,657	38,261	+3,396
Quarterly average	16,756	17,501	−745	12,028	11,773	+255	13,359	13,717	−358	10,414	9,565	+849

1969	I	17,446	18,260	-814	12,111	12,283	-172	13,755	14,312	-557	11,523	9,980	+1,543
	II	15,317	15,925	-608	10,838	10,712	+126	12,065	12,482	-417	9,603	8,704	+899
	III	13,873	14,882	-1,009	10,204	10,011	+193	11,464	11,664	-200	9,150	8,134	+1,016
	IV	15,499	15,771	-272	10,897	10,609	+288	12,090	12,361	-271	8,874	8,620	+254
Annual total		62,135	64,838	-2,703	44,050	43,615	+435	49,374	50,819	-1,445	39,150	35,437	+3,713
Quarterly average		15,534	16,209	-675	11,013	10,904	+109	12,344	12,705	-361	9,788	8,859	+929
1970	I	17,863	17,958	-95	12,157	12,080	+77	13,833	14,075	-242	10,075	9,815	+260
	II	19,284	19,351	-67	13,443	13,017	+426	14,755	15,167	-412	10,628	10,576	+52
	III	15,889	16,477	-588	11,040	11,084	-44	12,688	12,914	-226	9,863	9,005	+858
	IV	17,559	17,534	+25	11,898	11,794	+104	13,274	13,743	-469	9,923	9,583	+340
Annual total		70,595	71,319	-724	48,538	47,975	+563	54,550	55,899	-1,349	40,489	38,979	+1,510
Quarterly average		17,649	17,830	-181	12,135	11,994	+141	13,638	13,975	-337	10,122	9,745	+377
1971	I	20,497	19,913	+584	12,956	13,395	-439	15,031	15,608	-577	11,316	10,884	+432
	II	29,932	27,526	+2,406	18,056	18,516	-460	20,058	21,574	-1,516	14,614	15,044	-430
	III	24,550	24,180	+370	15,882	16,265	-383	17,817	18,951	-1,134	14,362	13,215	+1,147
	IV	28,731	27,541	+1,190	17,732	18,526	-794	19,985	21,586	-1,601	16,257	15,052	+1,205
Annual total		103,710	99,159	+4,551	64,626	66,702	-2,076	72,891	77,720	-4,829	56,549	54,195	+2,354
Quarterly average		25,928	24,790	+1,138	16,157	16,675	-518	18,223	19,430	-1,207	14,137	13,549	+588

Notes and sources

(1) Predicted values for the number of payments assuming constant proportions in each age group (1966 base year) were calculated by applying the average percentage in 1966 in the various age groups to the figures for total male redundancies (see Table 16). In 1966, the proportions in each age group were 33.3 per cent (under 40 years); 22.4 per cent (40–49 years); 26.1 per cent (50–59 years) and 18.2 per cent (60–64 years). Thus for the first quarter of 1967, the predicted value in the under 40 age group is total for age groups 1967, I × 33.3, that is, $\frac{49{,}119 \times 33.3}{100}$. For the 40–49 group the predicted value is $\frac{49{,}119 \times 22.4}{100}$.

For the 50–59 age group it is $\frac{49{,}119 \times 26.1}{100}$.

(2) The error is the difference between the actual volume and the calculated values.

Table 24 Number of stoppages of work caused by redundancy disputes, 1966–69 [1].

Year	Total stoppages from all causes	Stoppages from redundancy disputes	Redundancy stoppages as per cent of all stoppages	Index of stoppages caused by redundancy disputes (1965=100)	Index of redundancy stoppages as per cent of total stoppages from all causes (1965=100)
1960	2,832	47	1.7	84	71
1961	2,686	70	2.6	125	108
1962	2,449	114	4.7	204	196
1963	2,068	70	3.4	125	142
1964	2,524	51	2.0	91	83
1965	2,354	56	2.4	100	100
1966	1,937	53	2.7	95	113
1967	2,116	53	2.5	95	104
1968	2,378	47	2.0	84	83
1969	3,116	68	2.2	121	92

Notes and sources

(1) More recent data for stoppages solely from redundancy disputes are not available. See also notes and sources for Table 9.

Table 25   Number of workers involved in redundancy disputes, 1966—69 [1].

Year	Total number of workers involved in stoppages from all causes	Workers involved in stoppages from redundancy disputes	Workers involved in redundancy stoppages as per cent of total workers in stoppages from all causes	Index of number of workers involved in stoppages from redundancy disputes (1965=100)	Index of workers in redundancy disputes as per cent of workers involved in stoppages from all causes (1965=100)
1960	701,500	22,791	3.2	62	58
1961	672,900	72,819	10.8	195	196
1962	4,296,600	343,499	8.0	920	146
1963	455,200	26,154	5.7	70	104
1964	701,500	16,569	2.4	44	44
1965	673,500	37,322	5.5	100	100
1966	415,400	24,679	5.9	66	107
1967	551,800	21,440	3.9	57	71
1968	2,074,000	45,844	2.2	123	40
1969	1,426,600	47,930	3.4	128	62

Notes and sources

(1)   More recent data for number of workers involved in stoppages solely from redundancy disputes are not available. See also notes and sources for Table 9.

Table 26 Number of statutory redundancy payments (quarterly, 1966–71)[1] and number of redundancies notified in advance to the Department of Employment[2] (quarterly, 1969–71).

Year	Quarters	Number of statutory redundancy payments[3]	Number of redundancies notified in advance[4]
1966	I	24,130	–
	II	24,130	–
	III	33,792	–
	IV	55,157	–
1967	I	58,713	–
	II	62,218	–
	III	55,669	–
	IV	64,981	–
1968	I	67,500	–
	II	66,500	–
	III	65,292	–
	IV	65,208	–
1969	I	69,925	33,400
	II	62,447	35,000
	III	59,698	38,400
	IV	58,694	42,700
1970	I	63,954	53,900
	II	75,415	55,300
	III	69,907	51,300
	IV	66,287	60,400
1971	I	70,642	97,400
	II	102,057	88,900
	III	103,601	71,900
	IV	93,921	78,000

Notes and sources

(1)(2) These quantities are graphed at Figures 9 and 10.

(3)   Quarterly figures published in Department of Employment Gazette, see discussion in Chapter 6 about relationship between payments and number of people made redundant.

(4)   Monthly figures made available by the Department of Employment have been added together, quarter by quarter.

Table 27 Changes in output and employment during recessions in manufacturing industries in Britain and the USA, 1951–71.

	BRITAIN					USA			
	1951–52	1955–56	1957–58	1966–67	1970–71	1953–54	1957–58	1960–61	1969–70
Per cent decline in output	8.7	3.1	3.4	2.2	1.2	9.7	12.2	7.3	1.3
Per cent decline in numbers employed	1.7	0.7	2.0	3.3	5.3	6.2	9.3	2.9	0.9
Per cent decline in numbers employed for 1 per cent decline in output	0.20	0.22	0.59	1.50	4.42	0.64	0.76	0.40	0.69

Notes and sources
Derived from Nield, *Pricing and Employment in the Trade Cycle*, NIESR. The same series for output and employment in Britain has been used and updated for 1966–67 and 1970–71. Data from NIESR tables for production and employment. For the USA, the figures for 1953–54 are taken directly from Nield. For later periods a new series has been used from Survey of Current Business, US Dept. of Commerce, Office of Business Economics.

Bibliography

In order of year of publication

1947 – Conservative Political Office, *The Industrial Charter*.

1953 – Ministry of Labour, *Positive Employment Policies*.

1956 – British Productivity Council, *Productivity and Redundancy*.

– Ministry of Labour, *Policies Impeding the Full and Efficient Use of Manpower*.

– US Department of Labor, 'Layoff, Recall and Work-sharing Procedures', *Monthly Labor Review,* December 1956, January and February 1957.

1958 – Acton Society Trust, *Redundancy – Three Studies* and *Redundancy – A Survey*.

1961 – Ministry of Labour, *Security and Change – Progress in Provisions for Redundancy*.

1962 – W.H. Franke, *Long-Term Labor Force Adjustment and Sources of Income of Displaced Workers*, University of Illinois.

– S. Goodman, *Redundancy in the Affluent Society*, Fabian Tract.
International Labour Office, *Unemployment and Structural Change*, Geneva.

– International Labour Office, *Termination of Employment (Dismissal and Layoff)*, Report VII(1) and (2), ILO Conference (46th).

1963 – Ministry of Labour, 'Redundancy in Great Britain', *Ministry of Labour Gazette*, February 1963.

– National Economic Development Council, *Growth of the United Economy to 1966*, HMSO.

1964 – Hilda Kahn, *Repercussions of Redundancy*, Allen and Unwin.

– L. Lucas, *International Trade Union Seminar on Active Manpower Policy*, Supplement to the Final Report, OECD, Paris.

– Dorothy Wedderburn, *White Collar Redundancy – A Case Study*, Cambridge University Press.

1965 – A. Fox, *The Milton Plan*, Institute of Personnel Management.

– Alan Touraine, *Acceptance and Resistance – Workers' Attitudes to Technical Change*, OECD, Paris.

– Dorothy Wedderburn, *Redundancy and the Railwaymen*, Cambridge University Press.

– US Department of Labor, *Major Collective Bargaining Agreements: Severance Pay and Layoff Benefit Plans*, Bureau of Labour Statistics, Bulletin No. 1425.

1966 – 'Manpower Aspects of Automation and Technical Change', European Conference, OECD, Paris.

– A.D. Smith, *Redundancy Practices in Four Industries*, OECD, Paris.

– US Department of Labor, *The Operation of Severance Pay Plans and Their Implications for Labor Mobility*, Bureau of Labour Statistics, Bulletin No. 1462.

1967 – International Labour Office, *Labour and Automation: Manpower Adjustment Programmes*, I (France, Federal Republic of Germany), II (Sweden, USSR, United States), III (Canada, Italy, Japan), ILO, Geneva.

– *Technical Change and Manpower Planning – Coordination at Enterprise Level*, OECD, Paris.

1968 – Department of Employment and Productivity, *Dealing with Redundancies*.

– Caroline Miles, *Lancashire Textiles, A Case Study of Industrial Change*, Cambridge University Press.

1969 – Yves Delamotte, *The Social Partners Face the Problems of Productivity and Employment: A Study in Comparative Industrial Relations*, OECD, Paris.

– R.L. Rideout, *Reforming the Redundancy Payments Act*, Institute of Personnel Management.

– R. Thomas, *An Exercise in Redeployment: Report of a Trade Union Group*, Pergamoon Press.

1970 – W.W. Daniel, *Strategies for Displaced Employee*, PEP Broadsheet 517, January 1970.
  – *Ryhope: A Pit Closes – A Study in Redeployment*, HMSO.
  – Institute of Personnel Management, *Executive Redundancy and Obsolescence*, IPM Information Report 5 (New Series).
  – R. Martin and R.H. Fryer, 'Management and Redundancy: an Analysis of Planned Organizational Change', *British Journal of Industrial Relations*, Vol. VIII, No. 1, March 1970.
  – Trades Union Congress, *Automation and Technological Change*.
1971 – M. Bulmer, 'Mining Redundancy: A Case Study of the Working of the Redundancy Payments Act in the Durham Coalfield', *Industrial Relations Journal*, Vol. 2, No. 4, Winter 1971.
  – Cyril Grunfeld, *The Law of Redundancy*, Sweet and Maxwell.
  – L.C. Hunter, G.L. Reid and D. Boddy, *Labour Problems of Technological Change*, Allen and Unwin.
  – D.I. Mackay, D. Boddy *et al.*, *Labour Markets under Different Employment Conditions*, University of Glasgow Social and Economic Studies, Allen and Unwin.
  – Office of Population Censuses and Surveys, *The Effects of the Redundancy Payments Act*, HMSO.
  – G.L. Reid, 'The Role of the Employment Service in Redeployment', *British Journal of Industrial Relations*, Vol. IX, No. 2, June 1971.
1972 – *Managerial Mobility and Redundancy*, British Institute of Management.
  – W.W. Daniel, *Whatever happened to the workers in Woolwich?*, PEP Broadsheet 537, July 1972.
  – US Department of Labor, *Characteristics of Agreements Covering 2,000 Workers or More*, Bureau of Labor Statistics, Bulletin 1729.

Index